THE GR[illegible] EXPERIE[illegible]CE

TOOLS FOR ACCEPTANCE, RESILIENCE, AND CONNECTION

KELLY DAUGHERTY

FEATURING: KARYN ARNOLD, KATHLEEN BANICKI, ALAINA BULLOCK, KRISTI CAPRIGLIONE, KIRBY KAY L. CLARK, CHERI DAVIES, DEB DECELLE, BRITTANY DEMARCO-FURMAN, JULIE FUNKHOUSER, GEORGE GARCIA, APRIL HANNAH, REBECCA JOHNSON, MISTI KLARENBEEK-MCKENNA, AMY LINDNER-LESSER, CAROL S. MILLER, LISA MILLIS, DR. GABRIELA MINISCALCO, BRITTANY NELSON, CHERYL NIX, REBECCA RAINSTROM, SUSAN SETTLER, TIFFANY THOMAS, JEAN TREWHELLA, KAREN ANN WHITE

FOREWORD BY DR. LUCY HONE

TOOLS FOR ACCEPTANCE, RESILIENCE, AND CONNECTION

KELLY DAUGHERTY

FEATURING: KARYN ARNOLD, KATHLEEN BANICKI, ALAINA BULLOCK, KRISTI CAPRIGLIONE, KIRBY KAY L. CLARK, CHERI DAVIES, DEB DECELLE, BRITTANY DEMARCO-FURMAN, JULIE FUNKHOUSER, GEORGE GARCIA, APRIL HANNAH, REBECCA JOHNSON, MISTI KLARENBEEK-MCKENNA, AMY LINDNER-LESSER, CAROL S. MILLER, LISA MILLIS, DR. GABRIELA MINISCALCO, BRITTANY NELSON, CHERYL NIX, REBECCA RAINSTROM, SUSAN SETTLER, TIFFANY THOMAS, JEAN TREWHELLA, KAREN ANN WHITE

FOREWORD BY DR. LUCY HONE

The Grief Experience

Tools for Acceptance, Resilience, and Connection

Kelly Daugherty

Published by Brave Healer Productions

Paperback ISBN: 978-1-961493-17-9

eBook ISBN: 978-1-961493-16-2

Disclaimer

This book offers words of wisdom with regard to physical, mental, emotional, and spiritual well-being and is designed for informational and educational purposes only. You should not rely on this information as a substitute for, nor does it replace, professional mental health advice, diagnosis, or treatment. If you have concerns or questions about your health, or mental well-being, you should always consult with a qualified mental health professional, a physician, or other healthcare professional. Do not disregard, avoid, or delay obtaining medical or health-related advice from your healthcare professional because of something you may have read here. The use of any information provided in this book is solely at your own risk.

Developments in research may impact the health and life advice in this book. While we aim to include the most relevant findings, we cannot assure that all information will always reflect the latest developments. The personal experiences shared may not apply universally, as grief is a unique journey for each individual. The insights and perspectives in this book, brought by various authors with their own beliefs, faiths, cultures, and backgrounds, highlight that there is no definitive right or wrong way to navigate through grief. This book's diversity of experiences and viewpoints is intended to foster understanding and respect for the multifaceted nature of grief and loss. While offering insights and strategies, it may not cover every aspect of each individual's experience with grief.

Having said all that, know that the authors here have shared their tools, practices, and knowledge with you with a sincere and generous intent to assist you on your grief journey. Please contact them with any questions you may have about the techniques or information they have provided. They will be happy to assist you further!

JOIN THE "SUPPORTING GRIEVING STUDENTS/CHILDREN" FACEBOOK GROUP

Are you dedicated to helping grieving students thrive?

Connect with like-minded individuals
who share your passion for supporting young hearts.
In this group, we discuss practical strategies, share resources,
and offer specialized grief trainings, fostering a compassionate community.
Whether you work with children in a school therapy practice or
seek valuable resources and training to help grieving children,
join this group today.

JOIN THE "GRIEF EMPOWERMENT" FACEBOOK GROUP

Discover strength in shared experiences.

In the "Grief Empowerment" group,
we embrace the power of connection and resilience.
This is a safe space to share your grief journey,
find support, and access empowering resources and tools.
Whether you've experienced the death of a loved one or want to learn how
to navigate grief more authentically, our community is here for you.
Join us today.

Dedication

To my mom, I dedicate this book to you.
Although you may not be here physically to hold it in your hands,
I know you are with me in spirit, watching over me as I navigate this world without you. I honor your memory and find meaning in my grief through every word I have written. Your legacy lives on through me and my work with grieving individuals.

In Memory of Eileen Barry

2-14-43 to 7-28-94

TABLE OF CONTENTS

Foreword

Dr. Lucy Hone, Author of *Resilient Grieving*

It was an unsuspecting Saturday afternoon when grief truly got me. This wasn't the first time, and it wouldn't be the last, but it was definitely the day that changed my life forever.

Eating dinner in a remote backcountry lodge, the owner came to tell us a policeman was on the phone, asking to speak to us. We'd been waiting for the arrival of our 12-year-old daughter, Abi, traveling in a friend's car to join us. Yes, they were late, but we'd conjured innocent explanations, a bit of traffic, or they'd stopped for a meal perhaps. This can't be good, said the look on my husband's face. He was right. Twenty agonizing minutes later, the same policeman stood in front of us, relaying the news that our beautiful Abi, her 12-year-old friend, Ella, and Ella's mum, Sally, had all been killed in a tragic car accident. Killed. Instantly. Car. Accident. Dead. Gone. Gone. Gone forever. What?

I won't dwell on the immediate aftermath. Instead, I'd like to share what happened in the days, months, and years since our precious girls died. Because my story has lessons relevant to us all.

I was already an academic researcher when our girl died. Want to guess my field? Resilience psychology. *Oh, the irony,* I remember thinking. Accustomed to helping others navigate their darkest days, never did I think I'd be the one blindsided by such an extreme loss. Yet that's the point, isn't it? None of us know what's around the corner, what we might need resilience for. But, as my personal life, my professional work, and the stories in this book reveal, adversity doesn't discriminate. One way or another, sadly, tough times come for us all: if you're alive, the chances are you've already had to, or are going to have to, journey through some form of loss.

A recent study confirmed this, estimating that 71% of adults are exposed to a potentially traumatic event in their lifetime. That's the bad news, but fortunately, there is good news, too.

Thanks to my familiarity with findings from my field, I was well acquainted with the large body of science showing humans are hard-wired to cope with bereavement. The skills and knowledge of coping with loss reside deep within each and every one of us. Resilience is your birthright, baked into your DNA. While we hear so much about complicated grief, and bereavement is frequently pathologized and medicalized, the science couldn't be more clear: most individuals demonstrate resilience in the face of loss, generally exhibiting a stable trajectory of healthy functioning across time. Some studies suggest the majority even grow.

I'm not saying adversity is something we should wish for or that surviving such tough times is easy, but please take heart and draw hope from the fact that not only do the odds predict you will somehow survive this loss, but study after study demonstrates surviving requires very ordinary processes. By that, I mean things like leaning on your friends, bravely asking for help, continuing to get outside and soak up the sun, dialing back your inner critic, and increasing self-compassion, forgiveness, bravery, gratitude, hope, and what we refer to as realistic optimism.

This means that rather than being an elusive fixed trait, resilience is a 'capacity' that can be built, both in ourselves and others. Isn't that incredible, that you truly can develop your own resilience? And by genuinely caring for others, you can build their resilience too. These are the messages we need to be spreading, particularly in the current climate of ongoing challenge, disruption, uncertainty, and change.

Studies show each and every one of us has the capacity to build our personal resilience in the ways we choose to think, act, and be in the micro-moments of our days. Resilience is in many ways a choice: a choice to survive, to get out of bed each day and take that next step forward, to identify the help you need most and bravely ask for it, to focus your attention on the things that are still good in our world, even on our darkest days.

In the work we do in our *Coping With Loss* programs over the last decade, I have seen first-hand the transformational shift sharing the tools of resilience creates. Learning about resilience enables our bereaved clients, many of whom have struggled for years, to rediscover hope and to identify both inner strengths and outer resources they hadn't realized were there. This work has literally been life-changing for so many.

It has changed me, too, bringing me back to life and providing a clear path forward. I'm on a mission to transform the way people grieve, putting them back in the driver's seat of their lives, reducing the awful sense of overwhelm, and returning a sense of control. It's my belief that each and every one of us needs to find out what works for us in grief and that our needs are highly individual. I am deeply moved to be part of that incredible process, watching people heal.

I trust that reading the stories and tools within this book will demonstrate that you, too, can heal. You *can* and *will* survive this loss. That learning more about resilience—discovering the capacity that's your birthright—will have a profound impact on you, too. I trust you'll find the ways of thinking and acting that work for you and the language that resonates. I hope, too, that you'll join us in making this a less death-phobic, death-awkward, and death-illiterate world by joining our community.

Together, we can change the narrative around grief so that people all over the world discover it is possible to live and grieve at the same time.

See https://www.copingwithloss.co/ to find out more about our programmes/resources and how to work with Dr. Lucy Hone.

You can follow Dr. Lucy Hone here:

https://www.linkedin.com/in/drlucyhone/

https://www.facebook.com/DrLucyHone/

https://www.instagram.com/drlucyhone/

INTRODUCTION

"Just like the lotus, we too have the ability to rise from the mud, bloom out of the darkness, and radiate into the world."

-Unknown

Grief can swallow you whole. Yet, in the struggle to make sense of loss and find meaning in grief, you possess an inherent capacity to emerge from the depths of despair, blossom amidst the darkness, and radiate your light into the world.

May this book be a source of support and connection as you navigate the complexities of your unique grief experience, realizing how potently grief can open doors for personal growth and empower you to discover newfound strength and resilience in the face of adversity.

Tragedy struck in July of 1994 when my mother lost her battle with breast cancer. I was 14 years old. Returning to school in September after her death, the back-to-school mass had an unexpected prayer that twisted the knife in my wounds.

"Let us pray for Kelly Barry's Father, who died over the summer," they said.

Shocked and furious, my face flushed with anger. *How could they pray for the wrong parent?* Strained relations with my father amplified my resentment towards the misplaced condolences. Throughout the day, classmates offered misguided sympathy, saying, "I'm sorry about your dad."

Angrily, I corrected them, "It was my mom who died!" This was on the heels of the words from my biology teacher just a handful of months prior (before my mom died).

"I don't care if your mother is at home dying; you need to have your biology lab book."

As tears welled up in my eyes, mingling with burning humiliation, I couldn't help but gaze down at my black lab desk. Just fourteen and a freshman in a new school, I found myself caught in the turbulent sea of teenage emotions when a heartless remark from my teacher pierced through my fragile existence.

These pivotal experiences were the catalyst that formed the foundation of the Center for Informed Grief LLC, with a mission to educate therapists and educators about grief. It's astonishing that grief often receives little attention in undergraduate and graduate programs for social workers and counselors, leaving a staggering 60% of therapists inadequately trained in grief and loss. The lack of grief education is even more pronounced among teachers. This book is now extending this education to the masses.

As a society, we remain ill-prepared to understand and empathize with the grieving process, struggling to find the right words and provide meaningful support. Those who have yet to encounter profound loss grapple to comprehend the emotional, mental, cognitive, physical, and spiritual toll it exacts.

If you find yourself delving into the pages of this book, chances are you intimately understand the difficult journey of grief and the crushing weight it places upon your heart and soul. My purpose in writing this book is to foster a culture of grief awareness, equipping individuals with the knowledge to recognize various forms of grief and empowering them with tools to compassionately support those who mourn. My hope is that if you're grieving, you'll find solace in the shared narratives of the authors, understanding that you're not alone in your unending grief journey.

Grief is a universal experience, touching each of us at some point in life. It's a normal, natural response to loss, manifesting in a wide range of emotions. From the depths of sadness, guilt, and anger to the "grief brain," which impacts us cognitively, grief can manifest itself in various ways. Its effects are not solely confined to emotions; they extend to physical manifestations, including fatigue, stomachaches, headaches, sleep issues, and more. Grief doesn't adhere to a predetermined timeline. It's not a condition to overcome but rather a process to be integrated into our lives, something we learn to coexist with. The journey of grief is far from linear or predictable; it's like a turbulent whirlwind of oscillation between focusing on our loss and adapting to our new normal.

This book gathers 25 authors who've weathered a diverse array of losses, including the death of loved ones, the end of relationships, struggles with infertility, disenfranchised grief, anticipatory grief, ambiguous grief, delayed grief, and more. Each chapter dives into a specific type of loss, written by an author who intimately understands that type of grief. These authors, representing a wide spectrum of beliefs, faiths, cultures, and backgrounds, acknowledge that grief is deeply personal and unique, lacking a definitive right or wrong way to navigate it. As you read their stories, you'll likely find comfort in connecting with at least one of them, knowing that you're not alone in your journey through grief.

Within each chapter, you'll discover a treasure trove of tools and strategies to navigate your own grief experience. These resources encompass mindfulness practices, thought-provoking journaling prompts, self-care techniques, and practical advice for managing the waves of emotions. The tools provided in this book aid us in accepting the reality of your loss by offering practical guidance and support throughout your grief experience. These tools assist in navigating the complexities of grief, helping us acknowledge and process our emotions, find moments of solace and self-care, and gradually integrate our loss into the fabric of our lives, also known as resilience. It's essential to recognize that this process of acceptance is not a one-time event but an ongoing and evolving experience as we continue to grow and find new ways to connect and honor the memory of what we've lost.

Through the diverse perspectives and practical guidance presented in this book, you'll find solace, connection, and renewed resilience as you navigate the journey of grief.

The Grief Experience offers a compassionate and supportive outlook on the grieving process. I urge you to treat yourself gently and with self-compassion as you navigate your own unique grief journey, encouraging you to seek support and forge connections as needed. The book also underscores the importance of self-care and provides insights on ways to honor and remember what has been lost.

Comprehensive and all-encompassing, *The Grief Experience* serves as an invaluable resource for anyone grappling with grief, regardless of the nature of their loss. By presenting a multitude of tools and perspectives, this book offers unwavering support as readers navigate their grief journeys, fostering acceptance, resilience, and profound human connection.

I invite you to join us on this journey through grief to find acceptance, resilience, and connection amidst life's losses.

CHAPTER 1

TREASURED PAWPRINTS

NURTURING SELF-CARE WHILE NAVIGATING GRIEF

Kelly Daugherty, MSW, FT

MY STORY

"I think it's time to call the vet," my husband's voice quivered as he gazed at our little cairn terrier, PJ, struggling to walk and collapsing on the frigid ground. Less than 48 hours ago, I was joyfully playing with our nearly 15-year-old pup on the living room floor, surrounded by toys, unaware that PJ would die only two days later, shattering our hearts.

The passing of a beloved pet evokes a depth of grief often difficult for others to comprehend. It's a unique form of loss, intensified by the lack of understanding and support from those who haven't experienced the profound love and bond shared with an animal companion. Pet loss falls into the realm of disenfranchised grief, where society fails to fully acknowledge or validate the pain it entails. This can be disheartening, leaving grieving pet owners feeling isolated and misunderstood.

It was almost nine years ago when I first met my husband, Kevin, and shortly after, I was introduced to PJ and Boomer. He adopted them when they were a mere eight weeks old. Kevin was apprehensive about me meeting PJ, as he had a reputation for having an attitude and being unfriendly towards new people. However, it didn't take long for PJ to warm up to me, and I quickly fell head over heels for his unique charm. It was only a year since my beloved Tally, a retired racing greyhound, and my first dog, crossed the rainbow bridge. The pain of losing her was still fresh, and I wasn't sure I was ready to open my heart to another dog until I met Boomer and PJ. They quickly became an inseparable part of our lives, and I was grateful to be their mama.

Our schedules and plans revolved around being the best pup parents we could be, spoiling them with specialty foods, including "big yummies" that I cooked for them, treats, cozy blankets, and an abundance of love. People often speak of unconditional love, and I firmly believe that dogs embody that boundless affection. They greet us with unbridled joy and excitement, regardless of how long we've been away. They become our whole world, and we become theirs.

Since the summer of 2021, Boomer, our Boston Terrier, has required extra care and attention due to a life-altering injury. We began mentally preparing ourselves for the possibility of Boomer dying before PJ. However, fate had a different plan. Caring for two senior dogs had its challenges. There were sleepless nights filled with potty breaks. PJ, a small and low-to-the-ground pup, needed a set of puppy stairs to reach his cherished King PJ chair and required assistance to get on and off the bed. During these tender moments, I showered him with kisses, hugs, and heartfelt declarations of love. PJ possessed a one-of-a-kind personality that shone through his expressive eyes and repertoire of sounds, which conveyed his happiness, annoyance, or longing for a treat.

On a chilly evening just after Christmas, I returned home from a long day at work, yearning to be with my husband and our beloved furry companions. Exhaustion weighed heavily on my shoulders as I trudged through the front door, and there was PJ, his tail wagging weakly, making his way toward me. But something felt amiss. Kevin's solemn expression revealed the unsettling truth—PJ wasn't feeling well.

Kneeling down, I gently caressed PJ's head, planting a tender kiss on his furry forehead. Deep down, I sensed this was no ordinary ailment. Unfortunately, my intuition proved correct. During PJ's nightly potty time,

I noticed a chilling sight—blood in his stool. A wave of dread washed over me, and my heart sank. *Is this the beginning of the end for our sweet PJ?*

That night, Kevin and PJ slept together in the living room while I sought comfort in our bedroom with Boomer. But sleep evaded me as I was consumed by worry about PJ's condition and thought *Is he going to die in his sleep? Maybe he will be better tomorrow?* The next morning, I eagerly rushed to check on him, hoping for a miraculous recovery. Instead, I was met with a heartbreaking sight—PJ panting heavily and disoriented, a far cry from his usual self. Instantly, I knew, *I can't go see my friends, I can't leave him.* Leaving PJ in such a distressing state was unthinkable.

I quickly went to a doctor's appointment that morning and returned home, weighed down by the heaviness in my heart. Although Kevin reported no major changes, PJ's demeanor spoke volumes. We took him outside for the customary family potty time with Boomer just a few hours later, but PJ struggled to walk, stumbling and falling on the frozen ground. I thought *he is struggling so much, we need to do something, but I can't be the one to say it.* Then in that poignant moment, Kevin uttered the words that I couldn't say: "It's time; we need to call the vet."

My mind rebelled against the cruel reality before me. *This can't be happening, I don't want to have to make that call. He was fine just two days ago.* As his condition continued to deteriorate, I reluctantly accepted the painful truth that his time to cross the rainbow bridge was approaching. The decision to contact the vet and consider euthanasia was agonizing. Neither Kevin nor I wanted to face such a heart-wrenching choice. We were torn between wanting to end his suffering and not wanting to let him go, but ultimately, we made that decision out of love for him.

My voice trembled, and tears welled up in my eyes as I made the call to the vet and scheduled the appointment for the next day. *Every second matters now; we have to make the most of these last few hours with him.* We took turns cradling PJ in our arms, pouring out our love, and sharing cherished memories. Boomer sat beside us, sensing the somber atmosphere, bidding a silent farewell to his lifelong companion and the bond they shared. PJ's eyes held a mixture of sadness and acceptance as if saying goodbye to his beloved brother.

When the vet finally arrived, her kindness, compassion, and understanding enveloped us in a soothing embrace. As PJ lay in his king PJ chair illuminated by the soft, golden touch of sunlight shining through the kitchen window, PJ crossed the threshold with grace and peace, offering only a glimpse of his usual grumpiness. As he took his final breath, I whispered, "Run free, PJ. Go be with Tally and my mom."

Kevin, Boomer, and I sat there in silence, bidding our last goodbyes. It was important for Boomer to have the chance to say his farewell, even if he couldn't fully comprehend the gravity of the moment. With utmost care, Kevin wrapped PJ in his favorite blanket and gently placed him in a basket. Overwhelmed by grief, I retreated for a moment, overcome by a flood of tears and heart-wrenching sobs, unable to witness the sight. But I knew I couldn't hide forever. I needed to stand beside Kevin as he carried the basket to the vet's car.

Planting one final kiss on PJ's head, I whispered my deepest affection, cherishing every precious memory. As the car disappeared into the distance, carrying PJ's lifeless body, a suffocating silence descended upon us. Our family was forever altered, consisting of Kevin, Boomer, and me. It felt unbearably cruel that our beloved PJ was no longer there, an integral part of our lives—a cherished member of our family.

The days that followed were cloaked in a heavy blanket of grief. Our once vibrant home became a haunting reminder of PJ's absence. Every corner held memories of him—the untouched toys in the basket, the food bowl in the kitchen, and the empty space where his "King PJ chair" once stood. It was as if a piece of our souls had been torn away, leaving an irreversible void.

As time wore on, the rawness of our grief began to soften, but the ache in our hearts remained. We gradually adjusted to this new normal, where PJ's physical presence was replaced by cherished memories and enduring love. We found comfort in sharing stories of the moments we spent together. Although PJ had crossed the rainbow bridge, his spirit continued to dance within the walls of our home. We felt his essence in the gentle sunlight that filtered through the windows or in the soft rustling of the trees outside. Some nights, I awakened with a start, momentarily convinced I heard his barks or felt his presence at the foot of the bed, only to be reminded once again of his absence.

PJ's departure marked the end of his earthly existence, but it could never extinguish the flame of his memory that burned brightly within our hearts. He was an integral part of our lives—a source of unwavering love and companionship. Although the pain of his loss was raw and overwhelming, we knew the love we shared with him would endure. PJ's memory will forever be etched in the tapestry of our family's story.

In the wake of our deep grief, I discovered solace in the act of creating a tangible tribute to PJ—a testament to the unbreakable bond we shared. Reflecting on the healing power of a scrapbook I previously made in remembrance of my Tally, I embarked on a similar endeavor once more. This time, however, an unexpected gift from my nephew added an extra layer of comfort and significance to our tribute.

A few days after PJ's passing, my nephew arrived with a hand-drawn picture he lovingly crafted—a heartfelt portrayal of PJ. As I held the artwork in my hands, tears welled up in my eyes. It captured the essence of our dear companion—the twinkle in his eyes, the spirit that radiated from his being. This simple yet heartfelt gift brought immeasurable comfort to both Kevin and me and now hangs prominently in our living room. Every time our gaze falls upon that artwork, our hearts fill with a bittersweet mix of longing and gratitude, a tangible symbol of our beloved PJ's enduring presence. PJ's spirit lives on in that artwork, forever imprinted in our hearts and displayed proudly for all to see—a cherished memento of a beloved companion who will forever hold a special place in our lives.

Over the course of a weekend, I immersed myself in the vast digital archive of our shared memories, selecting precious photographs that captured PJ's vibrant spirit. I painstakingly printed and framed these moments, ensuring that each image reflected the love and joy he brought into our lives. Meanwhile, Kevin compiled lists of PJ's endearing nicknames, jotting down memories and the unique behaviors we affectionately dubbed. Together, we crafted a book—a testament to PJ's unforgettable mark on our lives. Each page was a treasure trove of cherished memories and heartfelt sentiments. I also sat down just two days after PJ's death, opened my computer, and let my thoughts and feelings flow into a document, a portion of which now compromises this chapter. I needed to express my emotions to preserve my memories of PJ.

For us, PJ and Boomer were not simply pets—they were cherished members of our family, our babies. Their presence completed our household, and their absence left a void in our hearts. Adjusting to this new normal was a painful and arduous journey as we grappled with the complexities of grief and sought understanding and validation amidst our intense sorrow.

I turned to online communities, joining pet loss Facebook groups to find empathy and a sense of connection. In these spaces, I discovered a shared grief—a community of individuals who understood the magnitude of our loss and the depth of our love for our fur babies. Engaging with others navigating the same journey provided a source of comfort and validation, and I could openly express my emotions without fear of judgment or dismissal.

Seeking reassurance took other forms as well. In my quest for connection and a glimmer of hope, I explored the realm of animal mediums—individuals gifted with the ability to communicate with animals in the spirit realm. While some may view this as unconventional or far-fetched, for me, it represented an opportunity to receive a message from our beloved PJ. I wanted to know that PJ was still with us in some form.

In my journey through pet loss, I realized that finding understanding and support may require seeking unconventional avenues. It's a personal and unique path that may lead us to online communities, spiritual practices, or alternative healing methods. The important thing is to honor our grief, to surround ourselves with individuals who validate our emotions, and to find solace in the ways that resonate.

Ultimately, we discovered our grief journey was as unique as our bond with PJ. While society may minimize the significance of pet loss, our grief was valid and deserving of acknowledgment. I embraced the support we found within online communities and through alternative means as we navigated the uncharted territory of our grief-stricken hearts. In doing so, I found moments of peace, connection, and a renewed sense of love for our PJ.

As a grief counselor, I advocate against comparing one's losses, for each person's grief is experienced at its fullest intensity. The pain and sorrow we feel are valid and should never be diminished. Each person grieves in their own way, and it's my mission to provide support, understanding, and tools to navigate these turbulent waters. The journey of grief is a winding path devoid of a destination. It's a journey filled with ups and downs, where healing and acceptance intertwine and where the memories of our loved ones continue to live on, inspiring us to cherish the love we shared and find gratitude for the legacy they left behind.

PJ's passing marked a pivotal moment in our lives that forever altered our family's landscape. The pain of his absence was searing, and our hearts carried the weight of sorrow. But within that pain, we discovered the resilience of the human spirit and the capacity to love and remember. PJ may no longer be physically present, but his spirit remains intertwined with ours. We're forever changed by the love and joy he brought into our lives, cherishing the memories and embracing the journey of grief, one step at a time.

THE TOOL

In the introductory chapter, I shared the experience of my mother's death during my teenage years. In this chapter, I delve into the sorrow of losing a beloved pet—two challenging experiences, each distinct in its difficulty. Self-care during both instances became paramount. On my personal journey, I've discovered solace through various self-care techniques. Following the loss of both my mother and PJ, I strongly felt the need for connection. During my adolescent years, I sought solace within a grief group. After PJ's death, my husband became my unwavering source of support and understanding, providing support as we navigated this shared grief.

While exploring these chapters and the tools from the 25 courageous authors, identify the tools that resonate with you. Download this self-care plan at https://www.centerforinformedgrief.com/navigatinggriefcourses to develop your own distinct plan. Take a moment to fill your self-care plan with strategies that harmonize with your personal journey. It's not about having all the answers but rather about honoring your desire for understanding and growth.

Remember, self-care plans are deeply personal and naturally evolve over time. These questions are meant to steer you in crafting self-care strategies that align with your distinct needs and circumstances. Creating a structured approach to navigating emotional challenges when we feel adrift becomes a lifeline. It's a poignant reminder that our well-being holds significance amid pain. It's a declaration: "I'm hurting, and I deserve care." This blueprint evolves into your personalized toolkit, bringing even the slightest comfort.

As you venture into the upcoming questions, bear in mind that you're crafting something meaningful—a method to nurture your own heart as it charts its course through life's storms. As you engage with the questions, keep in mind that you're creating something significant—an avenue to tend to your heart as it finds its way.

WHAT ACTIVITIES BRING YOU COMFORT

- What activities or hobbies have provided you comfort in the past? How can you integrate these into your current routine?

SOCIAL SUPPORT

- Who do you feel most comfortable sharing your feelings with? How can you reach out to them when needed?

PHYSICAL WELL-BEING

- How are you taking care of your body? Are you getting enough sleep, maintaining a balanced diet, and engaging in regular physical activity?

MINDFULNESS AND RELAXATION

- What techniques help you relax and stay present? Can you incorporate mindfulness exercises, meditation, or deep breathing practices?

CREATIVE EXPRESSION

- Do you enjoy any creative outlets such as writing, drawing, painting, photography, or playing music? How can you use it to express your emotions?

NATURE AND OUTDOORS

- Do you find solace in nature? How can you spend more time outdoors, whether it's taking walks, gardening, or simply sitting in a peaceful setting?

SETTING BOUNDARIES

- Are there situations or people that drain your energy? How can you establish healthy boundaries to protect your well-being?

PROFESSIONAL SUPPORT

- Have you considered seeking support from a counselor, or support group? How can you take steps to access professional help if needed?

MEMORIALIZING AND REMEMBERING

- How would you like to honor your grief? Are there rituals or activities that could bring comfort?

LIMITING STRESSORS

- What stressors can you identify right now? How can you reduce or manage these stressors to prioritize your well-being?

PERSONAL GOALS

- Are there small goals you'd like to set for yourself? These could be related to self-care, personal growth, or trying new activities.

GRATITUDE PRACTICE

- How can you incorporate gratitude into your daily life? Focusing on positive aspects can provide a new perspective during tough times.

For those seeking additional guidance and support in their self-care and grief journey, I'm delighted to extend an invitation to a free self-care grief class available at https://www.centerforinformedgrief.com/navigatinggriefcourses. This class comprehensively explores various techniques and strategies to navigate the challenging terrain of grief while fostering personal growth and resilience.

Allow this book to stand by you as a companion, providing insights and tools that, like mosaic pieces, gradually weave a portrait of hope and resilience. Remember, self-care is crucial for honoring your emotions and nurturing your well-being during grief.

Kelly Daugherty, a seasoned social worker with over two decades in the clinical field, is a Fellow in Thanatology: Death, Dying, and Bereavement. Anchored in Malta, New York, she owns Greater Life Grief Counseling and the Center for Informed Grief, LLC. Her commitment to the domain of grief stems from her personal journey, which began with her mother's death from breast cancer during her teenage years. This significant loss led Kelly to volunteer with a Hospice Children's Bereavement program and set the foundation for her career. Every day, Kelly finds meaning in her grief by helping both individuals navigate the complexities of grief and professionals aiming to understand it better.

Determined to revolutionize how grief support is provided, Kelly offers a wealth of tools and insights to those grappling with the death of loved ones and to the professionals dedicated to helping them. The Center for Informed Grief aims to create a more grief-informed society by benefiting individuals, families, schools, and broader communities. Through comprehensive training for educators and therapists, consultation with schools, online courses, and active social media communities, Kelly ensures that nobody faces their grief journey in solitude.

Kelly also co-owns Healing Strides, LLC, which blends emotional and physical well-being, culminating in a unique 7-week program that pairs therapeutic grief groups with 5K race training for women. The program aims to foster improved coping, emotional well-being, and physical fitness, leading to a richer sense of personal growth and meaning-making.

In addition, Kelly has contributed her expertise to the books "Holistic Mental Health, Volume 1" and "Brave Kids, Volume 1."

Outside of her professional life, Kelly cherishes time spent with her husband, Kevin, their dog, Boomer, and her seven nieces and nephews. She also enjoys DIY art projects, walking, and running, and loves visits to zoos, the beach, and Disney World.

Connect with Kelly for innovative trainings on grief and loss with the Center for Informed Grief at

https://www.centerforinformedgrief.com/trainings-consultation

Learn more about Kelly at: https://linktr.ee/kellydaugherty

CHAPTER 2

Unlocking New Depths of the Heart

How to Transform Loss

Julie Funkhouser, B.S.

MY STORY

I did it again.

I stuffed pain. And stress. And worry. And fear. It's wild how my brain tells me I'm not holding onto it. What a sneaky and relentless jerk. My mind often operates like an overworked and underpaid elf up at the North Pole on Christmas Eve. And I'll tell you, that makes one grumpy, terrified, and tired magic maker.

I know my mind tries to keep me safe. It wants to plan and project the next eighteen moves in front of me to prepare for the twenty-seven possibilities of things that could happen, leading to the loss of someone or something I love. At the very least, it'll brace me for something bad that may happen.

I can give myself grace because I know I've experienced some heavy stuff in my life, but there's a part of me that still gets so frustrated.

Why do I keep doing this? I've got 15 years in recovery. I practice yoga almost daily. And I'm a Reiki healer for goodness sake. I must not be doing this life thing right.

Then I remember.

Because pain hurts. Stress is overwhelming. Worry is unnerving. Fear is scary. That's why.

Because I am human.

And because I know grief.

*

On September 11th, 2018, grief arrived at my door—literally.

My best friend and I just opened our first recovery home. I was overjoyed by seeing our vision come alive, supporting other women on their recovery journey from addiction. We birthed a space of promise, hope, and connection.

The sun glistened, and the air felt warm that day. It was a picture-perfect landscape, a haven of new beginnings.

And I felt hollow inside.

My husband Danny was unraveling over the last week, spiraling in his addiction. After almost six years of recovery and a wonderful life built together, the disease slowly dug its ruthless claws into him.

Many moments within those last two years were spent with trembling hands and eyes glued to the phone. It often felt like I held my breath until he walked in the door. I grew used to this way of life, coasting on tiptoes and picking apart every way I could keep our family intact.

As a person in recovery myself, I rationally knew I was powerless over the disease. I knew this wasn't a matter of love or lack thereof. I knew it wasn't my fault. These were the same sentiments I shared with others when addiction and relapse entered their homes.

So, when it showed up in my family, I tried to adopt those attitudes. In some moments, I did. But mostly, I took on the role of professional overthinker, worrier, and control freak. I just couldn't stop my incessant and panicked mind, swirling in a cyclone of fear.

I can save him. I can fix this. He will stop for me and the kids. I can keep him safe. I know what to do; I'm an addict too. We'll just get him back into treatment. This is what I do for a living anyway. Plus, I'm the mom. I'm the wife. I keep everything in order and everyone together. Everything will be okay.

It felt easier and safer to spend time spinning up in my brain than it was to feel the pain in my heart, watching him slowly disappear. It was as if I was witnessing the light of his spirit grow dimmer. I knew he was in there, but no matter what I did or said, I couldn't reach him.

But whenever he walked in the door each evening, I exhaled.

It was the exhale of relief. The exhale of a moment's calm. The exhale of transient peace.

But the last night and the few prior, he didn't come home.

I came to work after dropping the kids at daycare on this picture-perfect landscape day. I figured I might as well obsess at our new company instead of at the house.

My muscles hurt from tensing as I stared down at the dark red carpet, uncontrollably bouncing my knee and tapping my pen on the desk. Suddenly, I heard three loud knocks at the door.

I saw the police uniform from the window and figured we had a situation with a client. But strangely, my mom was standing next to him. Her body was stoic, and her hands were clenched. I don't know if she even blinked.

Weird. Mom must have driven up to help me with the kids amidst this insanity.

"Are you Julie Funkhouser?" he asked.

"Yes, I am," I answered. I couldn't wait to feel that exhale of relief.

Oh my gosh, thank goodness. He must have been arrested.

"I'm sorry to tell you this," he paused for the longest two seconds of my life.

Then four words stripped my soul bare.

"Your husband passed away."

The whispering of the wind went silent. The backdrop of nature's colors in the front yard went hazy. My legs buckled. I gripped onto the doorframe, clenching for dear life, unable to stop my collapse to the ground. I remember crying out over and over, "No!" as the officer stood over me. I couldn't stop shouting that word. I'm not sure how many times it came out of my mouth; it's all I could create.

I heard noises and voices, and yet, everything sounded quiet.

I saw people around me and cars driving by, and yet, everything looked blurry.

My thoughts were racing, and yet, everything was still.

I felt everything, and yet, I felt nothing.

My mom and my friend physically lifted me up, my legs too wobbly to maneuver myself to a chair. With my eyes glazed over, I stared blankly into space.

And I exhaled. I felt my entire body loosen. The exhaustion of the last two years washed over me. And in quiet, hidden corners of my heart, I felt relief. No more fighting, no more terror, no more worry, no more bracing.

Immediately, I felt nauseous, sickened, and shameful.

How can you feel any bit of relief? What is wrong with you?

I swiftly shoved those parts back into their corners and locked them in (I didn't unlock this part again until much later when I realized it was safe to acknowledge and honor this piece of my grief).

My understanding of life was flipped upside down in a millisecond, and I questioned everything. With grief digging its way into unexplored crevices of my soul, Danny's death shook me more alive, more awake, and more connected than I ever thought possible.

I became a new person that day.

I didn't know it at the time, but this was to be the cornerstone of my own spiritual transformation.

This was my rebirth.

*

That night may have been the hardest night of my life. I was faced with an unanswerable question.

How do I tell them?

It was dark and quiet outside as I pulled up to my house. Each step toward the front door felt like pulling my feet out of quicksand.

I walked inside, and there he was. Our son, seventeen months old, bouncing in his jumper. His giggles sent glimmers of warmth to my skin. As I leaned down and held his cheeks in my hands, I felt a lump in my throat. My chest began to ache. My muscles tensed as I took a deep breath and turned toward the playroom.

There she was, our four-year-old daughter, creating magic in her playroom with her baby dolls.

"Hi, baby. I need to tell you something," I whispered.

"What is it, Mommy?" she asked.

I struggled to find the strength to speak. I inhaled.

"Daddy went to heaven today."

Silence.

"So, Daddy's never coming home?" She wiggled closer to me.

"No, baby. He was sick in his mind and in his heart, so God took him to heaven where there is no more pain."

I grabbed her and held her tight as she nestled her head on my shoulder. I tried to hold it in and swallow that lump in the throat. Then, I felt a soft tug from those quiet corners of my heart.

Show her it's okay. Show her it's okay to feel this.

Tears flowed down my cheeks like a river's current.

That night, I crawled into bed with her to watch her sleep. Her eyelashes fluttered while she danced in dreamland.

All I heard was the torture and verbal assault of my mind. I replayed over and over everything I could've done to stop this.

Suddenly, she gasped and reached her arms straight up toward the sky, just holding them there. With her eyes still closed, a huge smile spread across her face like a ray of sunshine illuminating the room. She took a huge, deep breath and then dropped her arms, snuggling back into the covers.

I never saw anything so divinely and inexpressibly beautiful. And I knew.

Danny visited her. He was right there within arms' reach.

I cried. I prayed. And I exhaled.

*

The months to follow were filled with blackout periods I still don't remember, except for a few fleeting memories.

I remember how exhausting it was to chew and swallow food.

I remember being paralyzed on the floor as I literally tried to coach my brain on what body parts to move in order to stand up.

I remember my refrigerator constantly overflowed with delivered dinners from family, friends, and the community.

I remember an average of fifty unread texts at all times.

I remember the silence when the funeral ended.

I remember the first night alone after my parents moved back to their house.

Everyone's lives went back to normal, and I felt angry and bitter.

And here I was, a widow and a single mom at thirty years old, swirling in unanswered questions and no sense of direction.

But, I remember my elliptical. That nifty piece of equipment became my first release tool and my path toward soul excavation, spiritual exploration, and my heart's transformation.

I was so unbelievably exhausted all of the time and yet had so much energy that I felt like I would explode if I didn't move.

So, every night after I put the kids to bed, I went to the basement, blasted music, and cranked that elliptical until my clothes were covered in sweat, my skin was vibrating, and I couldn't move my legs a second longer. But every time I got off that elliptical, I felt reprieve.

And every time, I cried, I prayed, and I exhaled.

In the undercurrent of pain's intense grip, divine love whispered hope into my heart. It didn't click until later that this desperation to get to my elliptical every night was my intense craving to feel peace.

Running my butt off on that elliptical was, in essence, me running to God.

I ran to God in every way I could.

*

I was guided to church, yoga, meditation, and energy healing along this journey in search of lengthening those divinely and powerfully fleeting moments. I was learning that in the expansiveness of loss, therein lies the opportunity to access and explore parts of the heart I never knew were there.

For so long, my baseline was maxed out on the stress meter, operating outside of my body and all in my mind. So, whenever I broke down, those soul-cleansing moments brought me to full presence and in direct contact with pure love.

Losing Danny cracked me wide open and raw. I literally don't know if I could've stopped the torrential tear tidal waves. There were plenty of times I tried to hold it in, but my body literally said, "Nope. You can't stop it. Here it comes."

I am so grateful for that today.

My kids often saw me cry. I didn't hide it. I couldn't. I may have held the heavy breakdowns for my elliptical time, but I let them see me grieve. In turn, they saw me as human and felt safe to be human, too. Those cleansing tears helped give their dad a clear channel to show his unwavering love through all kinds of signs, the biggest being feathers. We have one mighty fine collection. We learned to lean into the love that exists within us, between us, above us, and around us.

I've learned that the heart can not only heal, but it can grow in size, unlock new depths, and cultivate an endless space for love. And in divine timing and clearly on purpose, God brought someone into my life whose heart holds space for mine in a way that regularly reminds me that it is, quite literally, a match made in heaven. Bringing our families together is one giant "God-wink," as I like to call them.

I see the world from a softer lens, with a new respect for the human experience. I feel more deeply for others, I seek more meaningful connections, and I grow gentler with myself (which is the toughest task).

I'm also a human who has had some traumatic and painful experiences.

So, of course, I slip back into panic and obsession. I do it more often than I'd like to admit.

It's quite the paradox to feel so energetically sensitive and connected to God while simultaneously feeling deep fear and worry creep in and out.

So, then I release. Again. And again. And again. Sometimes, I hold it longer than others. Sometimes I shove it deep without realizing it, and it starts to come out sideways.

But every time I let go, I set my soul free and give myself permission to live life wide open, allowing myself to feel it all deeply.

I know grief leaves a unique imprint in every heart. I know healing is messy. And I know how powerfully beautiful it feels when we let go and ride the waves.

This is the space where loss can be transformed into connection with self, God, others, and humanity itself. It's where the heart opens up all of its hidden pockets to expand our capacity to love and be loved in this world and beyond. Love is the highest vibration in the universe.

In our essence, that is exactly what we are. Love.

This is the key to unlocking new depths of the heart.

It's okay if I forget, as long as I remember.

I am doing this life thing completely and perfectly right.

Because I am alive.

Because I am awake.

Because I still exhale.

THE TOOL

Our heart center is our divine path through which God communicates with us. Our heart center is the portal through which we feel God's pure and perfect intentions. Our heart center is our key to freedom and awakening.

As the grief experience presses its weight onto our hearts, we can feel blocked. Stuck. Heavy. We collect and hold onto this grief with tremendous terror at the thought of releasing it. The idea of rumbling with this profound pain can feel unimaginable.

Honoring these emotions and acknowledging their presence in our hearts is important. And feeling and releasing them is vital to heal. By cleansing this heart space, our spirit grows lighter. Our energy feels softer. Our heart slowly begins its journey to vibrancy again, perhaps more radiant than ever before, as we cleanse all of the deep pockets and crevices of our divine connective source.

So, breathe with me. Cleanse with me. Release with me.

And unlock new depths of your heart you never knew existed.

VISUALIZATION MEDITATION

Visit https://www.instagram.com/two_real_chicks/ for the guided meditation.

Settle yourself into a seated position with your spine straight and your sit bones nestled into the Earth. You may close your eyes or cast them down, whatever feels right for you.

Begin to bring focus to your breath, inhaling deeply through the belly and lengthening your exhales to slow your central nervous system. Enter into the present moment.

Now, bring your focus into your heart. What do you see?

Perhaps you see dark, murky colors or sense a hardening around the heart like dry clay. Maybe it looks sluggish and stuck. Congested.

What do you feel?

Does it feel heavy? Slow? Stagnant? Cluttered? Messy? Do you feel sad? Angry? Whatever is coming up, it is meant to come. It all belongs.

Now, place one hand over your heart. On your inhale, envision a bright, white light entering your heart from the middle of your back. Breathe it in from the back of the heart. Say to yourself, "I allow Divine love into my heart."

On your exhale, envision that dark, low, stagnant energy leaving through the front of your heart center as it becomes absorbed by the universe. Feel the sorrow, the pain, the fear, the worry clearing. Say to yourself, "I release the pain to allow more love."

Check in with your body and your heart center after each cycle. Repeat this breath as many times as you need to until you feel your heart center feel lighter, open, and vibrant. Perhaps you see it growing in actual size, changing colors, pumping rhythmically. You may cry, feel a deep sense of gratitude, or sense loved ones in heaven close by. Everyone's experience of what they see, hear, feel, and sense is different. Trust what is coming up for you.

When you feel that it's time to finish this practice, you may rub your hands together, creating warm, loving, healing energy in your palms, and place both hands on your heart.

Say to yourself,

"I am safe to release.
My heart is opening.
I receive God's pure love.
I deserve to heal."

Honor yourself for your bravery in this practice. By cleansing the deep corners of your heart, new depths of abundant love and light fill your spirit. Feel the peace in the exhale.

Julie Funkhouser's own personal grief experience not only inspired the chapter within this book, but has profoundly changed her life and the way she shows up to live every day. It's her commitment to continue transforming tragic loss into a deeply connected, heart-centered life. She is also a co-author of another Brave Healer Production piece, "Brave Kids," a story of grief and healing through the eyes of her daughter.

Driven by her own story of addiction and recovery, Julie is the Co-Founder and Chief Executive Officer of The Recovery Connection, a substance use treatment center in Winchester, Virginia. A holistically-focused, trauma-informed program, TRC aims to provide a meaningful healing experience on the path to freedom. With close to a decade of experience in the industry, Julie finds deep fulfillment not only in the strategic development of the company with her visionary spirit but also in building impactful relationships and supporting a mission-driven culture rooted in compassion and true authenticity.

She is also a Certified Reiki Master who finds bliss in the opportunity to share the gift of energy work and holistic healing with those around her while simultaneously focusing on her own spiritual growth and continued evolution. Some of her favorite things include practicing yoga, catching sunsets, and spending time with family and friends. Julie resides in Middletown, Virginia, with her fiancé, Jimmy, and their five amazing children.

Connect with her: https://linktr.ee/juliemarie3751

CHAPTER 3

When a Client Dies

Creating a Safe Space to Grieve

Brittany Nelson, PsyD, LMFT, RPT-S

MY STORY

In my office, I can hear the pitter-patter of little feet running up the stairs as I sit waiting for my new client.

The door opens, and the most beautiful head of golden, bouncing, perfectly shaped curls appears, surrounding a round face, cherub cheeks, and a wide grin.

"Hi, I'm Alex."

"Hi, I'm Ms. Brittany."

And so, our client-therapist journey began.

"What's this? What's that?" she asked as she assertively toured herself around my office, making herself right at home with the toys and the books on the floor.

Her smile and laugh lit up the room as she played games. Her little giggles were contagious as she found ways to integrate her sarcastic humor into her drawings. I didn't know how much sarcasm could be trapped inside a little six-year-old body until I met Alex.

We all have clients that stick with us, and she is one of mine.

Little did I know, almost ten years later, I'd feel a wave of grief smash upon me as I was hit with her unexpected death. It felt like I was washed out to a deserted island, screaming "SOS" but painfully realizing that I was alone in my grief. I kept asking myself the same question over and over: -When I met Alex, she was sassy and smart, far beyond her years. Every session had hard work but lots of laughs. One thing I admired the most was that she was ready to do her work.

"Ms. Brittany, what's this book?" Alex casually asked one day while looking through my bookshelf during our session.

"It's called *The Children's Place…At the Heart of Recovery.*

"What's it about?"

"Come look. It has drawings and pictures from children whose parents struggle with using drugs."

"Just like me."

"Just like you."

"I want to make a book like that." So, she did. Alex could do anything she set her mind to. We laid out a timeline of life events. She looked so studious as we went over her life from birth to age six, identifying critical moments she wanted to include in her story. She drew a picture of each event, and we worked together to write the narrative of her life.

We worked on her story for months. One event a session.

On some days, the door to my office would burst open, and I would hear, "Ms. Brittany I thought of something I want to add." We'd find the right spot in her narrative. It was inspiring to me to watch her process. I was a witness to her healing journey, and it was amazing. Alex had such a passion for sharing her story. She didn't shy away from any feeling or topic. She was brutally honest about her experiences and how she felt in response. She put so much effort into drawing out each picture so thoughtfully. As any true author does, she finished her book with a front cover, back cover, biography, ISBN and UPC code, and price (her book was not cheap).

I was so inspired I ended up laminating the pages and spiral-binding the book, and at our last session, she shared her narrative with her mom. I watched as Mom held back the tears in her eyes as her daughter recounted her life experiences, the good and the bad, culminating with this beautiful, bright family portrait at the end with the client, mom, and her siblings, all holding hands, with a shining sun and colorful flowers. That was where Alex saw her family now—healed and together in the sun.

It was such a beautiful process. Being the inspiring child she was, she even permitted me to keep a copy, names redacted, to use with other children in therapy as a support, just like the book on my shelf inspired her. After about a year and a half of therapy, at seven years old, a "published" author, this youth completed her therapy process and left behind a part of herself to help others with their healing journey.

Alex's book did help others. I used it with other clients over the years and reminisced back on that sassy little girl with the golden curls whose bravery to face her life story helped others.

About five years later, life got rough for Alex, and I found that same head of golden curls back in my office. The drama of junior high. Dad relapsed on drugs. Separation from a sibling she loved dearly.

"Do you remember me?" I asked.

"No."

"I used to meet with you when you were younger, and I still have something here that you made."

"Really? Can I see it?"

I found the book on my bookshelf. I sat back and watched her face as she read through it. Her expressions changed from pensive to remembering and then to throwing her head and body back on the couch with laughter at a particular picture where she drew a lot of cat poop.

"I wrote this?"

"Yes."

Although she didn't remember me or the work we did together, that book seemed to break down any walls of resistance about coming back into the therapy process.

Over the next two and a half years, we continued to work together until she moved.

About six months later, on a telehealth session with Alex's sibling, Aubrey, whom I was also seeing for therapy, Alex popped into the background.

"Hi."

"Hey there, Alex, I didn't know you were back."

"Yup, I moved back home."

And then she was off. Mom would later tell me Alex was introduced to drugs by some family, and when Mom discovered this, she brought Alex back home and enrolled her in drug treatment.

I finished treatment with Alex's sister. Overall, the family was doing well. Alex was still struggling, but she was getting the services she needed. I never could've guessed what the future held.

Less than a year later, sitting at my desk working on a Friday morning, I received a call from an unknown number. I don't normally answer unknown numbers, but for some reason, this morning, I did.

"Hello?"

"Is this Brittany Nelson?"

"Yes." It was a social worker from the local hospital.

"Are you the therapist for Aubrey? It's a crisis."

"Yes, what happened?"

"Aubrey's sibling just died, and I want to know if you can resume seeing them?"

"Yes, of course. Which sibling?"

"Alex."

Gut punch. I felt like I couldn't breathe. I couldn't think. I couldn't process it.

What happened? How could this be happening? She is just a child.

I called Alex's mom.

"Christina, I don't know what to say. Sorry isn't enough. But I'm here if you need it." I found myself struggling to get out any words. Words seemed insufficient to express condolences for something no parent should have to experience.

Mom explained it was a suspected overdose. It was too late when she found Alex in the morning, and she died in the hospital.

Again, I couldn't help but think: *How could this be happening? She is just a child.*

I tried to focus on work, but my mind just kept going back to those little golden curls and vibrant smiles.

She is just a child.

I began to feel claustrophobic in my house. My mind was racing, wondering how this could happen. *How is this wonderful child no longer with us?*

I had to leave. I had to move. My body wanted to race as much as my mind was.

I went to the beach and walked. I breathed in deep breaths of the air, heavy with salt and ocean spray. I walked back and forth for hours, thinking everything and nothing. I felt everything and nothing.

Should I feel everything or nothing? This was not my child. This was a client. A client I had known for ten years and watched grow up from a young girl to a young woman.

She was just a client.

But some clients are not *just* clients. Some connect more. Some connect less.

After a few hours, I left the beach and went home to my curly-haired child who was not much younger than Alex.

She was just a child. As a mother, I cannot even imagine.

I hugged both my kids a little tighter that night.

I did not go to the funeral. In therapy, Alex's sibling was talking about the planning process for the funeral and the details, and my work was to support them in preparing for experiencing the funeral of their older sister.

I will be honest. I was hoping I'd be invited. I felt like I needed to go to the funeral as a way of helping to process my grief, a way of helping with the finality of it. I never received an invite.

My clinical brain said: *You are the last thing on this family's mind when a mother is grieving the unexpected loss of her child.*

My grieving brain said: *You need to be able to be in a space with others grieving the same loss.*

I think this is one of the challenging things to battle with as a grieving therapist: the head vs. the heart. The head is the clinician who knows what's clinically appropriate, but the grief is in the heart. This was a part of my process of feeling so alone. As the therapist, I couldn't ask if I could attend; that would be focusing on my own needs and not the needs of the family or the client, but the grieving part of me longed to ask to be a part of the group grieving this vibrant young woman together. I needed a connection to others experiencing the loss of her, and yet it was a connection I was unable to seek out.

I've experienced many intense things in my time as a therapist, but never have I felt so acutely alone.

Therapists have an interesting job. We're taught that the most crucial component of the therapeutic process is the relationship. The relationship is professional; there are boundaries to maintain, and yet, we're not machines; we are all human, and we come to truly care about our clients.

We are the safe space, the containers, for the deepest, darkest secrets, most intense feelings, and incredible traumas. Things clients have never, and may never, share with anyone else. There are times when we may come to know our clients more intimately than any other person in their life and may be the only safe person in theirs. In this line of work, we're bound to make connections and be impacted by our clients and their stories. It only makes sense that when a client dies, we grieve.

When my client died, feeling lost, I turned to Google—looking for books, advice, or anything to support me through this process. I'm not the only one who has gone through this experience. The minuscule amount of information I found was disappointing. In a line of work full of trauma and grief work, where we talk so much about self-care, burnout, and secondary trauma, how could I not find more information about how clinicians can deal with the death of a client?

So, how does a therapist grieve?

A therapist needs to grieve with self-compassion, without judgment, and with a lot of self-care. I had to let go of a lot of "shoulds" in my process:

I should not have such strong feelings about this since this was a client.

I should have better boundaries than this.

Letting go of the "shoulds" was a crucial part of my self-care journey to healing and growth, both personally and professionally. I also had to accept that I was far more isolated in my grief of a client than in my other experiences of personal grief, which made self-care more important.

THE TOOL

The goal of my tool is to create a safe space that can be utilized for self-care during the grieving process. Many of us are likely familiar with calm spaces and containers, which I combine to create a safe place. Safe spaces are visualization exercises that can be created either through strict visualizing, creating a drawing, constructing a sand tray, recalling a memory, etc.—whatever medium speaks to you to help you with this process. The goal of a safe place is to create an outlet for times when we may be experiencing our grief, which is either becoming overwhelming, or we're not in a space to safely feel, and we need a place to reset.

When constructing your safe place, the first piece is to create a visual of a place in which you feel calm, comfortable, and safe. This visual can be only in your mind, or you can create an outward expression of your safe place that you can hold in your visualization. The place you create can be real or imagined. Next, we're going to further develop our safe space by integrating all of our senses. What do you hear? Smell? What are the things you can reach out to touch and feel around you? Is there anything you can taste in your safe place? With all the senses engaged, take a slow, deep breath. And again. And again.

Now, close your eyes and visualize your safe place and all the sensations associated with it as you continue to breathe slowly. I want you to imagine a container in your safe space. This can be any sort of container you like. Construct it however it fits into your safe place. Ensure your container is strong enough to hold any thoughts or feelings of grief that may come to your mind.

Now, imagine using this box whenever a thought or a feeling of grief becomes too much. Hold that thought/feeling until you can come back to your safe space and sit with your grief. Continue to breathe until you feel a sensation of calm, then take one more deep breath and open your eyes.

During sessions with clients, it would be challenging to close your eyes and go through the whole process. But when you can practice the calming piece routinely, during the session, you can take a slow breath and visualize your safe place and your container, and it can support in bringing you back down to a more grounded place in the moment. For example, there have been times when I've been in sessions with clients, especially in the early sessions with my client's sibling, when I was triggered and needed to find a way to quickly regroup. Being able to take a few deep breaths, think of my safe place, and place my feelings into my container was helpful for me to quickly shift back my focus, knowing I'd come back to my feelings for processing when I could.

References

Moe, J., & Ziegler, R. (1998). A Children's Place...At The Heart of Recovery. Acid Test.

Brittany Nelson, PsyD, LMFT, RPT-S, specializes in working with at-risk youth for the past 16 years. Brittany's extensive experience includes working with youth and families who have complex trauma histories and/or struggle with addiction, leading to various grief and loss issues. Brittany dedicates her full-time work to managing multiple mental health programs supporting youth to remain in family-based settings over incarceration, foster care, residential treatment centers, hospitalizations, etc. Brittany also supports growth in the mental health community by providing supervision to clinicians, associates, graduate students, and other mental health staff. Aside from her full-time position, Brittany also has a small private practice where she continues her therapy work with clients and families. Brittany also provides training on various mental health topics locally and on a state level.

Connect with Brittany:
Email: BrittanyNelsonPsyD@yahoo.com
LinkedIn: https://www.linkedin.com/in/brittany-nelson-lmft53290/

CHAPTER 4

FIGHTING FOR MEMORIES

ANTICIPATORY GRIEF, RESILIENCE, AND ALZHEIMER'S

Cheri Davies, MSW

MY STORY

There is an old saying, "Life can turn on a dime," but my life changed on a clock. There was nothing special about Oct 11, 2018, except I went with my husband to see his primary care physician because he was having some issues with his memory. I convinced myself it was nothing, and he wasn't paying attention to details. After 20-plus years of marriage, I didn't expect him to know every time I went to Target or the hair salon. We had a comfortable routine, and as annoying as it was when he forgot what I was doing, it wasn't a marriage-ending event. Even when my son came home from school in his junior year of high school and said, "I think something is wrong with Dad. I think he has Alzheimer's. We learned about it in school today, and here's a pamphlet." I responded with, "Your dad doesn't have Alzheimer's. He just doesn't pay attention."

The following summer at camp, one of my husband's close friends raised more concerns. "Cheri, I think there's something wrong with Chris. He kept telling me the same thing and doesn't realize he had already told me that." Two people I loved had raised the alarm about his memory problems for the second time in over a year. So here we were, sitting in a bland, pale, beige room on uncomfortable chairs, waiting for our family physician to tell me he was fine. *Everything's fine* was my mantra. *He doesn't pay attention. It's nothing.*

The first part of the conversation went as I expected. *Nothing to worry about. This will turn out to be a nice half-day off from work.*

My brain kicked into reality when my husband said, "I have a coffee fairy that keeps putting cream in my coffee. I don't think I do it, but it's magically in my mug. Like four days a week."

What did he just say? Did he say coffee fairy? That's not normal. What is going on?

I'm certain I had 100 thoughts going on simultaneously. The doctor gave him a brief mental status exam and then came the clock test. It was a simple task in theory. Three steps were all his doctor gave him. "Draw the circle for a clock, insert all the numbers in the correct position, and then place the hands at ten to eleven." Patiently, our doctor repeated the directions when my husband had a mix of confusion and determination on his face. Sitting six feet away, seeing what he was drawing was almost impossible.

What I could see was the concentration on his face. *This shouldn't be this hard,* I thought. Panic started to move from my stomach up to my chest. I caught myself holding my breath and had to consciously work on getting air into my lungs. *Breathe.* I repeated this to myself as I tried to keep my composure. I wanted to run out of the room to stop whatever it was that was happening from being confirmed. Instead, I grabbed the sides of my small metal chair, actively trying to stop myself from being the one needing a doctor. *If I start to cry, I may not stop,* is all I could think. Pushing the panic down, I waited to see what he drew.

After what seemed like 20 minutes, which was more likely only five minutes, my husband turned the paper towards the doctor and said, "I had some trouble with putting the time you said on the clock." I leaned over, looking at the drawing. I felt panic stick in my throat like I swallowed a golf ball, and it was slowly cutting off my airways. Fear, it was most definitely fear. The clock was somewhat oval-shaped. It looked like a lopsided egg, not a circle. Numbers twelve through six were close to their correct placement, but seven through eleven were bunched together where nine should be.

Why does that clock look so messed up?' My thoughts started to race.

Is he having a stroke? Is this a joke? No, he wouldn't play a joke like that. Get a hold of yourself and stop panicking.

But then I noticed the hands of the clock. What should've been straight lines on the face of the clock looked like shaky squiggles with pointy hats. I couldn't even tell exactly where the misshaped hands pointed because my brain shut down. I just knew they weren't in the right place. I felt the tears starting to well up in my eyes and all I could think was, *I was wrong all this time, something IS wrong.*

The doctor started planning on how to discover what was happening to his short-term memory. "Get an MRI, a PET scan, a neurological evaluation." I heard the words coming from the doctor's mouth, but they sounded like a foreign language. My fight-or-flight response was in full flight mode. All I wanted to do was run from the room and pretend I hadn't seen that misshapen clock with the scrambled numbers. I wanted to have a do-over. It was magical thinking at its finest.

If I leave and come back, maybe this won't really happen, and everything will be back to normal.

The social worker in me finally kicked in, and I got the information we needed. I found out who to call and started the ball rolling toward finding answers about his memory issues. It took another eight months to get a definitive answer. My son was right. It was Younger Onset Alzheimer's. He was 51 years old.

My life changed in a single moment and became two distinct segments, before October 2018 and after. Alzheimer's permeates every facet of my life. I make decisions every day based on how it impacts my husband.

How do I keep him active and engaged in life when he sometimes struggles with basic tasks? How do we take advantage of our time to live our life to the fullest under circumstances beyond our control?

These things feel very conflicting and overwhelming at times.

I didn't understand all my emotions because I had no one I knew dealing with their young, active, vibrant spouse slowly dying from a terminal illness.

I didn't understand grief. I thought grief was something that happened when someone you love dies, not when they are still alive. I'd never heard the phrase "anticipatory grief," and now I live in that world. Mourning our dreams for the future and our retirement plans became my new normal.

My grief is unpredictable and messy. Some days, it stays in the background of my life; other times, it's front and center, taking my breath away and bringing me to my knees. I have to pull myself back up and start over because I have responsibilities to my family and myself. I consciously work to maintain my sense of joy despite the diagnosis. Some days are easier than others, but I work hard not to lose my sense of happiness in all the sadness. I don't want to regret missing out on the time we have left. It's taken time to figure out what works for us, but we're doing the best we can. We focus on the now and make as many memories as possible.

As my life changed in that non-descript doctor's office, everything around me remained the same. It was as if everyone around me was living in color, and somehow, my world had turned black and white. I was acting my way through my days, pretending I was still the person I was before that lopsided clock knocked me down and broke my heart. I was a school social worker working in a special education program at the time. My students and teachers needed me, yet I felt disconnected from what everyone else expected of me. I felt an enormous sense of guilt for not being enough of what everyone needed from me. My colleagues were very supportive of me, but there was an invisible wall separating us, which only I could feel. They needed me at school, and all I wanted to do was be at home. It was exhausting trying to be everything to everyone around me.

Because of the overwhelming emotions I experienced, I put unrealistic expectations on myself. I had the misguided belief that I should manage everyone around me to keep them from feeling what I was feeling. It was a burden that I could not carry long. I had to face my feelings, which were incredibly painful, so that I could focus on what my son, husband and I needed to live the best life possible in the time we had left together. There was enormous freedom when I quit my full-time job and started my part-time private practice. I could still do the job I loved and have the time I desperately wanted at home. We're incredibly fortunate to have a robust circle of friends and family to support us on this journey. They each have their own form of anticipatory grief to process, but they show up for our family in beautiful ways.

Now, grief and I walk hand in hand. Sometimes, we walk together, but other times, I'm ahead, feeling like I can conquer the world. I forget that my grief is behind me. Other times, it trips me and drags me down to my knees, stepping on me like a bug on the pavement. I'm bound together now in both sadness and hope. I feel grief every day, even if it's a whisper in the background of my thoughts. I experience grief over the death of our future dreams together, even though he is physically here with me. Every time I must decide my future without my husband, I mourn what could've been.

What am I going to do without the person I planned so many retirement adventures with? Do I keep this house? Can I manage financially? Why do I already feel lonely when he's sitting here with me? Will I be alone the rest of my life?

It's a curious place to be emotionally because I intellectually know it's essential to be practical about big life decisions. However, it feels disloyal, like I'm moving on already while he's still alive.

I also had to grieve the changes to our social life, like having to go to a friend's wedding or 40th birthday party alone because he was no longer comfortable with people he didn't know well. It's a bitter pill to swallow when you know how much fun you have together, and then it disappears. I feel sad for my son, who won't have his father in his later adult years, to go fishing and watch their beloved New York sports teams.

There are days when I want to bury my head in the sand and pretend this isn't my life, but I give myself those moments without judgment. I consciously make sure not to stay in that space for long, however, because I know it will be harder to manage my emotions if I remain in denial. This is my real life, and I've found ways to stay in the moment, most of the time, which has enriched our lives in ways I couldn't have imagined before the diagnosis. Even when it's hard to feel joyful, there's an urgency to make memories now while we still have the time. Grief helped me discover the joy in small moments we often dismissed. Laughing at a TV show together, riding in the convertible, and holding hands on a walk all have new meaning and joyfulness. Alzheimer's forced me to prioritize what is important. For me, the priority is time. I've found strength in my soul that I didn't know I had, where I can access the happiness I couldn't find early in his diagnosis. I no longer take for granted the opportunities to be happy, present, and joyful with the people I love.

While navigating my new normal, I became connected with the Alzheimer's Association. A fantastic care manager spent several hours guiding me on navigating things I would need to know now, plus ideas for the future. It was incredibly hard for me to access any hope in the early days. Simply letting me know I wasn't alone in this journey was a start. It also became essential to channel my pain into a productive outlet. I became an advocate for the Northeastern New York chapter of the Alzheimer's Association. I used my voice to spread awareness in television appearances, podcasts, social media, and with our congressman. Without the support of our local staff, whom I now consider friends, I don't know that I would've been able to find my way through all the complexities of a disease like Alzheimer's. I do know that finding hope in my grief may have taken a lot longer without the many friends and family in my life who have been by my side through this journey. Alzheimer's has reshaped my life profoundly, but my resilience has been the guiding force that keeps me focused on living each day to the fullest.

THE TOOL

To manage all the information that comes with an Alzheimer's diagnosis, I kept all the documents, imaging, and reports in a convenient binder that I took to all the doctors' appointments. It was an important step for me to be able to communicate with the various specialists we would be having on our care team. Going to these specialists could be intimidating, so having the information on hand helped me answer questions confidently and accurately. This binder has been a lifeline that reduces my stress in already emotionally challenging appointments.

This checklist is a way to navigate any medical journey a person may be facing. It's convenient to have all your information in one place, and, in my experience, doctors appreciate you being able to give them information when they don't have access to it.

This happens frequently when you see providers in different groups' practices. You may have imaging done at another facility, see a holistic provider, and access services like speech or occupational therapy, all of which may not be connected to your doctor's network. Any records you can keep will help you advocate for whatever you need for your or your family member's care. Also, keep a notebook with all your questions for your doctor.

These appointments can be stressful, so be sure to give yourself time afterward to process the meeting if you are overwhelmed. Don't be surprised if appointments bring up feelings of grief. Take time after each appointment for some self-care.

Purchase these items from your favorite office supply store:

- A 3-inch, 3-ring binder: I chose purple, which is the color of the Alzheimer's Association.
- Sheet protectors for your paperwork.
- Folder tabs to separate the sections.

You can use a small composition book to write notes in the appointment.

Set up of sections: I suggest keeping them in chronological order in each section for easier access.

- Primary care provider: even if you have a digital portal, print your reports so you can refer to them in an appointment.
- Specialist (for us, it was the neurologist): print these if they are on a portal.
- Testing (this includes blood work): you may have other tests that can go in this section, like neurological testing, genetic testing, etc.
- Imaging (MRIs, X-rays, scans): After your appointment, you need two things from imaging. Ask for a copy of the report and a disk of the imaging. On the cover of the disk, write "Do not destroy." If you ever have a doctor's office make copies of the disk, it will remind them to return it to you.
- Insurance (keep paperwork of any prior approvals). Things like MRIs may need prior approval, and having a copy of the document will save you a headache if there is a dispute.

- Living will and health care proxy: This section is crucial to discuss with your family and doctor. I suggest everyone does this, even if they're in excellent health. Life is unpredictable, and someone may need this information to fulfill their wishes in an emergency.
- A living will will spell precisely what you would like to happen in various scenarios based on different healthcare emergencies. This can help reduce the chance of confusion about the choices you would like made on your behalf. Many websites can help create this document, or you can consult an attorney. Be sure to give a copy of this document to all your providers and whomever you choose to be your healthcare proxy.
- A healthcare proxy names the person (or people) you have chosen to oversee your care if you cannot make your own decisions. Make sure you have a candid conversation about your wishes with that person.
- Social security: paperwork related to applying for or receiving any benefits.

Use a notebook or a notetaking app during appointments.

It's hard to process large amounts of information at the doctor's, particularly if it's an emotional appointment that doesn't go as you hoped. The notes will help you when you get home and have time to reflect on what was discussed in the appointment. You will be less likely to miss important points if you take notes, decreasing your stress.

- Write any questions you may have before you go into the appointment.
- Document all impressions the doctor has on that visit.
- Write all recommendations for testing, imaging, etc.

Being a care partner for a family member is a life-changing event, but working with medical providers shouldn't be your biggest stressor. This simple system can reduce stress and help you confidently advocate for your family members.

Cheri Davies is an experienced Licensed Clinical Social Worker with over 16 years in the mental health field. Holding a master's degree in social work from Adelphi University, her professional journey has encompassed diverse domains, including roles within hospitals, educational institutions, not-for-profit agencies, and private practice.

In 2019, Cheri embarked on her dream of owning a private practice, Birch Hill Counseling, nestled in the picturesque landscapes of upstate New York.

Beyond her clinical undertakings, Cheri is the president and founder of Cheri Davies Coaching, LLC. Here, she channels her passion for writing and her unwavering commitment to advocacy. Collaboratively, she has partnered with Kelly Daugherty of the Center for Informed Grief to create divorce-oriented training for educators. This led to being invited to write a chapter in "The Grief Experience." Cheri also co-authored the bestselling compilation "Holistic Mental Health Vol 1" in 2022. As an unwavering champion for the Alzheimer's Association, Cheri uses her platform through television appearances, podcasts, and social media presence to illuminate various facets of the Alzheimer's community.

Cheri believes deeply in a Life-Work balance and cherishes moments with her family, friends, and black lab, Tillman. She loves spending time in the Adirondacks, traveling with friends, doing DIY projects, and camping. Her digital presence revolves around mental health and Alzheimer's advocacy. You can follow her on Instagram at Birch Hill Counseling and on Twitter (X) at CheriDCoaching.

Connect with Cheri at https://cdaviescoaching.com/.

CHAPTER 5

UPROOTED

MY STORY OF IMMIGRATION GRIEF

Dr. Gabriela Miniscalco, PsyD, Licensed Clinical Psychologist

MY STORY

"Hey babe, have you ever seen this show, or was that pre-America?" My husband shouts from the other room. I giggle because, throughout our almost ten-year relationship, he's learned that, unlike his upbringing in America, my upbringing didn't include sports, pizza parties, Girl Scouts, or sitcom shows. Moments like that remind me that I'm different and that I'm not from here. I'm an immigrant. The seeds of my ancestors have been planted in Poland, but I have since been uprooted. I come from Olecko, a town so small I had to be born in a neighboring town. Olecko is in the Masurian Region of Poland, known for its magical, breathtaking nature due to the abundance of lakes and forests.

The American Dream was not my family's dream. We didn't fantasize about the concrete jungle or the stereotypical notion that in America, money grows on trees therefore, life is easier. Instead, my family knew that to raise a daughter, "it takes a village," and since they had that, they were content. It was the unexpected, heavy orange envelope that changed my family's fate. Like she did every morning, my mom strapped me into my stroller and pushed me through the cobblestone street to the community's mailboxes. Intrigued, she pulled out an overstuffed envelope, wondered for a second what it could be, and tucked it away in the side pocket of my stroller.

Once home, my mom opened the envelope and, to add to her confusion, realized everything was in a foreign language: English. After sharing the story of the mysterious orange envelope with my dad, they decided to pay a visit to the town's translator. Ridden with anxiety and wonder, they patiently awaited answers as the translator curled his face, flipped eagerly through the pages, and smiled. "Congratulations! You're going to America!" he exclaimed. "What? How?" Of all the answers they considered, winning a green card lottery to move to America was not one of them. How could they win a lottery without even entering it? Filled with skepticism, they looked over at each other with a "This must be a joke" kind of smirk. With redundant clarification and confirmation, as well as frequent reassurance that the paperwork was specifically addressed to them, they stepped out of the translator's office with a new sense of wonder. *How did this happen?*

In 1994, the United States Citizenship and Immigration Services created the US Diversity Immigrant Visa program to diversify American society by embracing multiculturality. The program continues to be one of several pathways to immigrate to the United States legally and is an important part of the country's immigration policies, claiming to reflect its commitment to inclusivity and the idea that immigration strengthens the nation by embracing individuals with diverse backgrounds, talents, and experiences. On paper, this sounds like a utopia; however, when things are too good to be true, they usually are.

Even though she "won," my mom was unsure about collecting the prize. Her desire to stay comfortable in Poland was strong, and she was skeptical of moving to a new world up until the very moment she did. "When I was just a school-aged girl, I stood in line at the bodega in the blistering cold, waiting to utilize the rationed food stubs provided by the government. Your grandma was working two or three jobs at the time, so it had to be me, or we would miss our chance at getting any food. Envisioning the warmth of the bread is what kept me warm enough to continue waiting, but when it was my turn to enter the store, all that was left was vinegar on the shelves," my mother shares.

I'm speechless at how different our childhoods were, and I expect her to be tearful as she reminisces about her struggle, but instead, she goes on to say, "It was like this for everyone, though, not just me. Knowing we weren't alone is what got us through it." The importance of community and connection was instilled in me and generations prior to me, and maybe that's why it hurt so much when we had to give them up to move. My mom wished for her daughter to pursue her dreams, but our small post-communist northeastern Polish town lacked the educational opportunities for it. Her heart knew she'd have to sacrifice her dream to allow me to fulfill mine. Overwhelmed with uncertainty yet optimistic for the future, my family proceeded with the visa process by passing interview after interview, screening after screening, and test after test, granting us entry into the new world. I knew I was leaving, but I didn't know where I was going.

The losses of immigration might seem obvious and maybe even surface-level to those who haven't experienced it. Yes, I had to say goodbye to my home, community, school, and the overall culture running through my veins. All heart-breaking and for valid reasons. I missed my friends and the silly little inside jokes we created in our childhood minds. I missed the comfort of walking down a recognizable sidewalk as my little feet tried to keep up with the pace of my parents. I missed the smell of the sea breeze that infiltrated the entire town. I missed speaking a language I was born to speak, and I missed people pronouncing my last name correctly. I missed the upbeat Polish Polka songs that came rumbling out of the few restaurants in town. There was no acceptable space to name or grieve these nebulous losses, as the pressure to be excited for a new life was too grand.

The immigration process is not always simple or linear, and it certainly wasn't for me. Even though my initial journey to Chicago, Illinois, started when I was five years old. I went back and forth between Chicago and Poland while my family settled, got established, and navigated immigration-related stressors. While my move to Chicago became permanent in the fall of 1998, when I was eight years old, I continued living in between.

Moving to a new continent comes with tremendous uncertainty. The template the generations of my family and ancestors worked so hard to create, memorize, and internalize was no longer accurate or relevant. Therefore, we had to start from zero. The human brain is naturally equipped with an alarm system designed to detect potential threats, prompting us to become aware of them and take action to ensure our survival. The human brain constantly monitors our environment for anything out of the ordinary or unfamiliar, and when it detects discrepancies, it signals us to react and protect ourselves. Our brains tend to lean toward caution in the face of uncertainty, interpreting it as a possible threat.

Moving to a new continent and country and adapting to a new society and culture entails an entirely unfamiliar landscape, which can trigger pervasive stress. Consequently, this constant novelty can lead to feelings of anxiety, fear, and exhaustion as we navigate this uncertainty. What is familiar is safe, and because I lost the familiar, I also lost safety. My heart beat out of my chest, and I felt on edge; I wanted to return to the last time I felt safe. "Mami, I want to go back to Poland" is scribbled with crayon on a note my mom found returning from her night job when I was only five.

Being my authentic Polish self in America was not safe. My differences were constantly highlighted and laid out on display. Day after day, I went to school surrounded by peers who gawked at me and whispered things like: "What is she wearing?" "What is she doing?" "Where is she from?" Being misunderstood, especially during school age, becomes unsafe and damaging to development.

I can still pinpoint the exact moment I realized it was unsafe to be me.

My lifelong love affair with Nutella began before I was even born, as my mom savored it by the spoonful during her pregnancy. Nutella, the European hazelnut chocolate spread, is to Poland what peanut butter is to America. When I was preparing to move from Poland to Chicago, I made sure to pack jars of Nutella in my small suitcase because I knew it wasn't available in the US at the time.

On my first day of school in Chicago, I packed a Nutella sandwich for lunch. Nutella represented a sweet and comforting familiarity in the midst of all the unpredictability that came with moving to a new country. However, as I unwrapped my Nutella sandwich, I couldn't ignore the silent stares from my classmates. Of course, I knew they'd be curious, but I didn't expect their looks to be ones of hate. Being ostracized and bullied sadly feels similar in any culture, and I didn't need a translator to pick up on the words they were screaming at me. "She's eating poop sandwiches!" While I understood them, I didn't have the language skills to respond. Their laughter was so loud and piercing, almost as if they were waiting for something of this caliber to entertain them. Like a scene in a movie that was going in slow motion, I was the character everyone was laughing at. I froze, and my heart sank with the recognition that this would be my last Nutella sandwich at school. If a thing as innocuous and innocent as comfort food would isolate me, what did I have left?

Contrary to my naïve belief and everything the diversity visa led me to believe, my differences were not celebrated or welcomed. My peers weren't interested in expanding their mindset. Instead, they wanted to push me down for being different, and with no language skills and no idea how to behave in an American social environment, they succeeded. I recognized that to make it in America, I had to blend in, not stand out. Determined to expedite my belonging, I rejected my Polish identity and prioritized becoming who I was expected to be. Full House and Britney Spears became my models for how to be American. I read teen magazines out loud for hours, clinging to the hope that my Polish accent would fade. I developed a hatred for being Polish because that was one more thing I could relate to my American peers on. The more American I became, the more I abandoned and lost myself, but also began to be more accepted, liked, and included, something I wanted and needed desperately. I was torn apart and puzzled by the pain it caused, as there was no one or nothing to explain or validate the confusion I experienced.

I was shamed for being me, the only thing a child knows how to be. We're biologically wired for authenticity and attachment. Authenticity means embracing our instincts, desires, and needs without reservation or suppression. Being authentic means our inward experience matches how we present to the world without conforming or holding back. Humans are inherently vulnerable, relying on others for survival. When we realize staying true to ourselves puts our attachments at risk and, consequently, threatens our ability to fulfill our needs, we often make the difficult choice to compromise our true selves to enhance our chances of survival.

I became a master at fitting in. I strutted around in my bell-bottom jeans, collected beanie babies, and requested hot dogs for every meal. "What is that?" "What does that mean?" and "What does this do?" were the reactions I received from my family when sharing something I was excited or proud of. My family had no reference for what it was like to be a kid or teen in America. This left us with little to connect on, as continuously having to explain, teach, or show them was becoming burdensome. Just like my peers in school who didn't understand my Polish culture, my family did not understand my American identity. I was always "too Polish" in my friend group and "too American" in my family. I couldn't win, further isolating me into a grief I didn't yet understand. *You're not good enough* was the theme of my thoughts because in whatever space I occupied, I had to be deliberate with how I presented as my belonging was conditional. I was exhausted from "code-switching" or switching languages to fit in with a particular culture.

My immigration grief shows up as a feeling of incompleteness. I'm not one or the other; I'm not whole; I'm in-between. In American society, grieving is often reserved for losing a loved one to death. There's an immediate sense of sadness when we hear of someone's passing, and we are quick to empathize with the person's experience. "My condolences" and "Please let me know how I can help" are often the caring phrases we share to offer our support. I agree that the death of a loved one is the absolute most painful thing one can experience; however, other types of losses can initiate deep grief as well, and that pain also needs love and attentiveness. Disenfranchised grief, also called hidden sorrow, is grief that isn't recognized or validated by society as it doesn't fit into a box and is not by any means clear-cut. The message to immigrants is clear, however, and it's also loud and cold. We're expected to be grateful for the permission to live here, and the expectation is we conform and align as a means of demonstrating our appreciation for the opportunity. There's no interest in where we came from, only where we're going, and the slightest reminiscence of our country of origin is perceived as not being "proud to be American."

My immigration grief feels like a void, or a hole I try to fill with the wrong substance, only for it to be drained repeatedly. While I was aware I'd lost my natural connection to my culture, country, familial and ancestral ties, as well as the parts of myself I abandoned to fit in, a space to acknowledge these losses was non-existent. I did what I was told. I suppressed my tears, loneliness, anxiety, and inner chaos. I learned that since there was no space for it, then it must not be important or even real. I faked it until I made it, and I was successful. I recognize that I spent so much of my life making others feel comfortable, that I am now uncomfortable. My unspoken words became sources of pain I carried for decades. I wonder, *would my heart feel less broken and my void smaller if a caring person attended to me and said, "That must have been hard for you"?*

Like Edward Scissorhands or Wednesday Addams, I've always carried the feeling of being wrong. I felt like an outsider or an alien that could never truly belong. Not coincidentally, *alien* is also a word used to describe someone who is not a native or citizen of the host country. Despite my family being promised inclusivity and a celebration of our differences, we'll always and forever be labeled as aliens. I feel divided, and a deep sadness begins to swallow me as I long for a fix that doesn't exist. I crave the safety of my motherland, the one that bears my ancestral seeds. I do what I learned through my mom's childhood story: remember you're not alone and seek out community to connect with. So, I pick up the phone and call my mom to discuss the incongruence I feel when decorating for Thanksgiving, a holiday that doesn't even belong to me. My mom normalizes my feeling of disconnection and ache and says, "Nie da się być w dwóch miejscach naraz," which translates to "It's impossible to be in two places at once." I smile at the sense of relief I feel because I know she understands the discomfort I feel due to the split.

THE TOOL

A deep sense of isolation, hyper-independence, and, ultimately, ambiguous grief surrounds my immigration experience. The tool I've used throughout my healing has been connection to those who identify as immigrants, second or third-generation immigrants, children of immigrants, newcomers, foreigners, or those who have experienced life in the "in-between" of two cultures. As social creatures, we find consolation in sharing our stories of pain, survival, and grief with others and allowing them to respond with care and compassion.

Think about the people in your life who've experienced multiculturalism, whether in your native country or elsewhere, and reconnect with them. While all our stories of immigration are unique, it's our grief that binds us. I empower you to share your stories of loss instead of hiding them and them hiding you but also to celebrate your country of origin through enjoying food, music, and movies.

I recognize it may be a privilege to have connections to family members, friends, or even acquaintances from your country of origin therefore, if you find you do not have access to those people, seek out a therapist with your cultural background or experience in immigration or multiculturalism, for example, someone like myself. If therapy is not something you're ready for, connect with your younger self or your inner child. Imagine yourself at the age you were acculturating or adjusting to your new culture, and ask yourself, "What was it that I needed back then?" It's never too late to give your inner child, or your past self, the attention, love, and empathy you may have lacked. Embrace the differences that made you, YOU, with confidence and grace, despite what the general culture states.

My immigration story is only one of millions, and I'm proud of the vulnerability and courage it took to write it, and I hope it inspires others to share theirs.

Dr. Gabriela Miniscalco, PsyD, is a Licensed Clinical Psychologist and owner of Mini Mental Health Services, a private practice offering therapy services to those looking to understand and heal their emotional wounds. She recognizes the impact different forms of oppression have on our mental well-being and utilizes warmth, authenticity, and compassion to build a therapeutic relationship that can be used as a tool for healing. She creates a safe, validating, and introspective space for people to explore the roots of their pain, all while accepting them unconditionally. She believes everyone's unique story deserves to be heard. Her PsyPact Certification allows her to offer therapy services across the United States. Dr. Miniscalco is also an Adjunct Faculty member in the Clinical Psychology PsyD program at Adler University, reflecting her dedication to educating future generations of psychologists. Prior to establishing her private practice, Dr. Miniscalco dedicated herself to working in complex systems and institutions. Her career path included roles in correctional and residential settings, therapeutic day schools, community mental health, and higher levels of care like inpatient, partial hospitalization, and intensive outpatient programs. She has extensive experience in community engagement and outreach, program development, crisis management, supervision, and training. Dr. Miniscalco is actively involved in her community through volunteer opportunities and is a freelance writer, presenter, and speaker.

As an immigrant from Poland, Dr. Miniscalco understands the intricacies of living between two cultures and emphasizes the pivotal role that culture plays in an individual's development and mental health presentation. Her personal experiences have empowered her to help individuals make sense of their own multicultural identities. While being a mental health advocate is her biggest passion, she loves the forest and finds peace in spending time with her dogs, cats, and chickens.

Connect with Dr. Miniscalco here:
Instagram: @ Mini Mental Health Services
Website: www.minimentalhealth.com
Phone/Text: (847) 986-5688
E-mail: drminiscalco@minimentalhealth.com

CHAPTER 6

EVEN IN DEATH, WE CANNOT BE SEPARATED

DEVELOPING CONTINUING BONDS AFTER A DEATH

Rebecca Rainstrom, LMHC

MY STORY

It was another Wednesday. I hadn't slept in days. My mind was racing with thoughts of my dad. It had been five days since I was allowed to spend time with him, and updates were sporadic. The night before, I was granted five minutes. I had five minutes to say my goodbyes. I had five minutes to lay next to my dad to whisper my final words in his ear, to kiss him one last time, to smell him one last time, to hold his hand one last time.

How do you take in the magnitude of a final goodbye with an audience of strangers watching you? With strangers counting your final moments with the most important person in your world, as they point to their watch and say, "Your time is almost up."

I was sick to my stomach but forced myself to go to work the next morning.

Oh, please do not let this be the day.

I had a full day of clients scheduled. I remember the sunshine was so bright that morning. My eyes hurt as I squinted to see the road as I drove my familiar route to work.

How can it be such a beautiful day when I feel so miserable?

I felt sick. I knew my father's days were limited, and each day brought fear that this would be *the* day. I settled into my office with my stack of charts and prepared for my first client. I had 30 minutes before my day started. My phone rang and I jumped. I looked at the caller ID, and it was my sister. I hesitated to answer. I thought: *I'm not going to answer. Let it go to voicemail. I'm not ready.* I fumbled to hit the answer button. There were no greetings, only "Dad died this morning."

As I'm writing this, it's Father's Day. My tenth Father's Day without my dad. I loved Father's Day growing up. I loved all the rituals that went with preparing for it, like baking a cake, making my dad a gift in school, and, in later years, buying him something I knew he'd want but never buy for himself. And then, when I became a mother, helping my kids to make my dad homemade gifts to add to his collection. My father saved everything we ever made him. He used to say, "You kids will be shocked by all the gifts you made, and I saved after I die." Much to my dismay, I was never able to look through those artifacts after my dad died, but they existed and were cherished.

My father told me being a father was his proudest accomplishment. He told me "I love being your dad, it's the hardest job I ever loved." He used to say that "the best feeling is sitting in a room and hearing someone say "Dad" and knowing they were talking to me." My dad loved fiercely and with his entire heart, and was the glue to our family. He loved family dinners, knowing we were all there for him and because of him.

On the morning of July 25, 2012, I received the worst call of my life, the one from my sister. My visceral reaction was to vomit. *I'm not ready. I wasn't with him. I missed it.* I promised my dad he wouldn't die alone and that I'd be with him. I hadn't been able to keep that promise.

My kids were only seven and nine, and I feared they'd forget him. *I still need him. I never want to forget, not a single moment. I want to die.* I didn't want to go on without my touchstone, my hero, my friend, my advisor, my dad. In one moment, after a single phone call of one sentence, "Dad died this morning," I was orphaned. As I sit here almost 11 years later, a woman with two college-aged kids, I still feel like an orphan. Everything changed. I changed. And the trajectory of my life was guided by that moment.

My father went from healthy to dead in nine weeks. He went from playing golf and wiffle ball with his grandkids to dead in nine weeks. He went from walking and talking, singing, and laughing to frail, weak, silent, to dead in nine weeks. He was diagnosed with lung cancer and never had a chance to fight it or even try treatment. The silence after my dad died was deafening.

At the time of his death, he was married to his third wife, a woman who was not a mother to any of his children and kept my father's daughters from him during his last five days alive. This woman stole the precious gift of bearing witness to my father leaving this physical world from me. At the age of 18, I was with my paternal grandmother when she took her last breath. It was both the most beautiful and devastating moment in my life. My dad and I talked about that moment many times. My dad told me, "I don't want to die alone." I assured him, "I will never let that happen, you will never have to be afraid because I will be with you. I will be the last thing you see on this side. I will hold you, hug you, kiss you and talk to you. I will be with you when you cross, telling you it is okay to go." My dad cried and thanked me. Not being allowed to be with my dad for this moment haunted me for years after he died. I felt I'd failed him, that I lied to him. I wondered who was with him. *What were the last words he heard? What was the last thing he saw? Did he know it was okay to let go?* There were no do-overs; that was the final show, and I missed it.

As I reflect, one of the most difficult barriers I faced early in my grief journey was letting go of the belief that I could've controlled that moment. The anger and hatred I felt towards my father's wife consumed me. Yes, hatred; I never felt that intensity of an emotion before. This was different. In the past, my father was always there to help me through, pick up the pieces, rebuild, lift me up, care for me, and love me. And now I was alone. I was a failure.

I was numb for the first three years after my father's death and felt a total disconnect from life. Colors were no longer vibrant. Laughter took effort. Nothing interested me. Food lacked taste. I lost 40 pounds in the months after. I was just existing. I went through the motions of being a mother, wife, and friend. I have few memories from those years. I slept a lot. I laid in bed a lot. I said no to all social invites. I cried tears of sadness and anger. My life was not what I wanted. Every moment was measured in "before Dad died" and "after Dad died." And I was drowning in the quicksand of grief. I wasn't living. I missed the beauty of raising my children and creating my own legacy as a parent. I spent all the energy I had trying to right the wrongs done not only to my father but also to me and my sisters. But the truth is, I couldn't. No matter what I did, my dad was gone. Really, my dad was dead, not just gone. There is a finality to the sentence, "My dad is dead." Healing began when I relented to this truth. My dad was dead, and it was final. I began to lean into my grief.

I leaned into the world without my dad and the hope of him returning. As I began to wake up and feel again, I realized everything my father ever taught me was for this very moment—that he was preparing me for this moment his entire life. He taught me life lessons my entire life. When I was growing up, he always asked, "What did you learn?" I hated that question. Why did I always have to learn a lesson? My father said, "There are no mistakes. The only mistake is missing the lesson." So now I had to stop, feel, really feel, and find the lesson in this. What was the lesson in my dad's death?

I started to ask myself what I wanted my kids to remember and know about my dad. What was his legacy to myself, my kids, and our community? It was these questions that led me to start to do what I affectionately call "spreading a little Rainstrom in the world." I shifted my focus from how awful the world was without my dad to how could I keep him alive. *How can I make sure that the world remembers him? How can I bring him along on the rest of my journey?* And with a shift in that mindset came a shift in my behavior. I started to honor my dad, to laugh, to share his stories and jokes. I found ways to spread kindness. During this time, I also began to have conversations with him. I invited him to come to me. My dad had always told me, "Rebecca, even in death, we cannot be separated." I began to listen to the quiet. I practiced lucid dreaming. I learned to tolerate the discomfort of having two opposing experiences simultaneously, like having a dream so real that my dad was with me, hearing his voice, hugging him, and touching him while also being acutely aware that he was dead. I began to practice the art of noticing or bearing witness. I noticed the visitations from my dad without looking too hard or leaning in for more. I learned early on that that stopped the process. I developed an openness to possibilities I never believed in, like my father saying my name as I slept, or feeling a tug on my covers at night, or seeing my dad's face in my doorway. I know these are real because I experienced them and many more. My dad was right; even in death, we could not be separated. It was just different. And I had to allow myself to appreciate the differences.

I shifted my focus from the death of my dad to how he lived.

I wanted to bring him on my journey.

I wanted to carry on his legacy.

I wanted his life to remain an integral part of my life moving forward. And so began new traditions. Each year on Christmas morning, my kids get a letter from Papa. The letter highlights their year—successes and struggles. The letters are words of wisdom from my dad and reminders that he is still a part of them. My kids also receive letters at every monumental moment (graduations, big birthdays, going off to college). These letters offer the wisdom my dad offered me when I was their age.

Dollar questions: my dad would ask all of the grandkids dollar questions, maybe a complicated math problem, a geography question, or a piece of family history. If you answered correctly, you got a dollar. I have carried on this tradition with family history as a way to keep past generations alive for my kids.

I taught my kids to play the card game pitch. It was how I learned to count and do math when I was a kid.

Sharing my dad's love of music: Music was something my dad and I always bonded over. Today, my kids are avid music lovers and can sing songs from the 1960s to today.

And a final favorite is the act of giving. My father was a generous man to his family and strangers alike. My kids and I made a commitment to "sprinkling a little Rainstrom" within our community whenever possible. We have donated to public libraries (my dad loved to read, and he passed his love of local public libraries to me), paying it forward when we see someone in need, choosing a charity and volunteering, smiling at a stranger, or offering forgiveness to another person. Let me say this: grief is never easy. Grief never gets smaller. But we can learn ways to stand taller in our grief.

There are no right or wrong ways to grieve. But there are healthier options. Practice leaning into your grief. Allow all your emotions, big and small, to rise to the surface. Practice learning how to ride your grief waves. And I really mean practice. This means learning emotional tolerance. Grief is a lifelong process. Grief is normal. Grief is not a sign of weakness but rather the cost of great love.

THE TOOL

How can you develop continuing bonds as you learn to live in the aftermath of death? The first step is to honor your grief. Grief is not a sign of weakness or something to be ashamed of. Say your loved one's name. Share what made that relationship so special for you. Embrace the moments, big and small, that remind you of your loved one. Think of the life lessons you've learned and find ways to pass them on to future generations. Explore ways to carry on their love through acts of kindness, sharing their interests, cooking their recipes, keeping their pictures out, or keeping their memory alive through storytelling. In this way, you can find comfort in the enduring connection you still have with your loved one, even though they have died.

Then, I challenge you to ask yourself:

- What is my loved one's legacy to me?
- How do I want to honor that legacy in the world going forward?
- How can I bring them on my journey? What hobbies or activities did you share with your loved one, and how can you continue to enjoy them in your loved one's memory?
- What do I want the world to remember about my loved one?
- How do you find comfort in the everyday moments that remind you of your loved one?
- How can you incorporate the lessons you learned from your loved one into your daily life in even small yet meaningful ways?
- Are there specific places that hold special memories of your loved one? Can you continue to connect in those places?

You do not have to have the perfect starting point. You just have to start in whatever way feels right to you. This was your person. They may have died, but they have not left you. The beauty is in learning how to carry them within you.

Rebecca Rainstrom is licensed in New York State as a mental health counselor (LMHC). With 20 years of experience in the mental health counseling field, Rebecca spent the first half of her career working for community agencies, working in the field of addictions and specializing in trauma-informed care. In 2018, Rebecca opened her private practice, Infinity Counseling, in Malta, New York. In 2012, Rebecca's father died suddenly from lung cancer. This experience was the start of Rebecca shifting her focus to grief counseling and becoming a grief-informed therapist. Rebecca is trained in research-based best practices to aid her clients in finding a new realm of comfort and happiness after the death of a loved one.

Rebecca is a married mother of two children, Noah and Olivia. Rebecca is also a dog mom to her beloved Golden Retriever Bear Bear.

Connect with Rebecca here: rjrinfinitycounseling@gmail.com

CHAPTER 7

SOUL FRIEND

THE MIRACLE OF HEALING THROUGH PRAYER

Kathleen Banicki, BS

MY STORY

"Are you happy, my child?" "No," she answered. "God took my godmother away from me when she died."

We embraced while weeping tears of sadness. *Even a miracle doesn't soften the pain of grief.*

The child is my daughter Kathryn.

The godmother is Jean Marie.

The story is about a miracle of powerful healing.

On a beautiful sunlit day, my life changed forever. I met Jean Marie on a riverbank. We both signed up for a white-water rafting trip organized by a twelve-step recovery group. The day was perfect. The sun warmed the air in a cloudless light blue sky. On arrival, we broke into groups of six, were given a raft, oars, life jackets, and some instructions, and off we went. The water was cold, clean, and powerful. The river looked like it would challenge even the most experienced rafter. My team had a wonderful time navigating the rocks, water surges, small waterfalls, and the much-needed calm of the river.

When we completed our journey down the river, it was time for a break. I noticed a woman alone on the bank of the river. She was carefully trying to exit a white-water raft. She looked startled and a little scared. I was eager to help. I delighted in showing off my sea legs and all my nautical knowledge. I've always loved every moment of boating, rafting, and swimming. The energy of water has always called to my inner spirit.

I went to help this beautiful woman who looked very out of sorts. Her skin was alabaster white and looked untouched by the wind and water. She wore white clothing to protect her soft skin from the sun. *She would be perfect in the Victorian Era.* As I approached, I introduced myself. "Hi, I'm Kathy," I said, "excuse me for saying this, but you look very out of sorts."

She immediately smiled and said, "I'm Jean, and I feel very out of sorts."

I helped her out of the raft, and we sat on a boulder to enjoy lunch. Little did I know our adventure had just begun. Our friendship was formed on that rock.

This remarkable woman changed my life and my children's lives, especially my daughter Kathryn.

Her name is Jean Marie. She was an esteemed lawyer and an award-winning amateur photographer. She was very active in her church, community, and political party. Jean was honest, loyal, and discerning. She was a woman who loved her faith and prayed every day. Her photography was so stunning she created photographic greeting cards, and her greeting card company was successful. She developed a loyal customer base. The cards were her magnificent signature work. I saved every precious card she has sent over the years.

Her family was a jovial bunch who belly laughed a lot. I loved being around them; laughter was foreign to me as a child. I was always told, "Laughter brings crying," and to be perfectly honest, growing up wasn't a fun experience.

Jean taught me the meaning of unconditional love. Having been the recipient of this love, I now pray to understand how to give this unconditional love to others. I have learned that "agape" love is what we humans should develop in our lifetime. This agape love is pure and without any self-benefit. This kind of love is imperative in the act of forgiveness. Can you imagine how enamored I was of Jean Marie? My background was full of painful rejection and a tremendous weight of judgment and criticism.

I married a wonderful man, Raymond, and birthed two beautiful children, Sean and Kathryn. Jean volunteered to be the photographer at my wedding. Her generosity and love didn't stop there. When my children were born, she affectionately adopted them into her family, always treating them as her nephew and niece. When the time arose for Kathryn's baptism, Ray and I asked Jean Marie to honor us and bless Kathryn by accepting the invitation to be her godmother. Jean stood with my brother Glen, the chosen godfather, and presented Kathryn to the priest for her baptism. On a bright and calm Sunday afternoon, Jean and Glen became her godparents. From that day forward, Jean was affectionately referred to as Aunt Jean.

I watched as Aunt Jean nurtured Kathryn's spirit, spent quality time with her, listened attentively to all her concerns, and showered her with the same unconditional agape love she gave to all. It's no coincidence Aunt Jean was affectionately known as Kathryn's second mom. It's funny when I ponder their relationship; when Kathryn came to me for advice or direction, she always called Aunt Jean right afterward to ask the same question. I thank God Jean and I were aligned in our words of wisdom to her.

When I was with Jean, I was always learning. She was smart and could converse with people on any topic. I admired her confidence, knowledge, and self-esteem. She knew her worth as a precious child of God. Jean loved exploring. The family and I went with her to parks, beaches, nature preserves, and her favorite place, Maine. She camped with us every summer.

Sharing our life with Jean was so easy. I never met anyone who approached life by giving unconditional love. It was easy to adore her. Much was revealed as Jean and I continued to share our lives and families with each other. We laughed together, explored emotions, shared our family struggles, prayed together, and helped each other with situations that seemed baffling and confusing. She nurtured all of us, and I felt emotionally safe for the first time in my life. Our relationship was built on trust and mutual respect.

Jean was always bringing fun into ordinary moments. We became traveling companions because we agreed that being in each other's company was a pleasure.

Before I was married, Jean and I went on a pilgrimage that changed our lives. We boarded a 747 airplane out of JFK and landed in Dubrovnik, Yugoslavia, now known as Croatia. We toured this beautiful countryside by bus and arrived at our final destination, Medjugorje, Yugoslavia, now known as Bosnia and Herzegovina. Croatia and Yugoslavia were at war at this time, and we actually heard the horrific sound of the distant bombing. At the same time, we enjoyed and discovered the culture, people, agriculture, simplicity, and peaceful lodging in this blessed land. Medjugorje is named an "Oasis of Peace" because the Blessed Virgin Mary is said to have appeared there to three children. Our Lady has been giving the children messages on how people should pray, live their lives, open their hearts to God's love, and meditate on Jesus's life while praying the holy Rosary daily. The Rosary prayer deepens our understanding of Jesus' life.

During the time I spent in Medjugorje with Jean, I realized I found my "Anam Cara." Anam Cara is a Gaelic term for "soul friend." Anam Cara is the "essence of true friendship."

When we returned, I stood at mass beside my dear friend, Christine, in an oak pew. I turned towards her and handed her a rosary with silver links. As she held that rosary in the palm of her hand, we both watched each individual link turn the color gold. A testament to the power of prayer at work in her hand.

Life wasn't always smooth sailing in our family. At the young age of eight, Kathryn was diagnosed with chronic osteomyelitis of the distal radius bone of the left arm. In layman's terms, inflammation of the bone. We grieved as she suffered. She had surgery after debilitating surgery. She was homeschooled, had visiting nurses three times a week, and suffered with IV antibiotics that I administered in our home three times a day. The antibiotics were inserted into a PIC line placed in her right arm. Her left arm was bandaged in a cast. We constantly contacted her doctors and drove to the hospital in Manhattan to visit a team of doctors for weekly follow-up appointments. The ride from our home in Long Island was long and tiring. We spent up to six hours a day commuting in the car because of the heavy traffic patterns.

Kathryn tried to find joy in a day filled with chronic, unbearable pain. Unrelenting pain hurts the spirit, prevents sleep, slows concentration, dulls the senses, and is exhausting. Five surgeries over three years yielded no results. The entire ordeal left Kathryn with scars and pain. Ray and I dragged her to every healing mass we could find and begged God to heal her, to no avail. Oh yes, Kathryn was angry at her God. "Why me?" she asked. I could never answer that question. I never lost my faith. I prayed she wouldn't lose hers.

Then, in 2015, the doorbell rang, and I opened it to find Jean Marie looking pensive. She said, "I have cancer." Five years later, Jean Marie died from that awful disease.

Knowing that cancer would take her life, Jean spent time with every family member. She planned her funeral mass, paid for her wake and burial, and traveled first class to Africa with her cousin Beth. Jean had a plan. We spent quality time together. We traveled to Maine, Gurneys Inn in Montauk, Greenport, where we rode the carousel, and New York City for fine dining and a show. Jean never stopped being positive. She had a bucket list of plans, and together, we lived her final wishes. She was generous, prayerful, and kind to everyone. When the final stages of cancer left her bedridden, I visited her often. We prayed together every time. I loved pampering her. I gave her foot baths and pedicures, brought her favorite foods, and sat by her bedside, trying to anticipate her every need.

Now Kathryn and I suffer a different kind of pain together. Her dear Aunt Jean, my dear "soul friend," died on January 20th, 2020. Grieving, at times, is fraught with tears, memories, and emotional pain searing the heart. We all miss her generous human presence in our lives. Kathryn is dealing with the agony and ecstasy of Aunt Jean's death.

The day her dear godmother died, Kathryn's arm pain vanished. It was gone, no more pain! No medication was needed after seventeen years of suffering and constant pain management supervised by doctors. We believe Jesus answered Jean's prayers upon her death. I believe Jean offered up her pain and suffering for Kathryn's healing. A true miracle and saintly godmother in the truest sense of the word.

Now, what do I do? My heart feels like it's broken. I've lost a love on Earth that was pure, honest, and unconditional. I miss her voice every day.

I pray.

It's the only thing I know how to do. Through prayer, I feel comforted and mourn her death. I feel spiritually close to Jean. For the first time in my life, I cry freely. My heart opened. Crying was never easy for me. I now pray to give others the unconditional love that was so freely given to me.

Most mornings upon awakening, me, my trusty dog, Mishka, a large cup of freshly brewed coffee, and my rosary beads accompany me outside to my yard. There, I recline on my comfortable cushioned lounge chair, but not before I walk into my garage with my red cardinal bird feeder and proceed to fill it to the brim with bird seed. Now, surrounded by a concrete bird bath and colorful wildflowers, multiple species of interesting, colorful birds come to my bird buffet and spa. I relax with Mishka on the padded lounge chair. We watch the birds fly, feed, and bathe. I pick up my rosary. As I meditate on the mystery for the day, the life of Jesus comes alive in my mind. While praying, I spot the magnificent red cardinal. Lo and behold, when the cardinal appears, it's symbolic to me. My soul friend has arrived in spirit.

I buy one gift for Sean and Kathryn each year and place it under our Christmas tree with a festive gift tag that reads, "Love, Aunt Jean." I keep her memory alive in our lives!

For my son Sean's birthday this year, I wrapped a beautiful gift for him and delivered it to the doorstep of his apartment. It was a 16" by 20" canvas print of lobster traps hanging on a fence, with the backdrop of fishing boats harbored in a picturesque marina. Sean is a gentle soul, and he recognized Aunt Jean's photography. He called me and said, "Mom, thank you. I cried when I opened the present and gazed at the work of art. I miss Aunt Jean so much."

My grieving process for my Anam Cara (soul friend) is centered on the power of prayer. I talk to Jean every day. I know she's watching over me and my family. I've come to recognize that grief is good. As I allow myself to feel, I allow my tears to flow down into my heart, where they rest to soothe the ache. Crying is healing my wounded heart. Grief is a form of validation. Jean's death shouts out to me that I matter, Jean mattered, our relationship mattered. My grief validates Jean's life.

Our relationship was the purest form of love I've ever known. Now, I turn to Jesus. Agape is the love that Jesus offers. Agape is unselfish love, asking nothing in return. I'm also in touch with the love that Jesus has for me. As I bring Him my sorrow, He is nurturing me spiritually. I'm becoming a softer, more compassionate woman. I now realize that Jesus can handle everything in my life, including my emotions. I let go and let God. It's getting easier to turn to Him. Jesus supports my emotions and deep sadness. He helps me navigate a course of healing just like I use my instruments to navigate a safe sailing course on the vast sea.

Since her death, I experienced a deepening of my spiritual connection with Jesus and his blessed mother, Mary. I cherish the time I spend in prayer and love the graces I feel I received since her death. My heart has been opened! I laugh more often, cry more tears, love unconditionally, and enjoy every moment of every precious day! Through her example, I embraced and love the Eucharist, the true body of Christ, and pray the Rosary daily. The Rosary is my "stairway to heaven" until we meet again in heaven.

THE TOOL

The practice of the Rosary is accessible to people from all walks of life and can be adapted to individual needs. Whether you're seeking solace in times of grief, moments of reflection in your daily routine, or a way to strengthen your spiritual connection, the Rosary can be a flexible and personal experience. It's a timeless tradition that has brought comfort and spiritual growth to countless individuals throughout history. So, don't hesitate to explore this prayerful journey, as it can be a source of deep inner peace and understanding.

HOW TO PRAY THE HOLY ROSARY

The Holy Rosary is a prayer that allows you to reflect on the life of Jesus Christ. Each day of the week is associated with specific Mysteries:

- Monday and Saturday: Joyful Mysteries
- Tuesday and Friday: Sorrowful Mysteries
- Wednesday and Sunday: Glorious Mysteries
- Thursday: Luminous Mysteries

Here's a step-by-step guide:

1. Begin with the sign of the cross and recite the Apostles Creed.
2. Say the Our Father.
3. Follow with three Hail Marys.
4. Recite the "Glory Be to the Father."
5. Announce the First Mystery and say the Our Father.
6. Meditate on the Mystery while saying ten Hail Marys.
7. After each decade (a group of ten beads), say the prayer requested by the Virgin Mary: "Oh, my Jesus, forgive us our sins; save us from the fires of Hell. Lead all souls to heaven, especially those most in need of thy mercy."
8. Repeat steps five to seven for the remaining Mysteries.
9. Conclude with the "Hail, Holy Queen" prayer on the medal after completing the five decades.

Those unfamiliar with these prayers can find guided Rosary prayers in this Facebook group: https://www.facebook.com/groups/745786165568413/, making it easier to meditate and focus.

Praying the Rosary deepens your understanding of Jesus and His sacrifice. Mary, his Mother, offers profound insights into his life and death. As Jesus hung on the Cross, he entrusted Mary to all humanity, emphasizing her role as the Mother of all. Praying the Rosary brings wisdom and spiritual enlightenment.

THE JOYFUL MYSTERY

The Annunciation- Gift: Humility

The Visitation- Gift: Love of Neighbor

The Birth of Jesus- Gift: Poverty in Spirit

The Presentation- Gift: Obedience

Finding the Child Jesus in the Temple- Gift: Joy in Finding Jesus

THE SORROWFUL MYSTERY

The Agony in the Garden- Gift: Sorrow for sin

The Scourging at the Pillar- Gift: Purity

Crowning with thorns- Gift: Courage

Carrying of the Cross- Gift: Patience

The Crucifixion- Gift: Perseverance

THE GLORIOUS MYSTERY

The Resurrection- Gift: Faith

The Ascension- Gift: Hope

Descent of the Holy Spirit- Gift: Love of God

The Assumption- Gift: Grace of a Happy Death

The Coronation- Gift: Trust in Mary's Intercession

THE LUMINOUS MYSTERY

Baptism of Jesus- Gift: Openness to the Holy Spirit

Wedding at Cana- Gift: To Jesus through Mary

Proclaiming the Kingdom- Gift: Repentance and trust in God

Transfiguration- Gift: Desire for Holiness

Institution of the Eucharist- Gift: Adoration

Introducing **Kathleen Banicki,** a truly remarkable woman who is currently living a life "beyond her wildest dreams." Kathleen grew up in Long Island, New York, and graduated with a degree in Marketing/Management from St. John's University. At just 29 years old, she bravely surrendered to the first step of the AA program and has been living "one day at a time" as a sober woman ever since. With therapy, honesty, enthusiasm, faith, and prayer, Kathleen found the strength to push through and develop lasting friendships. She married a wonderful man in 1991 and, while working in the corporate world, raised two great children, Sean and Kathryn, with her husband, Ray.

Now retired, Kathleen has continued to make a difference in the lives of others. She has a certification in Alzheimer/dementia care and works part-time as a director in a Social Club for adults with these conditions. She has also discovered new passions, including making jewelry and creating Shell Art.

Kathleen's commitment to living life to the fullest is grounded in her faith and everyday prayer. She lives by the words of Padre Pio: "If you pray, don't worry. If you worry, don't pray." Whether she's soaking up the sun as a snowbird in Florida, captaining her own boat, practicing yoga, or volunteering with her parish, Kathleen is a shining example of what it means to embrace life with enthusiasm and grace. Her unwavering spirit and determination to make a difference are an inspiration to us all.

Connect with Kathleen Banicki at kathleenbanicki@gmail.com
Learn more at: https://linktr.ee/kathleenbanicki

CHAPTER 8

FROM LOSS TO CONNECTION

CREATING A RELATIONSHIP WITH LOVED ONES IN SPIRIT

Deb DeCelle

MY STORY

The very first time I realized children could die too, I was five or six years old. What I didn't know at the time was that one day I'd communicate with them and others across the veil. This is when Curtis died.

I can still see the sun shining beautifully all around me on the day the letter came home from school. "Debby, please come here," my mom called from the kitchen. She looked at me with love, pain, and tears in her eyes as she said, "Curtis has gone to heaven."

My world changed forever that day. Curtis was a kind and friendly boy in my class who was full of life on the playground and in the classroom. He had strawberry-blonde hair, bright eyes, and freckles. He always offered a big smile to the world. He used to drink chocolate milk at snack time. Back then, pints of milk were brought to our classrooms in a pail mid-morning.

My mom was a nurse and never let me get chocolate milk, so I had a special reverence for those who were allowed. It's funny the small things you remember. Curtis was my friend.

Curtis, a momentary light to the world, drowned. I felt sad but also very angry. I wanted to sense him around me, see his spirit. I wished he'd come to me in a dream, but unfortunately, he wouldn't come through until I sat down to write these words on this page.

As time went on, I felt angry all the time. There was a lot of turmoil at my house, and as an adult, I see this through a new lens. Grief isn't just something that happens when people or pets die; it happens when people experience trauma, illness, and the loss of themselves. Looking back at my childhood, I see myself in the students I've worked with who have social and emotional issues. The rage I saw in them awakened in me at a very young age. Although I dared not step out of line (which was often the case for those who were parented in my generation—proud Gen X'er here), it presented itself in a variety of ways. Most of the time, it was hidden and pushed deep down.

I wanted attention. I wanted to be included. I wanted to feel okay. Those feelings were met with nothing but dismissive laughter. That devastated me. It was grief in physical form, a longing to be okay, a longing to be accepted, and I felt like no one would understand. And so, the rage and self-loathing grew. I also began noticing things about other people. I felt their emotions, and they merged with mine. As you can imagine, this made me feel completely out of control in my little brain. On top of my already negative emotions, I felt everyone else's too. I had no idea what was happening, but I sure knew the intent and thoughts behind every word spoken and unspoken, which made me even angrier. People's words did not always match their feelings, actions, or intent. I noticed every nuance, not only the things said but the things left unsaid. The body language, tone, and expressions came at me every moment of every day. It was as if I was always decoding the true meaning behind the words. When were people lying to me? I knew it beyond a shadow of a doubt 100% of the time. I couldn't escape it. I had no idea that that was my psychic ability or that I was an empath. I wasn't aware for many years.

I grew up in a time when children often felt powerless. It's just the way the world worked at that time. We didn't have voices and we weren't encouraged to share. Grief took its toll on my physical body. I had severe abdominal pain with vomiting, and the doctors couldn't figure out what was wrong with me. The pain and confusion I experienced led to feeling like a prisoner in my own body with no escape. Fear gripped me in every moment as I begged my mother to make it stop. I couldn't imagine how terrifying it must have been for my parents and sister. I was hospitalized, eventually diagnosed with abdominal migraines, and put on medication.

As a young child, life continued, and at seven, my maternal grandmother died. She was unwell for a while and diagnosed with polymyositis. We visited her on Saturdays at her home about two hours south of us. We watched her struggle as my dad and grandfather lifted her to her feet to try to help her walk a little bit. Most of my memories of her are in her recliner in the living room, but I remember her laugh, smile, and fondness for Marmaduke cartoons on TV on Saturday mornings. It's my theory that her illness was also a result of her grief. Her youngest son, my Uncle Kevin, was killed in a car accident on February 6, 1970. In the prime of his life, 18 years old, set to graduate in June, he was instantly gone. Leaving work that evening, he was hit by two vehicles drag racing on the road and was thrown out of the car. Grandma would tell me, "You remind me so much of him." Dad shared that his injuries were so bad that the first funeral home refused to do an open casket. My grandfather immediately had him taken to a different one so my grandmother could see her son one last time. Although I wasn't born until four years later, losing him would impact my journey in many ways. My grandmother became weaker and weaker as time passed, but she always smiled for my sister and me.

The morning she died, my mom came to get us out of bed. It was still dark out, by my recollection, so I guess it was about 4 a.m. We put on our robes and slippers and descended the staircase. We walked into the TV room. My dad stood completely dressed in his overcoat, looking somber, and told us, "Your grandmother has died." Like that, my world once again shattered all around me. I cried until my head hurt. My father was a man of action, so he went to assist his father in whatever way possible. Shortly after, I was at my grandparents' house looking through Polaroid pictures of us with her, trying to pick one to help me feel comforted by her presence. I asked my grandfather if I could have one, and in his grief, he yelled, "Put it down!" I was shocked and felt lost. My great-grandmother was there and did her best to comfort my sister and me. Eventually, my grandfather gave me the photo.

At the wake, I thought: *She looks like she is still breathing.* This helped me because I could imagine she was just sleeping. A kind family friend took my sister and me to McDonald's for a happy meal with an orange drink to give us a break from the wake. She was kind and loving, and although I don't remember a clear picture of her face, I sense her faith and kindness around me even now. Later, at the funeral home, we were told my grandmother was with Jesus and could walk again. As I watched them lower her into the ground at the cemetery, I knew in my heart that I'd never see her in this physical world again. I felt a sense of brokenness and despair.

Upon returning to school, a boy sitting in our sharing circle began to mock me and made the sound of the song Taps by blowing through his lips, pretending to play the trumpet. I was full of rage and completely devastated. Once again, the flame of pain and loss burned inside. This despair and anger led me to my first experience with mediumship.

One day, I sat in my walk-in closet with my blanket. I often spent time there when I was in trouble or wanted to play with my toys. I rubbed the edge of my blanket on my skin, which often comforted me and still does. I called my blanket my "yee." I have no idea why; it just felt right. I found myself saying it repeatedly while rubbing the skin on my face, and it felt as if I'd drifted off and was out of my body, but I was still awake. As I said "yee, yee, yee," I felt my grandmother all around me and knew beyond the shadow of a doubt that she was with me. I sensed her with me. I couldn't understand it but knew it in my soul.

I learned, as an adult, that what I was experiencing was a trance-like state with clairsentience—clear feeling and claircognizance, clear knowing. I remember what felt like "coming back around" as if I were waking up from a light sleep, but I was still rubbing my face and saying a different word repeatedly. "Aspirin, aspirin, aspirin," I said. It made no sense, but I knew she was okay. It was revealed to me later in life that some drug interaction with aspirin and her illness led to her death.

As time went on, my anger continued to grow. No one understood me, this child who could feel and understand things others couldn't. This little girl knew when people were lying to her, which made the bullying she experienced even worse. I continued to feel the losses of others in a profound way. I felt everything of my own and others, especially grief. It often shut me down, so I cried at the drop of a hat. I was told that I was "too sensitive," a "crybaby," and a "brat" for making things "all about me."

In fifth grade, one of my classmate's sisters was hit by a car while walking to the mall. Only in junior high herself, her death impacted our entire community. I only met her a few times, but the loss affected me as if it were my own. I cried myself to sleep, worrying that my sister or mom would die. Often, people would say to me when such things came up, "Why are you so upset? That's stupid. It's not like it happened to you!" No one realized, even myself, that I felt the feelings of my classmates and the community around us. I didn't have the knowledge or tools to release it.

In sixth grade, the Challenger blew up on live TV. We watched this historic event in my classroom as the first teacher, Krista McCauliffe, was launched into space. A woman and an educator (as an entire country, we were so proud of that moment), and then there it was, the explosion. My teacher gasped and began to cry. I don't know how, but I held back my tears as I silently cried inside on that fateful day. My teacher needed to leave early that day as shock and grief overcame her. I experienced so many feelings I didn't know what to do with, so I wrote. I joined a gifted writing program to help me express my emotions.

Imagine living for 35 years not knowing you are truly a psychic medium and an empath. I became aware I was experiencing everything around me; I understood crying was how I coped, reset, and got it all out. I was also *finally* told by my primary care physician in 2023 that when it came on suddenly, and I couldn't stop it, that was my version of a panic attack. There's no controlling that, which is often very inconvenient in public and at work. Although I've experienced it for years, this was a revelation. And imagine someone like me trying to discern what was panic of my own, and what belonged to other people or Spirit. "Holy Shit" doesn't even touch it.

I firmly believe all of this played out due to the grief I experienced from losing my friend and feeling a complete loss of control over my life, body, and mind. Time marched on, and I experienced many more losses in my life. Sensing my loved ones around me felt easy, especially as I got older. I often smelled their scent, felt their presence (as if someone was standing or sitting near me and no one could be seen), and experienced signs that were unmistakably them. Certain songs came on, and I felt them near. I experienced unexplained divine intervention during a potentially tragic accident, being given nudges to go a certain way in traffic that helped me sidestep delays. I was guided to go to certain stores and always found exactly what I needed on sale (thanks, Mom). There were so many signs!

Although I sensed my own loved ones in spirit, the first time I truly stepped out of my comfort zone to share with someone else was one day over the fence in our yard with the neighbor. The conversation started with, "I hope you don't think I'm crazy, but your partner in spirit tells me that June 13th is important, and he shows me a diner-style white coffee mug. He also wants you to know that it's okay for you to move on and find a new love. Does that make sense to you?" She responded that June 13th was the day they met and that he brought her coffee in bed every morning in that very mug! I was floored.

As time passed, messages started coming faster and faster, and I knew I needed to do something with this ability to help others. In 2017, I began sharing this journey with others professionally. Nothing has given me greater joy than serving others in such a profound way. I have sat with the broken, smiled with the joyful, and laughed as loved ones in spirit bring through fond and funny memories. What an incredible blessing it is to help others heal by providing messages and memories from their loved ones beyond the veil.

THE TOOL

We can tap into our inner wisdom through meditation and introspection and create a profound connection with those who have died. This personal approach allows us to feel the presence and guidance of our loved ones in a deeply authentic way. By nurturing this connection, ourselves, we can find comfort and meaningful communication. It's about embracing our own unique abilities and understanding that our loved ones continue to exist in our hearts and memories, offering their guidance and love to us in our daily lives. This is a meditation that I use with my clients to help them connect with their loved ones. To hear this meditation, please visit: https://www.debdecelle.com

Before beginning to connect with your loved one, it will be helpful to release any physical tension by utilizing progressive muscle relaxation (PMR).

Here's a basic guide on how to practice Progressive Muscle Relaxation:

Choose a quiet environment where you won't be disturbed. Sit in a comfortable chair or lie down on a soft surface. You may do this with your eyes open or closed.

Start with a few deep breaths to calm your mind and focus your attention on the present moment.

Progressively work through different muscle groups in your body by tightening the muscle group (in the order below) as tightly as you can, holding the tension for about five to ten seconds, and then releasing it. Concentrate on the feeling of relaxation as the tension melts away. Relax for 20-30 seconds in between muscle groups. When you're finished, take a few deep breaths and gradually bring yourself back to full alertness.

- Feet and toes
- Calves, knees, and thighs
- Abdomen
- Chest and back
- Hands, fingers, arms and shoulders
- Face and neck

CONNECTION WITH LOVED ONE'S MEDITATION

Close your eyes and begin to focus your attention on your breath—breathe in through your nose and out through your mouth—breathe into the count of four, hold to the count of five (if it's comfortable for you), breathe out through your mouth to a count of seven. You may repeat this as many or as few times as you'd like.

Begin to envision yourself in a relaxing setting—a special place you shared with your loved one in the physical world or another place that makes you feel comfortable. We're not all visual people, so don't fret if you don't "see" anything.

Envision or sense your loved one approaching and joining you. Notice the details. Perhaps it's how they look or a scent they used to wear. What do they look or feel like now? Do they appear to you as they were in their younger years or the age at which they passed?

Imagine them embracing you or standing with their hands on your shoulders. As you experience this moment, feel or see their soul's energy. Often, this appears as light. Picture or sense it surrounding you both and see or feel your light merge with theirs.

Stay in this moment as long as it feels right to you. When your time with your loved one is finished, become more aware of your physical body. Move your fingers and toes, focus again on your breathing, and open your eyes to return to the physical world.

Rest in the knowing that Spirit is always with you in whatever form makes sense to you.

Deb DeCelle is a trauma-informed intuitive evidential medium, healer, meditation facilitator, intuitive arts educator, and psychic investigator. In addition to her work in the intuitive world, Deb formerly worked with at-risk youth and parents in the educational system for over 14 years. Her experience working with those who have been touched by trauma gives her both a sensitive and unique perspective.

Spirit has utilized Deb as a conduit locally in upstate New York, nationally, and around the globe. Her compassionate heart, humor, and healing are her hallmarks. You may find her literally laughing out loud when your loved ones in spirit provide humorous messages and memories from beyond the veil.

Although she wears many hats, the goal is always the same: to connect in a way that is meaningful for everyone's greatest and highest good. Whether it be intuitive guidance, mediumship, healing, mentoring, intuitive education, or investigation, she holds herself to a gold standard and has been educated by some of the most quintessential mediums around the world.

Deb offers gratitude daily for being able to serve by helping others connect, heal, learn, and discover in an incredibly magical way!

You can find her at www.debdecelle.com
Facebook@debdecellemedium and Instagram @debdecellemedium

CHAPTER 9

ISOLATED IN GRIEF

PRESERVING RELATIONSHIPS AFTER LOSS

Karyn Arnold, B.S.

MY STORY

Have you ever felt alone, even in a room full of people?

I did that night and have felt it many times since. But I didn't truly understand it was possible to be lonely when surrounded by friends until I found myself in the middle of a crowded party two weeks after my grandfather died.

It was August in Pennsylvania. I was 18 and just about to leave for college. My closest friends and I were at the house of someone whose parents weren't home. It was hot, crowded, and noisy. "Whoomp! There It Is" played loudly from a standing speaker someone was using as a coaster for their drink.

"Have you talked to your roommate?"

"What does your schedule look like?"

"Did you buy the stuff for your dorm room yet?"

These were the questions swirling about, and while I wanted to participate and feel the excitement and punchy nervousness that surrounded me, all I could think about was my family and the fact I was leaving them at such a sad time. The contrast this loss created sometimes felt just too much, with beginnings and endings happening all at the same time.

Growing up, I was close to my grandparents. They lived in Florida, and we visited them every winter at their small mobile home park. In the mornings, their house smelled like coffee and freshly squeezed orange juice, and I loved having breakfast at the kitchen table with the soft rolling chairs.

On one of these mornings, I came in to find my grandparents having a disagreement—a rare occurrence. As an adult, I now know it probably wasn't anything at all, but at the time, it felt significant. And something in me said: *They are having a fight, and they need to work this out.*

I invited them both to sit at the kitchen table, and I don't know if it was the fact that, as grandparents, it was their instinct/obligation to humor me no matter the circumstances, or the fact that they were generally curious, but regardless, they sat down, just as I asked.

I proceeded to talk to them about the importance of communication and how if they'd tell each other how they were feeling, they'd be able to work anything out.

They smiled with amusement, agreed to work on my suggestions, and thanked me for the therapy session.

I slid an invoice for five dollars under their bedroom door. I was eight years old.

Flash forward ten years later, and my beloved grandfather Charlie, who was bright, quiet, and funny, had just died, and it was time for me to go off to school. I did what I thought I was supposed to do—keep moving, keep busy, don't focus on the grief.

But it was there, and that, coupled with the connection to my grandparents and the love I found for therapy, quickly shaped my future.

I graduated with degrees in Psychology and Gerontology, moved to the Jersey Shore (also, I suppose, as a nod to my grandparents who had lived there for many years), and got a job at my local hospital's Senior Health Network.

One day, my boss walked into my office.

She was short, pretty, and always wore skirts, no matter how cold it was outside. She was a good first boss, even though later she told me having children ruins your marriage. Weird the things people say, and the things you'll never forget. But I wasn't pregnant yet. I was just out of school and not sure what I was doing except for what they told me to do.

"Want to start facilitating some of our bereavement groups?" She asked. I hesitated for a moment.

Bereavement groups?

I didn't know a lot about grief. I knew enough to know I didn't know anything, and a quick check told me I still hadn't processed the loss of my grandfather.

What did I know about running a grief group? After all, my job up to that point had been assisting our staff nutritionist in running healthy eating programs and doing registrations for the free blood pressure screenings we provided each week. This was the first thing my boss had asked me to do on my own, the first thing that would actually utilize the degree I worked so hard for, and I wasn't sure I was ready to do it.

But I was a young people pleaser (as opposed to the middle-aged people pleaser I am now) and figured: *I can't say no.* So, despite my hesitation and the fact that I had never run a group, I answered with a simple, "Sure!"

I did my research, waiting patiently in my little office while my computer dialed into AOL, and proceeded to read every article on grief I could find. I typed up a bullet-point list of topics, printed out some of the best articles I could find, and came to the group as ready as I could be.

I also arrived as nervous as I could be. I was young, and I looked young. I didn't know what I was doing, and I was sure they'd see right through it.

I walked into the room where the four long tables were set into a rectangle with a hole in the middle and set down my papers as I greeted each person who arrived. By the time we were ready to begin, there were ten people in total. A few men, but mostly women—a trend that I would see for the next 25 years.

"Welcome, everyone," I said. "I'm Karyn, and I'll be the facilitator for today's meeting. I have a lot of topics to cover, but why don't we start with some introductions? Tell me who you are and what brought you here today."

Two hours later, we never got to any of my articles. We didn't need to. These ten people were so raw and vulnerable yet so willing to talk. Actually, upon reflection, it wasn't that they were willing. It was that they needed to; they were *compelled* to. No one else was listening, and this was the only place they could share.

I won't say it was a calling, but it wasn't long after that first group that I knew this was what I wanted to do and also perhaps would feel compelled to do for the rest of my life.

"Isn't it sad?" is the question that has followed ever since. Every time I tell someone what I do for a living, I get that question, along with the sense that the person asking sort of wished they didn't ask, once they heard the answer.

Isn't it sad?

I've thought about that, too. And, of course it is! I work with the most wonderful people going through the worst possible time in their lives. But honestly, that's not what sticks out.

It's the love. That's what grief is, after all, and I get to be witness to great love every single day.

I became particularly close to one widow from that first group. Her name was Addie, and she was a great teacher. She showed me the duality of grief and helped me understand the depth and duration of it, why it's so hard, and why it lasts so long. She told me how ugly and beautiful grief could be, all at the same time.

I named my oldest daughter after her, and although several years passed and we were no longer in the group together, I called Addie to tell her. Not long before she passed away herself.

I have heard countless sad stories since. I witnessed people come into the room for their first group with rounded shoulders, crumpled in grief. I have said, "It's okay," a thousand times as a griever sniffles and apologizes for their tears. But what I've also seen is the shriveled griever straighten and strengthen as they surprise themselves with a resilience they never thought they were capable of.

The grievers have been my teachers, and with the passage of time and age, I have become one of them. I've since lost all of my grandparents and experienced three heartbreaking miscarriages; I've lost my beloved stepfather of 35 years, my favorite uncle, and my 25-year-old nephew, who was like no one else in the world, who we lost suddenly and much too soon.

Through it all, I never stopped working.

"Why are you doing that?" my friends asked me. "Isn't it hard?"

I guess their assumption was that coaching other people through loss while also grieving would be too hard.

But it wasn't hard. Or at least not harder. Because I was with my people. In the one-on-one sessions or groups I ran, the people I was working with and surrounded by *got it.*

I can't say they have all felt so lucky. I've heard so many stories of grieving people feeling lonely in a crowded room—that feeling I related to from so many years ago. It's the sense that everyone around them is on a different planet, or at least in a different life, with different concerns and worries—all of which can seem so trivial and unimportant to the griever.

It's this isolation in grief that's one of the biggest challenges for the people I work with, and it comes up again and again. Friends, family, coworkers—the people they expected to be there for them; the relationships they nurtured and cultivated for years. The expectation is that when we need people most, we can count on them to help and guide us.

Which brings me to a few fundamental "facts" I think every griever finds out eventually, and it's the education and validation of these ideas that I've made a central part of the work I do:

1. People are inherently disappointing. I know! This is a sad one, and I don't even like saying it. I love people, and I'm an optimist. But I understand this in ways now that I didn't when I first began this work. And you know what? It's surprisingly liberating. People are disappointing. They don't mean to be. But they can't help it. Because very rarely, if at all, do people live up to our expectations of them. And truthfully, and unfortunately, it seems to be revealed just in those moments when we need them most. Probably *because* we need them most.

2. People don't like sadness. They don't like being around it. They don't know what to do with it. They're spending all their time and energy trying to be happy. Or at least distracted. And when faced with another's deep and unrelenting sadness, they just don't like it. No one will admit this or say it out loud, but for the most part, it's totally true.
3. Your grief makes the people around you feel helpless. They have no idea, and I mean NO IDEA, what to say or how to act around you now. You seem different (and obviously, you are different). They may have had a few comforting words in their pocket to use in the line at the memorial service, but now they are fresh out of ideas. And they live under the assumption that what they say or don't say will somehow make a difference. When they can't find those words? Well, they decide, probably better to say nothing at all.
4. Your grief and your loss are reminders of the things that everyone is working so hard to avoid: mortality. If it can happen to you, it can happen to anyone, and no one wants to think about that.
5. Finally, it's important to remember that people don't understand grief. They think they do! After all, they more than likely also knew the person who has died, and they're thinking, *Oh, he was so great. It's such a shame he's not here anymore.* And then they get to go on with their day. Meanwhile, every part of your life has been impacted. Everything! People who haven't been through it just don't get it. They don't understand the depth or the duration, and honestly, until they've been through it, they can't or won't be able to understand.

But what can help, and how can you possibly get someone to understand this experience of grief when feeling so isolated and alone?

Tell them.

It's not easy, and probably not even fair to put the onus on you, the grieving person, but in some ways, it's as simple and complicated as anything can be in the way that it's really the only choice.

And here's what you need to tell them.

- **You don't have to fix this.** Take the pressure off right away and let anyone you're talking to know that you *know* they don't have the words or the power to make this better, and that's not what you're expecting.
- **You're asking me what I need, but I don't know what that is. But there is one thing I am certain I need, and I need a lot of it—time.** This is all it comes down to anyway because you don't know how long you're going to feel this way. And no matter what, if you feel like you're not being hurried through this process, you're going to feel more understood and supported.
- **You see my loss as a date on the calendar, and with that, the perception of it being a past event. But it's not. Yes, I lost my loved one (fill in the blank) weeks/months/years ago, but I felt the loss yesterday. I feel it today. And I will feel it again tomorrow.** Grief and loss are a present event. It's not a part of history or just a date that fades with importance with the passage of time. Don't let a timeline (or anyone else's perceived timeline) determine where you are or should be.

Finally, when speaking with the people in your life about your loss, express gratitude and hopefulness even if you're not feeling overly filled with either.

If you can start off by thanking them for their support and patience, they may feel more inclined to continue with that support and patience.

And last but not least, it helps those around you to know that you feel hopeful. You may not know this now, but there's something I know to be true and it's the one *and only* promise I'll make to anyone I work with: how you feel now isn't how you'll always feel. Know this, internalize it, and let the people around you know it too.

Because in the end, easing isolation is about feeling connected, seen, and understood by the people you spend the most time with. This journey is not for everyone. Find the people who you can trust this with (it may not always be who you think) and let them in on what you're going through. Isolation ends with communication. And today's as good a day as any to start.

THE TOOL

Use this template to organize your thoughts. You can fill it out and send it, or use it as a base for a conversation—whatever you choose. Share it with as many people as you like, and remember that the one who benefits most from better communication in grief is you.

Dear ________________________,

I'm writing because I need you to better understand this loss, my grief, and all that has changed since it happened.

You have always known me as a person who is ________________ (think of adjectives here: strong, funny, easy-going, optimistic...include as many as you like).

I'm sure you've seen the change in me, and I know I don't feel like that same person right now. While every day of grief is different, most of the time, I'd say I'm feeling ___________________ (exhausted, scared, angry, helpless, alone...again include as many descriptive words that you can think of).

This loss has changed everything. I have lost the life I thought I would have and a future that I hoped would be. I have lost every part of who I am and who I used to be. It has changed every minute and every hour and every part of my routine. I think about it all day and pretty much all night, too.

I'm just not myself right now. I say "right now" because I hope to be able to show you a glimpse of who I was again at some point, but there is no going back to normal. The me you knew before is gone, and in some ways, I guess we all have to mourn that loss as much as any other.

But I am ______________ (hopeful, confident, filled with faith or belief...try and think of at least one positive phrase or word here) that with your love and support, I will survive this.

I may not feel as strong a person as I once was, and I'm asking for your patience because I think this pain will be with me for a very long time. In many ways, I will carry it forever. In return, and as best I am able, I will also try to be patient as I recognize that you, too, are adjusting to the changes you see in me.

More than anything, I'm inviting a conversation between us. You can ask me anything, at any time. Please don't be afraid to make me sad, and don't be fooled into thinking that if I look "okay" and that if I'm back to work or at a party or returning to some kind of routine that I'm not thinking about it. I'm always thinking about it.

It helps me to know you are thinking about it, too. I want to hear ___________________________'s name. I want to know that you miss him/her too. I don't want this loss to be forgotten.

You don't know how much this will mean to me and how much it will help me to feel less alone...

Karyn Arnold was born on a bridge in Belmar, New Jersey (true story!) and raised in Bucks County, Pennsylvania, where she currently resides. She has a bachelor's Degree in Psychology and Gerontology, along with her 200-hour CYTT and Reiki practitioner certification.

She has worked in the field of Grief and Loss for almost 25 years. Eight years ago she created the website Grief in Common, an online community dedicated to connecting grievers based on background and similar circumstances of loss. Services include message boards, a live chat room, an online classroom, Zoom support groups, education programs, and individual support.

Karyn has worked with grievers worldwide and has encountered just about every grief and loss a person can experience. Her professional and personal experience with grief means she understands this process in ways that few people can, and through her daily work, she aims to provide education, validation, and support. Through a simple 3-part process, Karyn takes the griever from where they've been, to where they are now and tries to help them answer the question, "Where do I go from here?"

She is married to her elementary school sweetheart (if that's actually a thing) and has two amazing daughters who are funnier, wiser, and more fearless than she'll ever be. Together, her family loves to travel in their RV with their three dogs, ride ATVs, and listen to live music anytime and anywhere they can.

Connect with Karyn:
Website: https://www.griefincommon.com/
Facebook: https://www.facebook.com/griefincommon
Instagram: https://www.instagram.com/griefincommon/
Online Classroom:
https://www.griefincommon.com/online-support/grief-self study/

CHAPTER 10

MINDFULNESS IN DEATH

HOW TO USE NATURE TO COPE WITH GRIEF

Kristi Capriglione, MA, LPC

Feelings come and go, like clouds in a windy sky.
Conscious breathing is my anchor.

~ Thich Nhat Hanh

MY STORY

Mindfulness came knocking on my door when death came crashing into my world. Sitting mindfully, even if only for three minutes, hasn't always come naturally. Being consumed by my thoughts of the past and fears of the future is my baseline.

I lean into my breath as I sit on the weathered dock from years of unsheltered seasons. Everything begins to take shape. My attention begins to shift outwards, and my world comes alive.

Airplane jets overhead begin to fade as they fly off into the distance. Water in the lake dances with the early autumn wind. The sun's unseasonable warmth hugs my left side as I look towards the East.

As my mind shifts inward toward my thoughts of negativity, I gently turn it back to the present moment.

The soft singing of the bird invites me back into the world. Occasionally, a dog barks at the squirrels, gathering their feast for the impending winter. Through all this, I notice a slight uneasiness in the center of my gut. Not the same worry as when she was diagnosed, but nonetheless, I feel it knocking to be heard.

One month into my 32nd year of life, my biggest regrets were not starting college right after high school, not authentically being myself, and the fractured relationship with my mom. These regrets contributed to the repeated negative thoughts I heard: *Who will love you? You can't even love yourself or find a way to get along with your mom.* These thoughts about myself played into my inability to sit. Each time I neared quiet space, my heart pounded, fears surfaced, and emotions shut down. Needless to say, heading to the emergency room with my mom wasn't exactly effortless.

In my gut, the queasiness spoke loud and clear. *Shut it down. You can't handle this. Everyone knows you'll end up running.* Hearing these thoughts, I truly grappled with myself and what was about to unfold.

After gently pleading with my mother to head to the emergency room, she obliged. At first, she was resistant even after the doctor said, "If you start feeling sick or throw up, you need to head to the ER immediately." I wasn't the only one fighting my inner demons. My mom lived with anxiety most of her life. Hearing she needed an MRI sent her concern into high gear. Fear taking over, she hoped to wait until after the weekend. A local imaging center had a Monday appointment for an open MRI, lowering her fear of claustrophobia. Unfortunately, this was no longer an option. Off to the hospital we went.

Sitting in the cold, sterile examining room, few words were spoken. What appeared to be patiently waiting on the outside was fear coming alive on the inside. *It can't be that bad. What are the odds? It's probably vertigo. The doctor even said, 'Maybe vertigo.'*

Hours were spent in that room. At the time, distracting myself became the priority. So, I opened a book I bought the week prior, written by a well-known Zen master about meditating and applying mindfulness to your life. Unbeknownst to me, this book would guide me over the next seven months and beyond. The guiding principles consisted of breathing, saying hello to emerging emotions, and learning to be present as life shifts.

As the doctor slowly entered the room, there was a palpable silence. Being able to breathe escaped me. I felt myself dropping into the deep abyss of suffocation. *The book, Kristi, what did the book say? It said to breathe. Breathe in, two, three, four. Breathe out, two, three, four.* Breathing couldn't change what we heard next, but intuitively, I understood it was a form of survival.

"The CAT scan shows an unidentified mass on your cerebellum, which explains your balance issue. We'll have to admit you for further evaluation," his words lingered.

Once again, we sat in silence. We all thought it, but none of us spoke it. *Unidentified mass? You mean cancer.* Silence held us in the safety of life being paused.

On the drive home, my silence broke. The silence of my thoughts shifted to screams of terror. Reality gripped me by the throat, and every cell of me understood my mom faced death. Eventually, the medical team confirmed a stage four lung cancer diagnosis, which metastasized to the brain. The chance of a five-year survival was less than five percent.

What the fuck! I can't do this! I can't survive this! And I don't want to! My chest, so much pain.

Breathe. Remember to breathe. Focus on your breath.

Driving to the hospital after her second brain surgery, a conversation with my sister came to mind. As I left her house in sheer agony, she looked at me and matter-of-factly said, "We'll be okay." To be clear, she didn't mean everything would be okay and my mom would live. We all came to a place of understanding her days were limited. What she meant is we could survive.

But how?

My mind kept drifting back to the book. *Breathe,* I told myself each time I remembered. Hearing my mom fall and hit the bathroom floor, I reminded myself to breathe before I lifted her back up. Listening to screams of terror in my mind, I reminded myself to breathe, helping to quiet the noise. Feeling excruciating emotional pain, I reminded myself to breathe, comforting the pure sadness. While these breaths failed to make my mom healthy, they slowed my thoughts and racing heart. They let me sit with myself for a few more seconds than my typical baseline.

Breathe.

Surviving looked different now. It meant enduring the primal howl. It meant getting through an emotional conversation. It meant surviving what I once thought I couldn't. As I realized my survival ability, I began to take this breathing onto my walks. Walking and breathing allowed my attention to focus on something other than pain, grief, and terror. Slowly, I noticed trees changing colors. I saw ants carry twice their weight. I hadn't paid attention to most of this before, and now, it helped with a mental nap from the chaos of my mom.

Breathe.

Throughout my mom's seven-month illness, she endured two major brain surgeries, one potent round of radiation, and four months in hospitals and rehabs. At each sharp turn, my breath was there to accompany me. I wish I could tell you that in death, there was gentleness. However, this wasn't the case. Being mindful during my mom's illness didn't prepare me for her death.

Breathe.

Our last living memory is of me watching her take her last breath in the same spot where I gently pleaded with her to go to the hospital—my parent's living room. Except this time, she was in a metal hospital bed, not on her comfy green couch watching *Lifetime.* The pain of her dying tripled in comparison to the experience of her illness. Death is forever. No more chances, no more hugs, no more memories would happen.

After she died, my innocence was stripped away. Pain, from somewhere deep inside, surfaced at an uncontrollable rate. Once, when I straightened my newly washed duvet cover, I dropped. My knees buckled, and tears overflowed.

I'm so sad. I'm sad for not calling and spending time with you more. I'm sad you needed to experience this. I'm sad we all can't grow older together. I'm just so sad.

Tears streamed down my face, leaving a salty aftertaste on my lips. Slowly, they dripped from my chin and landed on my shirt, soaking the collar. *Has anyone died from crying too much?*

Mostly, the pain settled in my chest, and it could stop my breath immediately. All that work on mindful breathing was for nothing. I stopped. I forgot how to breathe mindfully, or maybe I chose not to. Breathing seemed pointless. *Why breathe if we're all going to die anyway?* I was confronted with the harsh reality of death and grief each morning.

This shit sucks! This is impossible. How do I bear this?

At some point, after my mom died, my sister signed us up for a 13-mile mud run. *Great, more torture.* I cringed at the thought but figured it couldn't hurt any more than grief. Most of the training came from running outside and increasing my endurance. While I was not too fond of endurance work, I found myself connecting back to nature. After each run, I walked around the park or sat on a bench. Tears streamed down my face at times, and at others, I searched my brain, thinking of ways to get through grief. While sitting in a tearful moment one day, a faint whisper came from deep inside: *We'll be okay.*

But how?

Breathe.

Mindfulness was a foreign concept until that dreadful Friday in the hospital. Often, I questioned its simplicity and actual effectiveness. *How will focusing on my breath help me through the most harrowing moment?* With nothing to lose, I gave it my all. Each day, I practiced pausing once and took a deep breath. Over time, I found myself pausing five times a day. Then, I paused and breathed each time I walked into a room. To say it took away my pain would be a lie. However, it helped me to be present even with the pain.

Mindfulness is truly experiential. To fully understand, one has to practice it. It's like joining a gym. A certain level of faith is needed at the start. When we begin to work out, we're not 100 percent sure we will get results. However, we have seen others do something similar, and we learn to trust the process. Once we begin to see results, we stay committed and motivated. The same applies to learning mindfulness. We need to trust the process. Once we experience the impact, we become more willing to stay with the practice. The more we practice, the more we gain.

Focusing on our breath isn't the only way to bring mindfulness into our lives. We can listen to guided meditations, intentionally pause to smell our coffee before each sip, and watch the trees bud on an early spring day, to name a few. These guide and teach us to bring our attention to the present moment mindfully and thoroughly. At first, it's challenging, especially if we are unfamiliar. With practice, it becomes easier.

While my practice wasn't, and still isn't, perfect, it was more than I was doing before. Over time, a mindfulness practice builds our endurance to sit with the uncomfortable, the pain, and everything else that comes with grief. Watching a parent die and lose cognitive functioning brings a tsunami of emotions. Suppose I were asked three months before my mom was diagnosed whether I could survive her having a terminal cancer diagnosis, her losing cognitive functioning, and me needing to switch the role of child to co-caregiver, I'd say, "Fuck no!" And yet, here I am.

THE TOOL

Here, allow yourself to be guided through this meditation and embark on the practice of mindfully being present. At first, it may feel unnatural, or you may question whether you're doing it right. Approach this with no judgment or expectation and focus on the overall experience. Remember, mindfulness is experiential, and each time, it will showcase something different.

While reading each paragraph, take time before moving on to the next. Let yourself relax into the words and bring the world around you alive. After each time you practice, the experience will brighten. If you prefer to listen to this guided meditation, visit my website https://daylightgrief.com/tools-and-resources to hear a recording where I gently guide you through this tool.

- Find a serene and secluded spot in nature where you can sit comfortably. Choose a place that resonates with you, whether it's a park, a forest, a beach, or a quiet garden. Allow yourself ample time, free from distractions. As you take your seat, close your eyes for a moment and take a few deep breaths, allowing your body to relax.

- Begin by grounding yourself in the present moment. Feel the firm support of the earth beneath you. Visualize roots extending from your body, sinking deep into the earth's core. These roots symbolize your strength and resilience during your grieving process. Connect with the steady stability of the Earth.
- Shift your focus to your breath. Take slow, deliberate breaths, inhaling through your nose and exhaling through your mouth. Observe the rise and fall of your chest with each breath. Let each breath become an anchor, gently guiding you into the present moment and calming the turbulence within.
- Open your eyes and take in the exquisite beauty that surrounds you. Allow your gaze to wander, taking in the colors, shapes, and textures of your environment. Observe the interplay of light and shadow on leaves, the graceful dance of branches swaying in the breeze, or the gentle flow of a nearby stream. Nature is a living testament to the interconnectedness of all life.
- Fully engage your senses. Focus solely on the sounds of nature—the birds singing, leaves rustling, water trickling. Feel the warmth of the sun caressing your skin or the coolness of a gentle breeze on your face. Use your sense of touch to connect with the earth beneath you. Let your senses become an intimate bridge between you and the natural world. Feel free to close your eyes for a moment and take in all the senses.
- As you continue to observe and engage with nature, practice mindful presence. Become aware of any emotion that arises within you without judgment. Allow your emotions of grief to exist in this very moment. Acknowledge them and know that they are valid, seen, and held.
- Contemplate the profound concept of impermanence, which is inherent in the natural world. Just as seasons change and trees shed their leaves, life moves through cycles of transformation. Similarly, your grief will evolve with time. Embrace the natural ebb and flow of emotions, trusting in the healing journey.

- Take a moment to express gratitude for the gift of connecting with nature during your grieving process. Gratitude is a potent tool for healing and finding peace. Reflect on the beauty and serenity nature generously offers, even amidst your grief.
- As you near the end of this guided mindful moment, take a few moments to reflect on any insights or feelings that arose during your time in nature. If any burdens or emotions are weighing heavy on your heart, imagine placing them gently in the hands of the natural world, trusting that it can hold and heal them.

As the guided mindful moment comes to an end, remember that nature is a reliant companion, always available to offer solace and support whenever you seek it. Your grief is your own, and it's crucial to honor your emotions and grant yourself the time needed to heal. Nature, with its timeless wisdom, is here to nurture and guide you on your journey.

When you're ready, slowly bring your awareness back to the present moment. Begin to wiggle your toes and your fingers. Take a few deep breaths. Carry with you the sense of peace and connection you've found in nature as you continue your path toward healing and self-discovery.

Kristi Capriglione, MA, LPC, is a compassionate and skilled licensed professional counselor, bringing over 15 years of invaluable expertise to the mental health field.

Throughout her career, Kristi has offered her support to individuals grappling with the profound grief that accompanies losing a cherished loved one. Her experience equips her with a unique perspective, informing her compassionate counseling approach.

Kristi's qualifications include a post-master certificate in Thanatology from Hood College, showcasing her deep knowledge of the intricacies of death, dying, and the grieving process. She has also completed comprehensive training as an end-of-life doula through the International End-of-Life Doula Association (INELDA), enhancing her ability to support individuals and families as they approach life's final chapters.

As the proud owner of Daylight Grief, a private practice in Denville, NJ, Kristi specializes in offering individual and group therapy for adults who have experienced the profound loss of a loved one. Her practice serves as a sanctuary where clients can safely explore their grief, process their emotions, and embark on a journey toward healing and renewed hope.

One of Kristi's innovative contributions to the field is her creation of the Hiking with Grief group at her practice. This unique program seamlessly integrates mindfulness and ecotherapy into the grief counseling process. This holistic approach fosters healing on physical, emotional, and spiritual levels, offering a sense of connection with nature and one's inner self.

Beyond her professional endeavors, Kristi is a nature enthusiast and an adventure seeker. She finds solace on the water through kayaking and paddleboarding, where the serenity of the waves mirrors the tranquility she brings to her clients. On land, she embarks on a delightful quest to discover the best ice cream and pizza, savoring life's simple pleasures.

Connect with Kristi: https://linktr.ee/daylightgrief

CHAPTER 11

A LOVE LETTER TO MY SONS, IN MEMORIAM

NAVIGATING THE RIPPLES OF LOSS, LOVE, AND TRANSITION

Carol S. Miller, LCSW

MY STORY

Dear Matthew and Daniel,

Growing up, I loved to throw pebbles into the lake near my grandparents' cottage. The pebble hit the water with a loud splash, and ripples would fan out from the point of impact. The water shifted and changed through the ripples. It would never be the same as it had been before the pebble hit. To me, loss and grief are much like those pebbles, the water, and the ripples. A death or other loss occurs and strikes the waters of your life with a resounding splash. From that moment, your life is changed in a multitude of ways—painful, jarring, challenging, and ultimately, often transformative ways. You, my sons, are two such pebbles in my life, and the ripples from your births and deaths continue to shift and change my life's direction in never-ending ways.

You, Matthew, my first son, would be 37 years old this year. And you, Daniel, my second son, would be 36. I can see you both in my mind's eye, just as I have seen you throughout the years. Like your younger sister, Jessica, now 35, I have no doubt you both would have been kind, intelligent, compassionate human beings. I enjoy imagining you with families of your own, at gatherings with your sister and her family. You would have been protective, loving big brothers and uncles.

So let me back up to where that first pebble hit the water, even before that, and recall our story. I was 32 years old when I met your father, Lynn. I was clear with him when we met—I wanted children, and I was ready to have a child now. We were lucky. Infertility was never an issue for us; we got pregnant quickly and easily.

The pregnancy with you, Matthew, was completely "normal," with no indications that there might be any problems. I went into labor in the early morning hours of February 21, 1986. I was so anxious I threw up in one of the ashtrays in the hospital waiting room soon after we arrived. Taken to a room, I was placed on monitors and left in the bed to labor; everything continued as expected. At some point, however, the doctor came in, frowned, and said, "There's meconium. Get her to the delivery room now." I recalled hearing that meconium might sometimes be expelled during the birthing process, and did not necessarily indicate a problem, so I didn't worry. You were delivered quickly; you came out blue. Doctors and nurses checked you out in a frenzy of activity. I was barely allowed to see you before you were whisked away to the NICU. A big pebble, a huge splash.

What the hell just happened?! Your father and I were in shock. This wasn't the way the story was supposed to be written! Yet, here we were, in a room with another woman in the next bed, cuddling and holding her baby. We had no baby to hold and no idea what was going on with you. Who knows how much time passed—minutes, hours? Eventually, the doctor came in and said, "Your baby is being helicoptered to Children's Hospital for emergency heart surgery."

What? How did we get here? What is wrong with my son? Lynn drove to Children's to wait for news; I had to stay behind to try to rest and recuperate. Fortunately, I was moved to a single room, so I didn't have to endure the continual heartbreak of witnessing another mother's joy with her living, breathing, healthy child.

You survived the surgery and were placed in the NICU at Children's. When I first saw you there, your little body in a huge adult-sized bed, connected to every conceivable wire and tube, I wondered, *How can I mother this child? How can I take care of him?* Our days were spent going back and forth from the hospital. I tried to pump breast milk for you. Your father and grandmother (a nurse) tried to read and explain the scribbled notes your doctors and nurses left on your chart. I could not take it in. I wanted to hold you and take you away and get back to a normal life, be your mom.

The daily back-and-forth was grinding, and I took a day off from going to the hospital. Later, I felt so guilty about that decision. What kind of a mother was I, anyway, not going to be with you every single day? After a couple of weeks, they finally said you could go home with us. They gave us a ton of medications and a list of things to watch for. Having no experience with a newborn, I worried. *Could we truly care for this fragile baby?* I felt helpless and unprepared.

We had you with us for about two weeks. During that time, I held you close and slept with you in my arms. Your large, brown eyes seemed to drink in every sight around you. They captivated and held me spellbound. Later, I wondered if you had known your time with us would be short. *Did you need every minute to live a meaningful life?* You couldn't breastfeed. You didn't grow. It was as though all your energy was spent on simply staying alive.

On your last day home with us, you were inconsolable, crying. I couldn't comfort you. And then you were back in the NICU at Children's Hospital. They tried to fix you. Yet they could do nothing. A day or so later, they called us at 3 AM to come. I knew. *They never call you at 3 AM if things are okay!*

Sure enough, a doctor greeted us at the doors of the NICU saying, "There's nothing more we can do for your son." Once at your bedside, they asked if I wanted them to remove the wires and tubes and put you in my arms. *Of course,* I thought, *give him to me. If he is in my arms, he will be fine. Everything will be all right.* Within seconds of laying you in my arms, you gave a soft little sigh, and I felt you leave. My heart broke. We had you with us for just 40 days.

Days and weeks passed. My brain was in a fog. I recall little of that time. Lynn had to make all the arrangements. I could barely breathe my way through the day, let alone think coherently. I obsessed about you, wondering what I did wrong, what I could have done differently. I felt empty and alone. Other than your father, I knew no one else who had gone through this experience. People—friends, family—would tell me I'd feel better. They said, "You're still young. You can try again," or "Well, at least you know you can get pregnant." The doctors all said, "It was a fluke. It won't happen again." Mother's Day came. All I could wonder was, *I have no baby in my arms. Am I a mom? How can I go on living without you in my life?*

In the next few months, I returned to work (great distraction). We met with a counselor. We started attending a support group for parents who experienced miscarriages, infant deaths, and stillbirths (MIS). Surrounded by others with similar experiences gave me a sense of community, validation, and recognition that what I was experiencing and feeling was normal. I wasn't alone. These things helped me to move forward again even though there were still many train-wreck moments and many more ripples.

For some time after your death, I thought I'd never want to be pregnant again. I could not go through that again. Yet, at some point, my brain took a 180-degree turn, and I thought: *It's time. I can do this. I'm ready.* A month later, I was pregnant again, this time with you, Daniel.

Was I anxious? Sure. But I kept holding onto the promise made by doctors that what happened to your brother was a fluke. An ultrasound showed you had a strong heart (Matthew's autopsy indicated a severely malformed heart). Turned out your heart was the only thing right with you! Toward the end of the seventh month, the doctors became concerned that you were not measuring as you should be. A stress test alerted them to potential problems, and they sent me to the hospital for another fetal stress test. Again, you did poorly. An emergency cesarian section was ordered. An epidural was injected. My arms were tied down. I was pumped full of morphine. You were taken from me, and this time, I wasn't even granted a look at you before you were whisked away to the hospital NICU. *Not again, God! Please, not again!* Another splash—expanding ripples.

The next day, a specialist arrived from Children's Hospital. Standing in the hospital room doorway, compassion in her eyes, she said, "We've drawn blood and sent it for genetic testing. The results will take a couple of weeks. However, I must tell you, based on my examination and experience, I believe he has a genetic condition known as Trisomy 13. Babies with this condition do not live very long. And if they do live, they require significant care in an institutional environment."

Nooooooo!

We agonized over a decision no parent should ever have to make—do we remove you from life support? The hospital staff brought you to me. You were not a pretty baby like Matthew. You had a cleft lip and palate; your forehead sloped back. You had six fingers and six toes. I felt deep shame. *What kind of a mother am I if I can barely look at you?* You were with us for only two days. Again, devastation, profound sadness, emptiness, loneliness, and helplessness. And this time, as well, deep, deep anger. *How could this happen to us again? What could we have done to deserve this? What could my sons have possibly done to deserve this? Why these ripples?*

Honestly, I don't know if it was sheer insanity or a stubborn sense of perseverance that allowed us to try again about six months later. I was an anxious basket case throughout that third pregnancy. I sought ways to impose some sense of control. I asked for every conceivable test. I needed assurance. I wanted them to schedule a c-section. My doctor agreed, although he insisted it was unnecessary. Even though your sister, Jessica, arrived looking perfectly healthy and sound, the doctor put her through a battery of tests to assure us that she was fine. The first night she was home with us, she came down with a case of diarrhea. Holding her, all I could think was, *She's gonna die. That's what my babies do. They die.* There are days I'm still amazed she managed to grow into the amazing woman she is today.

Many believe that our loved ones must be alive to have an impact on our lives. That is not my lived experience. Initially, after your deaths, the ripples I experienced in my life all felt negative—loss of faith in my body to perform as it "should," loss of a sense of control, loss of innocence and optimism, loss of relationships in my life, loss of a piece of my identity. And I feared so many other losses. *Would I ever be a parent? Could I ever find joy in being pregnant? Would I ever be happy again?*

Just as those pebbles rippled through the lake of my childhood, you continue to spread and pulse in and through every fiber of my being in so many ways. First and foremost, I recognize my capacity for unconditional love. Letting go of you both was one of the most difficult things I've ever experienced. Yet my love for you remains strong and true. You guided me to reach out to the facilitator of the MIS group, and with your father, we agreed to take on the facilitation of the group. Later, I chose to leave my job with a law firm and complete my bachelor's and master's degrees. Fresh from completing my master's degree, I chose to work for a hospice organization. You helped me to recognize that I can make choices in my life that better align with my values, including leaving difficult employers, taking risks in moving into private practice, and deciding to relocate to another area of the country. You've helped me to recognize my resilience, to see we're not alone, and to learn how to reach out and be vulnerable. You pushed me to learn and grow and understand how grief impacts us, our families, our communities, and our world. You've shown me the kind of compassionate support most needed to help ourselves accept the ripples that occur and find new ways to navigate our lives and grow.

I haven't always liked these teachings, but I've come to appreciate them and your presence within them. I need you both to know that I feel you at my side often. I will love you deeply forever.

Thank you for this most recent hug (encouraging me to write this chapter!).

Love, Mom

THE TOOL

Our culture still minimizes or runs from grief. This is especially true for losses through infertility, miscarriage, stillbirth, and infant death. These types of losses are often invisible to others. They represent "disenfranchised grief"—grief not usually openly acknowledged, socially accepted, or publicly mourned. Often experienced as a trauma because of their unexpected, sudden nature, they go against the grain of what we are expecting—to give birth, not to experience death.

Created by Cath Duncan, co-founder of The Creative Grief Studio, The Ripples of Loss is a tool for exploring and integrating grief. I've offered this tool to many of my clients and group participants. It's useful for death and non-death losses alike, and people always tell me they found it helpful for gaining greater insight into their loss and grief. I'm going to share a shortened version of The Ripple of Loss here so you can use it, too.

The tool is simple. I invite you to gather:

- One or more sheets of unlined paper (8½ x 11 or larger if you like!).
- Art supplies of your choice—pencils, colored pencils, crayons, markers, paints, pastels, whatever you enjoy working with.
- You may want to have a journal nearby to make notes as you go along.

You may wish to have some quiet, peaceful music playing in the background. I invite you to first settle or ground yourself in the moment before beginning to work. You might sit quietly, focusing on your breath. Pay attention to where and how it enters and leaves your body, the rise and fall of your abdomen as your breathing deepens. You might enjoy placing your hands over your heart and continuing to breathe into your heart space. Or select another grounding technique that calls to you.

When you're ready, select a piece of paper and a writing implement. Draw three concentric circles, like a bullseye: one small circle in the middle of the paper (perhaps 1.5 to 2 inches in diameter), a second circle around that (perhaps four to five inches in diameter), and a third large circle around these two.

1. In the center circle, write down or symbolically identify your loss. For example, I might write the names of one or both of my sons in the center circle.
2. In the second circle, using words or symbols, note your responses to this question: *What other losses have you experienced because of this death or loss?* I might write: *Loss of innocence; trust in my body; identity as a mother; faith in medical technology.*
3. In the third outer circle, again using words or symbols, note your responses to this question: *What other losses are you concerned about or fearful of experiencing because of this loss?* My responses might be: *The ability to parent in a joyful, easy, non-anxious way; being able to enjoy a pregnancy; losing relationships with others who don't get it.*
4. It is important to recognize that despite these deep injuries and losses, they do not define our lives completely. In the blank space that surrounds your circles, note your responses to these questions:

Despite this loss, what remains? What blessings or gifts are still present in my life? For example, I might write: *unconditional love; resilience; greater understanding and empathy for others who grieve; friends and family who stepped up and supported us.*

After completing your Ripples of Loss, you may find it helpful to journal. Here are some questions you might wish to reflect upon:

- As you moved through the process, what did you notice in your body? In your emotions? In your thoughts?
- What surprised you about this process?
- What did you learn about yourself and your loss?
- What invisible or ambiguous losses did you identify through this process? How do those losses impact your primary loss?
- What new meaning or meanings might have arisen for you through this process?
- What new resources came to light for you?

If you've found this Ripple of Loss process meaningful and you'd like to do a deeper dive using Cath's expanded Ripple of Loss journaling prompts and guided creative process, I encourage you to work through Cath Duncan's book, *Untangle Your Grief – Questions + Art After Loss,* which you'll find at her website, www.RememberingForGood.com. If you'd like to train to use The Ripple of Loss and many other wonderful creative tools in your work and become a Creative Grief Support Practitioner, you can do that with Cath Duncan and Kara Jones at The Creative Grief Studio (www.CreativeGriefStudio.com).

Carol S. Miller, LCSW, is a licensed clinical social worker and has worked in the field of loss and grief for over 25 years. Carol graduated with her master's in social work from the Virginia Commonwealth University. Throughout her career, she has worked as a therapist, bereavement coordinator, group facilitator, program manager, and educator in agency, private practice, and volunteer settings. Carol currently owns and operates her own private practice. She holds clinical licenses in Arizona, Virginia, Maryland, and the District of Columbia and enjoys working with folks in those areas of the country. Carol serves and supports grieving folks through all types of loss experiences, including death loss, pregnancy loss, infertility, divorce, job loss, loss of health, and many other non-death losses. She is certified as a Creative Grief Support Practitioner, a Grief Educator, and she is part of the teaching team for the Creative Grief Studio. Carol is also a Certified Daring Way™ Facilitator, and she enjoys facilitating Daring Way, Rising Strong, and Gifts of Imperfection groups at various times throughout the year. Carol lives in Tucson, Arizona, and when she is not working, she enjoys spending time with her spouse, Suzanne, their Russell Terrier, Holly, and the many good friends she has connected with over the years. She also travels frequently throughout the year to Massachusetts, where her daughter, son-in-law, and two grandchildren currently reside.

Connect with Carol:

Email: www.carolsmillerlcsw@gmail.com

Website: www.carolsmillerlcsw.com

Creative Grief Studio Website: https://creativegriefstudio.com

Grief Educator

Website: https://grief.com/grief-certified-counselor/name/carol-miller/

Daring Way Website: https://brenebrown.com

CHAPTER 12

My grief journey

CARVING A HEALING PATH BY LISTENING TO AND HONORING YOURSELF

Karen Ann White, MS, LPC

MY STORY

I cried myself to sleep every night for four months.

*

"Oh, Dad."

The words were instinctive. My sister and I were in his ICU room, and the nurse spoke what we knew yet didn't want to hear. Dad was dying. Through the fog that overtook my brain, I heard her say one of the medicines was the only thing keeping his heart rate up and that they couldn't give that to him for too long. "The doctor would like to meet with the four of you," she continued, her voice calm and quiet. "Are your mom and brother able to come now?" she asked, kindness and compassion etched on her face.

Kristi looked at me as I spoke the words and walked to Dad's bed. *How is this happening? What are we going to do?* Were her thoughts the same as mine?

We rode the proverbial rollercoaster of emotions during Dad's three-month hospital stay—his unexplainable pain, overlooked infection, broken MRI machines, a couple of almost-releases as he made improvements, his sudden inability to walk, a transfer late on Christmas Eve to the Level 1 trauma hospital for emergency spinal surgery, and even a good week post-surgery beginning rehab at the best facility in the state. *And now he's not going to make it?*

Rubbing his forehead with one hand and squeezing his swollen hand with my other, I looked at Kristi who moved beside me. Both of us were fighting back tears. Time froze. Somehow, the beeping machines, the stark white walls, and the bustle of ICU activity outside the door disappeared. And then reality: *We have to do this.*

We texted Mom and Kevin. Mom asked if we were sure because only two people could be there at a time. We were sure—the doctor wanted to talk with us together.

Leaving Kristi sitting next to Dad, I walked back to the lobby to share the news with his brother, who flew in early that morning.

Understandingly, the young doctor explained to the four of us, "Unfortunately, the staph infection has returned and taken over his body. I'm so sorry." We could continue the medications and the machines and let time and the infection wreak more havoc on Dad, or we could say our goodbyes and stop everything.

"What would you do if this was your dad or spouse?" Mom asked him, her disbelief not yet materialized into sorrow.

How is this happening?

Just two short weeks earlier, in the wee hours of January 10, as I was unsuccessfully trying to sleep in the plastic recliner in Dad's hospital room, I heard him fumbling for something. I sat up, and before I could jump to his aid, he said, "Happy Birthday, Toots." Astonished that he knew what day it was, let alone my birthday, I smiled and said, "Thanks, Dad. You win for being the first person to wish me happy birthday."

"You're 45 today, right?"

What? He has been in and out of lucidity for weeks now. Hospital psychosis they say. How in the world does he know how old I am?

"Yes sir, 45. That means we're both officially old now." We laughed, and I told him I loved him and was thankful to be spending my birthday with him. Later that morning, after my sister came to relieve me, we finally got the news that Dad was cleared to move to the rehab facility. *Best birthday present ever!*

I planned on visiting my mom's 96-year-old dad, Pappaw, that day. He was in another hospital and rehab facility most of the time Dad was sick and was recently released. He and I were always close and became more like friends in the last 15 years. Pappaw hadn't given me his traditional birthday spankings in decades, but we always talked on my birthday. I hadn't seen him since Dad had been sick—we hardly left Dad alone the entire time—and this year especially, I was longing to see him and hug his neck. Pappaw's wisdom and confident, steady faith meant so much to me since my grandmother died when I was 22.

However, I decided to stay and help get Dad moved. Even though we knew we would be traveling a long, hard road with his recovery, we were hopeful and excited amid the uncertainties. Also, due to COVID policies in place, only two people were permitted to visit for the entirety of his stay. This might be the last time I'd see Dad for a while, and I wanted to check out his new digs and spend a little more time with him.

As we waited for hospital staff to come get him, I asked Kristi to take a birthday picture of Dad and me. It's the last picture I have with him and the last one taken of him.

Back to January 24, 2022.

We spent the rest of that day with him. "Dad's not gonna make it," I told my mom's sister when she answered the phone. "Mom wants you to be here." She came, along with my sister's husband, my brother's fiancé, and my boyfriend of seven years. Taking turns alone and with each other, we said goodbye to Dad. We laughed, we cried, and we looked into his baby blues one last time.

The preacher came. The nurse asked us to step outside while they unhooked the machine that helped Dad breathe so his lungs could rest.

Circled closely around Dad's bed, sharing memories through our disbelief, we did the thing that no one prepared us to do.

I heard Mom's voice quietly ask, "Can we sing Jesus Loves Me?"

Slowly, and most of us with quivering voices (except the preacher, whose voice was truly angelic) we joined together and quietly sang that familiar melody we all knew since childhood.

"Jesus loves me, this I know, for the Bible tells me so. Little ones to Him belong, they are weak, but He is strong. Yes, Jesus loves me. Yes, Jesus loves me. Yes, Jesus loves me, the Bible tells me so."

As we were singing, Dad took his last breath and slipped quietly away from us.

I lingered for a moment after everyone filed out, willing myself to believe that this was the last time I'd see my sweet dad's physical body and be in his presence. I didn't want to leave.

Our glue was gone.

My safe person.

The one who helped my four-year-old self write a letter to the Oak Ridge Boys asking if they'd play at my birthday party—and was just as excited as I was that they might come.

The one who knew how I needed to be loved and did it so well.

"Oh, Dad." I left the hospital with my mom and boyfriend and walked into a world without my dad in it.

That's when the nightly tears came. Crawling into bed I thought, *not tonight.* I tried to pray and hoped sleep would come. Instead, I found myself talking to Dad. Out loud. Asking him questions. Telling him how I felt, and what was going on. Interweaving my conversations with Dad and conversations with God, I let go.

Pappaw died April 14, 2022.

A couple of weeks after Pappaw's funeral (where my tears flowed nonstop), I woke up one morning realizing I hadn't cried the night before. It freaked me out a little. Weirdly, I got used to it. I wouldn't say it made me comfortable, but it became my ritual. I'd lay there, take a deep breath, say, "Oh, Dad," and then the tears and the talking would come. It was healing. *What will I do now?*

July 22, 2023 - *What am I doing here?! Sometimes, I feel like I'm where I'm supposed to be, experiencing a new place, beauty, exploring, resting, and healing from the last year and a half. At other times I feel like I'm in some kind of psychological bootcamp that I didn't sign up for.*

Did it start with the break-up text or when Dad and Pappaw died? Was it before? After? Does it matter?

Here I am, regardless - in San Juan, Puerto Rico, sitting outside my cozy, peaceful apartment late at night, mesmerized by the sound of the coqui (local frogs whose sound resembles the pronunciation of their name). Although I can't see them, I have fallen in love with their sound and will miss it when I leave. I arrived on July 4, full of excitement, curiosity, hope, goals, uncertainty, and questions about the direction my life was headed. I knew I would be working while here, yet I was also craving rest, renewal, and adventure. Healing. Solitude. I wanted to experience that feeling I get when I'm somewhere new. Before my departure from Jackson, I crafted a list of what I hoped to work on during my two-month stay on the island. Part of me didn't know what I wanted or needed. I just knew I wanted to get unstuck - from the feelings, the rut, the uncertainty of the last year and a half. It hasn't gone exactly the way I planned (or some days even hoped) – it has been a different "format," as a good friend says, a different way of healing.

August 1, 2023 - I'm the only person on the beach this morning. Not sure why that hit me. I'm just glad I noticed it and stopped to be grateful. My heart is full. I'm glad I came back. Even with the additional questions and challenges that have come up during my time here, causing me to think about my entire life, I'm trying to be in the moment. Maybe that's the lesson, the reason everything fell into place for me to come back?

I wonder about Dad – what risks did he take that I never knew about? Which ones was he proud of, and which ones did he regret? How did he make decisions? Did he feel like he was in control of his life?

I catch myself wishing lately, more than usual, that Dad was here. I've been wrestling with where my life is going, and before he died, just knowing he was in the world made me feel safe.

There hasn't been one technique, method, or skill I've used to help myself wade through these murky waters that I've been navigating.

My dad died. And that changed my life.

I've been figuring it out one day at a time ever since.

Then Pappaw died. Ten months later, just a year after Dad's death anniversary, my boyfriend ended our relationship out of the blue with a text message. That sparked a myriad of feelings and questions, bringing my grief from the previous year back to the surface.

When I found myself in Puerto Rico this summer, asking myself how I got there, I realized that since Dad had gotten sick and throughout the last year and a half, when I thought I was flailing and directionless at times, I was doing the thing that felt right for me. I was choosing what I needed to do to keep moving forward and to heal amid my grief and feeling lost.

Even when it appeared weird or didn't make sense to others, it was normal for me. And that was okay.

I learned to listen to myself. To pay attention to what was happening inside me, how I felt, what I needed. To trust myself. To honor my feelings, my memories, my needs. To care for myself.

Nobody prepares you for death and grief—the feelings, the questions that arise inside you. Maybe because everyone experiences it differently. Who knows? It's certainly not something we sit around and talk about.

Death—and everything that comes with it that we label "grief"—changes us.

Adequately explaining what my heart and head have experienced lately seems impossible. Yet it's all normal.

I was talking with some other therapists recently about how death can be an accelerator, a motivator, and how it can wake us up and lead us to re-evaluate everything about our lives.

Honestly, a couple of life questions roamed around in my head before Dad died. I kept them on the back burner of my brain because life had become familiar, and acknowledging that they were there and that I needed to answer them was too scary.

Then death came.

Not only did honoring Dad's and Pappaw's lives and legacies become hugely important to me, but those questions came flooding back to the surface all at the same time.

I breathed a sigh of relief when one of those therapists said that death and grief can lead to identity reconstruction. I was glad to have a label for what I knew I was experiencing.

I'm not excited that these deaths gave me the courage to listen to myself and to start taking the steps I needed to answer the question, "Who do I want to be now?" Yet, I know both Dad and Pappaw are looking down at me and cheering me on, as proud of me as they've ever been.

And I'm determined to continue this process, whatever it might look and feel like. To lean into this courageousness brought on by their deaths, to live out their legacies, and to continue listening to and trusting myself, and ultimately God, to create the life and the identity that I was hardwired to live.

THE TOOL

I can't tell you exactly what to do because we all have different feelings and needs. What I can encourage you to believe is that everything you're feeling and experiencing after the death of a loved one or another significant loss is okay and normal.

It's okay if the loss creates a paradigm shift. Honor that. Embrace it if you can. Eventually, things will start making more sense. You'll feel better and stronger. You'll learn that grief and joy can coexist. Things will start lining up, and you'll start to see that reconstructed identity taking shape. It's not easy, and more questions will come. Take the time to feel the feelings, acknowledge the questions, and do what you need to do to find the answers. When you do, you'll come back home to yourself.

For me, listening to myself and honoring my needs looked like:

- Taking time off work
- Limiting time with people who felt draining
- Getting real with my closest friends
- Letting the tears fall, no matter where I was or who I was with—crying is healing y'all
- Meditating, breathing

- Writing a birthday card to Pappaw and reading it out loud at his grave
- Speaking at both funerals
- Enjoying a nice takeout meal and wine aptly labeled "Complicated" on my ex-boyfriend's birthday
- Dinner and toasting our dads' memories with two good friends on Father's Day
- Incorporating legacy and ritual into my life
- Therapy
- Taking a gym break. I used that time in the mornings to read, reflect, journal, and pray; this was invaluable for me
- Reviving a family tradition of going to Waffle House on Christmas even though my mom, boyfriend, and I were the only ones who went
- Going to Puerto Rico with two amazing friends the week my ex-boyfriend and I were supposed to be in Colorado — so freeing and healing and presented me with new opportunities and a door to return

To start listening to and honoring yourself, slow down. If you have to cut some things out temporarily, do it. This came naturally to me (like the gym and even church). I didn't want to stop these things, yet something in me needed that break. Don't worry, y'all. I've talked with my preacher about the church part, and we're good. I just couldn't go for a minute.

Breathe. Pay attention to your body. Move. Spend time outside. Put your bare feet on the ground.

Get a notebook. Write in it—your feelings, needs, those questions that keep popping up.

Step by step, do the thing that feels right for you—the thing you need to do. Just go with it.

This is how you honor yourself.

Don't worry about what other people think. If you're worried, do it anyway. You're on your own healing journey.

Some of the questions I've been answering are:

- I want to honor Dad's and Pappaw's lives and the good parts of my relationship. What are meaningful ways I can do this?
- What feels right to me? If I don't know the answer immediately, I'm acknowledging what's happening and my needs and feelings about it.
- What gives me a sense of purpose? How can I do more of this?
- Who are my people? Am I being real with them? How can they support me? Am I asking for this?
- What are my core values? Is the way I'm living congruent with them?
- Who am I?
- What do I want?
- What do I need?
- Where am I going, and what will life look like when I get there? What will I be doing?
- How can I live out the both/and that grief and loss present (e.g., sadness/joy, fear/courage, anger/gratitude)?

Word to the wise: don't tackle these all at once!

Use these like journal prompts, especially when you're feeling stuck. Focus on one at a time, and give yourself the time you need to reflect and answer them.

This is an ongoing journey. The waves of grief and loss ebb and flow, as will your healing path.

Come back to these questions and others that arise as often as you need. Get comfortable with uncomfortable feelings.

You might not be able to take a trip or move to a new city. That's okay. You don't have to.

Just do the thing, whatever you need to do. You'll be so glad you do.

Here's to growth. Here's to legacy and ritual. Here's to healing.

Long live Percy Campbell. Long live Jim White.

Long live you.

Karen Ann White is a Licensed Professional Counselor with over two decades of experience working with individuals, couples, adolescents, and families. Karen also has extensive experience providing counseling and consultation to military personnel and their family members. She loves working with people and is passionate about helping her clients grow into their potential, realize their worth, and live full lives. Karen believes that healing happens within the context of relationship, and she is committed to providing a warm, non-judgmental space where clients will be heard and supported as they work through their issues and journey toward healing, hope, and restoration.

As a teenager, Karen knew that she wanted to help people, and after personal experiences led her to counseling, she determined that this field was the best way to live out her calling. Karen successfully helps her clients navigate through relationship issues, grief and loss, life transitions, military work/life issues, and the wounds caused by addiction.

Karen Ann received both a B.S. in Psychology and an M.S. in Counseling from Mississippi State University and is a diehard Bulldog fan. She serves as the Chapter Captain for Team RWB Jackson, a health and wellness community for veterans, and is the Secretary for Mission Vigilant for the 22, a 501(c)3 organization for veterans, first responders, and their families. Karen is always up for an adventure! In her free time, she enjoys traveling and experiencing new cultures, book clubbing, running, and spending time with her friends and family. She currently maintains offices in Mississippi and Puerto Rico and splits her time between the two.

Karen would love to connect with you:
LinkTree: https://linktr.ee/kawhite28
Facebook: https://www.facebook.com/KarenWhiteLPC
Email: karenwhitelpc@gmail.com

CHAPTER 13

MINDFUL MOTION

THE ULTIMATE TOOL FOR HEALING

Lisa Millis, MA, CHC

MY STORY

I've always grounded myself in nature. From as young as five years old, whenever I was upset, I ran to a maple tree in my yard—one with low branches inviting me to climb up, catch my breath, and look down at the world from a fresh perspective.

This form of nature-based therapy allowed me to return home with a shift in energy. It was an early developmental version of emotional regulation. One I often returned to, in one form or another, in the turbulent years to come.

When I was eleven, I experienced the death by suicide of my 28-year-old Aunt Donna. She was the youngest of seven children whose parents, my grandparents, were both living with mental health issues. They lost custody of all their children when Donna was two, forcing her and her siblings to be separated and raised in foster care.

In the first decade of my life, I spent a lot of time with Aunt Donna, helping her care for my baby sister (who is eight years younger) while my parents worked full-time. This closeness gave me a unique window into Donna's chaotic life.

Though I couldn't have understood at the time, Donna suffered from her own trauma and significant mental health issues. But I knew Donna to be a kind, generous, sort of big sister who shared my love of "The Muppet Show" and offered me unfettered access to her awesome album collection.

In the days leading up to her death, I remember asking to sleep over so Donna wasn't alone. I witnessed what I now know were several manic episodes and when Donna wasn't behaving normally, I wanted to be with her more often to safeguard her, to protect her from herself. Donna confided to me that she felt alienated by her family, and although I assured her everything would be okay, I knew, deep down, something was wrong.

A week later, a police officer was at our door to inform us that Donna had tried to take her own life and was being taken by ambulance to the local VA hospital. Once there, she'd be placed on life support until my mother and her siblings could arrive to decide how to proceed. Mom was her primary caregiver. She was distraught by the situation and by the thought of having to unite with her estranged siblings to decide the fate of her baby sister. In the end, the consensus was to terminate her life support.

When those same siblings stood to speak at Donna's funeral, presenting an absurdly false narrative of their roles in her life, I couldn't handle it. And when my uncle, her eldest brother, announced he would throw the first shovel of dirt onto her casket, I turned to my grandfather—my father's father—and said, "Grandpa, I'm going to be sick. I gotta go home—now!" He explained that he couldn't leave because he was a pallbearer.

A wave of nausea surged through me as I bolted outside for some air. I ran down the steps—and kept running, nonstop, a mile and a half uphill, all the way home, where I climbed my tree, pulled my knees to my chest, and cried.

At 11 years old, I was already forming core philosophies about the stigma associated with mental health, coping with grief, and why it's important to live without regrets. If not, a person might find himself standing at a funeral, spinning a false narrative to mask a guilty conscience.

At the end of my sophomore year of high school, I started dating a boy whom I'll call James.

My parents weren't thrilled about our age difference. James had already graduated, was attending community college, and worked for a local contractor—whereas I still couldn't drive and had a curfew. Nevertheless, we managed to see each other almost daily, typically during my lunch period or after my sports practice. Even though he was my first serious boyfriend, I felt certain he'd be my last.

Two years into our relationship, James slid his Chevy Camaro off the road and into a tree. He was removed with the Jaws of Life and rushed by ambulance to the hospital. I was home, waiting for his call to say goodnight, when shortly after 9:00 p.m., his mother called to say that James had been in a very serious accident.

Seeing James in the Emergency Room, covered in wounds and blood, tubes tangled everywhere, was so overwhelming that even now, over thirty years later, I see it with perfect clarity. Once he was stabilized, James was transported to a larger medical facility, where he remained in a coma for two months. I spent every afternoon at his bedside holding his hand, talking with him about my day, exercising his legs, and wishing he'd blink or wiggle a finger. It took ten weeks for him to finally open his eyes. I was so elated just for him to be conscious that I couldn't see how badly the accident had affected his ability to process emotions or understand reality.

James couldn't walk, eat, or perform any personal care without assistance. As a 17-year-old high school senior, my focus should've been on applying to colleges and planning my future. Instead, I was focused entirely on helping James achieve his daily milestones and setting his future mobility goals. After six months of rehabilitation, it became clear that not only was he no longer the confident, sweet guy I fell for, but my hope of attending my senior prom or applying to colleges was not meant to be.

Through his slow recovery process, James became possessive, self-conscious, and an angry, jealous version of himself—a version I was confused to be around. Sadly, despite weekly physical and occupational therapy, it was never recommended that he attend talk therapy to discuss these changes or the feelings he felt.

When he was well enough, I spent spring break with him and his family in Florida. While there, he raged at me, grabbed my arms, and screamed, "You're not applying to any colleges! It's not happening!" That's when I felt scared.

Soon after, during my graduation week festivities, James's mother suffered her own mental breakdown that resulted in her psychiatric hospitalization. One evening, I received a frantic call from him screaming, "Lis, come now! It's Mom! I need help finding Mom! Help me find her!" I sped over in my car and as I arrived, the ambulance was just leaving. The front door of the house was open, so I entered and walked straight through to the back, calling out for him all the while. At the back door, I looked out over a wooded area that sloped down to a stream. Beside that stream is where I found him, holding a blood-covered knife, shaking and crying. I ran toward him, screaming for him to put down the knife. He looked utterly despondent. He let me take the knife from his hand and just hold him. In that moment, I had no idea how to help James or comprehend what just happened. I was very frightened—for him, his mom and for our future together.

James's mother survived the attempt and returned home, but, in my opinion, no one ever adequately processed or confronted what occurred. Looking back, it's clear to me that, after that event, something shifted significantly in James's mind. Our discussions about the future grew more threatening. He frequently tested my commitment to him by saying that if I loved him, I'd stop whatever I was doing to spend my time with him. I worried constantly that he was going to show up wherever I was and make a scene, so I stopped going places with friends. I felt trapped.

When those feelings got too heavy, I laced up my sneakers and went for a sprint around the block. At first, it was once around, then twice, and then I'd run deeper through my neighborhood. Week after week, as I kept running, his threats continued: "If it's over, Lis, then I have nothing to live for," he'd say. "What's the point?" All the while trying to maintain a hopeful outlook for his recovery and a possible future together.

Then, one day, he called me, ready to argue. "There's no other way!" he yelled. "If it's over, then it's over for both of us!" James told me that he was going to drive to my house, shoot me, then shoot himself. He wasn't cleared to drive, but, within the hour, he drove through the dark and pouring rain and was screaming and pounding on my front door.

My family was away on vacation, and I had a few friends over to watch movies, so I hurried us all into the basement, where we waited until he left. I was too embarrassed to explain the severity of the situation. A few hours later, he called again, this time to ask where I was. When I didn't answer to his satisfaction, he yelled, "You failed!"

Finding my voice, I screamed back, "I'm sick of being tested!"

Through tears, James said, "If I killed myself, would you go on living, or would you kill yourself too?"

I didn't know how to respond. I had no desire to end my life—or for him to end his. But when I didn't answer immediately, James hung up.

Nearly an hour passed before the phone rang again. It was James. He remained silent, and we stayed on the phone that way, listening to each other breathe, until finally, he said, "I can't do this anymore. You can just read about me in the paper tomorrow. I love you, and we'll see if you really ever loved me."

I did not call him back. I didn't call the police or his parents. I spent the rest of the night in denial but feeling very sad that our relationship was over.

The next morning, just after dawn, someone was knocking at my front door. It was James's uncle. Before he said a word, I collapsed. Alone in his basement, James had ended his life.

Reluctantly, James's family invited me to his calling hours. It was made clear that many in his family and their circle blamed me for James's decision. I attended the wake with a copy of my favorite picture of us. It was taken at my junior prom, between dances, both of us flush and smiling—pre-car accident, pre-trauma. I leaned down to kiss him goodbye, placed our picture inside his casket, and lost consciousness.

I awoke on the floor in another room of the funeral home, an EMT wafting smelling salts beneath my nose. Though my vision was blurred, and I was too disoriented to speak, I heard muffled voices telling my parents, "Get her out of here."

For weeks, I remained in a fog of grief. I felt physically ill and emotionally numb as a terrible headache thrummed in my skull. If I allowed myself to feel anything, it was always some form of guilt. I was consumed by the same inner monologue on repeat: *Why didn't I get him help? Why didn't I believe his threats were real? Why did I prioritize having friends over, then hiding, avoiding him, instead of talking? Why didn't I call his parents, or his brother, or 911? Why was I still alive? Did I not love him?*

With no access to drugs or alcohol, I made a safety plan with my family to allow me to leave the house alone once a day to exercise. I started by running my neighborhood loop as fast as I could, for as many laps as I could stand until my feelings of guilt were replaced by fatigue. I used this time as a way to gain control of my emotions and channel them toward positive memories of James and our time together. On some runs, I played old mixtapes on my yellow Sony Walkman, crying the entire loop. Other days, I thought about how I was still alive and how good that felt. When I outgrew my neighborhood loop, I drove to our local State Park to run the trails with my dog as my running partner.

The days strung together into one long, continuous run, and the more I kept moving through nature, the more I noticed the rhythms of the seasons, the passage of time, and the fact that I was still here. I listened to the water as it moved along the stream, the crushed stone crunching beneath my feet; I smelled the crisp air, and, in those moments, I wasn't feeling guilt or sadness. Moving in nature was rebooting my brain. I was searching for peace and harmony, and I felt, with every fiber, that I was searching in the right place.

Eventually, I could find joy in the simple things again: return home to my family to share a meal or discuss plans for tomorrow. The progress of my daily runs resulted in a psychological transformation—one I'd come to learn much later, as a professional clinician, was a healing foundation formed in nature, focused on the practice of mindfulness, resilience, and self-love.

When I did turn my attention back toward my education, I spent about a year floundering at community college before I course-corrected to the track that led me to earn my bachelor's and master's degrees and a long career in health and human services. Whether it has been as a community grief group leader, a Hospice bereavement coordinator, a crisis intervention clinician, or running coach, I found that taking my clients outside for a walk or run builds up their resilience, fosters gratitude, and, for some, transforms their lives entirely. The more I witnessed the growth of clients over the years, the more I reflected on my own journey and how I always turn to movement in nature when I'm hurting. It begged the question: Was this an actual therapeutic tool?

When I dove into the research, it led me to Dr. Thaddeus Kostrubala, author of *The Joy of Running* and the "father" of Run Therapy. When I discovered his work, Dr. Kostrubala was retired in New Mexico after a long career as a clinical psychiatrist. I contacted him, and he was invigorated. This began a year-long apprenticeship consisting of hour-long phone consults wherein Dr. Kostrubala read and reviewed case studies, guiding me through treatment plans and helping me incorporate Run Therapy into my work.

As my clients varied in age and fitness levels, with Dr. Kostrubala's blessing, I expanded Run Therapy to include a walking component; thus, Walk-Run Therapy was born. Assuming a client had no aerobic history, I could begin by offering a two-minute walk, followed by a sixty-second jog, perhaps building up, over time, to a thirty-minute sustained jog over six weeks or more.

Dr. Kostrubala also connected me to Wolfgang Schuler, an instructor at the Deutsches Lauftherapiezetrum (German Center for Running). The Center was founded in 1991 using the training practices found in *The Joy of Running*.

I feel extremely fortunate to have been mentored by the two individuals who pioneered the international clinical study and application of the positive effects of running on the mind. In 2013, I proposed a pilot program of Walk-Run Therapy for our clients to my friend and colleague, Kelly Daugherty, and we've been incorporating it into our therapeutic grief programming ever since.

I may not have a tree in my yard anymore that I run to and climb when I'm feeling overwhelmed, but I'm still running—and still finding my solace and my soul, and sharing my approach to healing in nature.

THE TOOL

The following Walk-Run Therapy practice combines the art of being aware with the movement of your body in nature. Our research shows that being present while moving decreases the body's stress response, reduces anxiety, lowers blood pressure, increases the ability to regulate your emotions, and improves your overall sense of well-being and peacefulness.

First, choose a Couch to 5K plan and a safe, familiar route to move on. Begin with a three-minute walk, transitioning into a one-minute jog at a conversational pace. Add 30 seconds each week to the jog time while subtracting 30 seconds each week to the walk. This strategy will allow you to slowly build your endurance, reducing your risk for injury while introducing you to the healing powers of mindfulness-based Walk-Run Therapy.

STEP 1—PREPARE YOUR BODY

- Wear comfortable shoes and non-cotton apparel/sports bra.
- Make nutrition choices natural, fresh, whole, and organic when possible.
- Properly hydrate with water throughout your day.
- Adopt a dynamic warm-up and static stretch cool-down routine

STEP 2—PREPARE YOUR MIND

Before Your Workout

- Take a slow, centering breath and determine your intention.
- Quickly scan your body to notice if you are feeling fatigue, sadness, and/or anger. Or are you energized and ready to move? Acknowledge the feelings you're having without judgment, and release them.
- Choose a mantra. For example: "With every step, I heal." Or, "I've got this."

During Your Workout:

- Practice raising your awareness by noticing how your feet feel when they hit the pavement or what you see or hear.

STEP 3—PREPARE YOUR SOLE

Use Good Form as a simple method for achieving a natural, efficient stride.

- Posture – Pull shoulders back, keeping a long, tall spine with chin up, eyes level with the horizon.
- Mid-foot strike – Minimize your impact and maximize your efficiency by landing lightly on the center of your mid-foot.
- Cadence (Stride) – Make shorter strides at a comfortable pace. An ideal stride doesn't break your posture and allows you to have a soft, unlocked knee.
- Lean – Use a subtle, forward shift of your weight from the ankle joint.

After Your Workout

- Congratulate yourself for your initial intention, no matter how many times your mind wandered or how difficult you thought the workout was. Practice becomes habit-forming, which cultivates gratitude and healing.

Lisa Millis (M.A. Psychology Counseling) is a Certified Health Coach and Wellness Counselor with the American Council on Exercise and a Certified Running Coach. Her grief work spans 25 years and includes Hospice Bereavement & Spiritual Care Coordination, Cindy's Comfort Camp, and Cindy's Retreat with the C.R. Wood Cancer Center through Glens Falls Hospital.

Lisa has always had an interest in fitness and mindfulness and credits the "father" of Run Therapy, Dr. Thaddeus Kostrubala, for mentoring her and helping her find a renewed passion in her approach to therapy. Coaching hundreds of individuals for their first 5k, 10k, half & full marathons, Lisa founded a private practice to merge movement in nature with healing the mind and body. Grief is a difficult road to navigate. Lisa understands that first-hand and believes that Healing Strides is the perfect balance of education and wellness to help people create a safe, supportive path forward.

Lisa also works full-time as a crisis clinician with Northern Rivers. She is certified in Mindfulness of Mortality and End of Life Planning. You can spot her most days out trail-running with her dogs or jockeying her vehicle into position in the pick-up line at school for her identical twin boys.

Connect with Lisa Millis or The Healing Strides Program:
Website: www.glgrief.com/healingstrides
Email: lisa@healingstrides.org

CHAPTER 14

Walking Through Divorce

Finding Grace, Forgiveness, and Acceptance

Tiffany Thomas, CADC-II, MA, LMFT

MY STORY

"Your pain is the breaking of the shell that encloses your understanding."

- Khalil Gibran

I was very humbled by the process of grief. As a therapist of six years, I still didn't know what to do, how to process it, or what that might look like. The end of my marriage was one of many significant losses of my life, but the one that has thus far made the biggest impact.

I walked into the room, exhaling, feeling relief mixed with anticipation about what the next few days would be like; I hadn't even finished unpacking the boxes in my new apartment. I started to unpack and put the food away in my rented condo when confusion set in. *That's weird. Where are my shoes?*

I drove six hours to Yosemite to start the next chapter of my life. I envisioned my gray running shoes in my gym bag, but they weren't there. I couldn't believe it. *What's happening with me? I'm usually so on top of things.* In an instant, I felt disappointed, frustrated, and confused. I was very aware of my new alone-ness, intensified when I looked down at my phone to tell someone, only to find I had no cell service. *Oh my God, no one can comfort me. I'm in this all by myself. I have to figure this out.*

I spent months enduring the signs of stress, starting immediately after I moved out. While the relationship ended two months prior, it took some time to find a new apartment and divide up our things. I remember immense mental relief from being out of the relationship and all of the emotions leading up to the end; it never occurred to me that the overwhelming emotional and physical impact was still yet to come.

Setting each box down with the help of my brother and dad to fill up my new apartment kept me mentally and physically occupied, the way I preferred to operate. My brother suspected my first night alone would be hard and offered to spend the night. We made the most of the night, catching up on stories from when we were younger, laughing, and connecting over the current events in each of our lives. He left early the next morning, and the silence was deafening.

There was nowhere for my body and mind to hide, no person or activity to distract me. My body was the first to react to everything I went through. I started feeling full-body pain and fatigue. Several times, I drove home and suddenly realized I didn't know where I was. I re-sent emails I'd sent an hour before, having completely forgotten I'd already sent them. I misplaced things at home and work. My body screamed at me to listen, almost as if it was saying: *You went through hell, but now you're safe. It's okay to let go.* I now know my body was in survival mode for years, barely holding itself together to keep me functioning. The shell of protection I built up was starting to crack.

The physical signs showed up first, but the emotional fallout forced me to look at the lessons I needed to learn that were triggered by my grief. Some of the most important ones are as follows:

MY STUBBORN INDEPENDENCE

I felt alone in the marriage for years, combined with my natural tendency to represent myself as independent and strong, so when I decided to end the marriage, I believed I could handle it on my own.

I'll just find a new place to live, get out of this situation, and then I will tell people what happened.

Only a few close friends knew what I went through, but my family was kept in the dark. Telling my family felt like the final acknowledgment of the death of the marriage as well as the relationship they built with my then-husband.

How will they respond? Will they think I didn't try hard enough? I didn't want to answer any questions.

I quickly realized I couldn't move forward as the date approached to move out; the secret was eating me up inside.

I drove to my father's house to surprise him to tell him the news. *Breathe. It's okay. He loves you and will understand.* My heart was beating out of my chest. The moment felt surreal, like bracing yourself for when you're about to pull the bandaid off. He opened the door, surprised to see me, and invited me in. The words spilled out, "Dad, I'm getting a divorce," and I just sobbed. *I can't believe I waited so long to tell him. Of course, he was going to support me.* I released some of the pressure I was holding on to for months. Shortly after my father and my brother heard the news, they both dropped everything to help me move (and yes, I was going to do it on my own!), which confirmed for me I didn't have to navigate this alone.

BEING UNDERSTOOD AND FORGIVING OTHERS

I experienced a range of reactions as I started to feel more comfortable telling people I was getting a divorce. Each experience of telling someone was a lesson in grace, although, at the time, there was a lot of anger. Some appeared to assume I must be happy since the divorce was my decision, and I was no longer in a relationship that caused me pain.

Because of that, I felt lonely. People weren't asking me how I was doing. *Why aren't people asking me how I am? I know so many people who have gone through divorce that there must be people out there who can relate to how*

I feel. Where are they? I didn't feel like there were a lot of spaces where I felt understood.

"Don't be angry. Stay friends with him," some said. *If only they knew what I had endured. I have a right to feel angry.* I shut down during some of these conversations, feeling misunderstood. "The best way to get over an old love is to find new love." The last thing I was thinking about was opening myself up to another person.

When I told my ex I wanted to separate and live apart, he responded, "What's the point of that? Let's just get divorced." I knew it was over, but I could only think of each next step; it was the only way I could process what happened. I wasn't thinking about having to fill out paperwork or go to court. When I was asked about whether I was planning to legally change my name, I couldn't think about what that daunting process was going to be; I was trying to get through the next day.

I learned my independence was only going to keep me isolated if I didn't initiate and tell people when I was having a hard day. I started to reach out and, in time, learned who my support system was.

Over time, I could make room for understanding that others were doing the best they could given what little information I provided. I also became aware that others have their own understanding of grief and divorce that influences how they interact and how much of that had little to do with me. The hurt and anger started to fade away.

FINDING CLOSURE

I found there were a couple of things getting in the way of processing my grief. I was looking for closure. "You're out of the relationship; what else do you need?" One person asked. I knew I wouldn't be able to fully move forward until the judge confirmed the marriage was over. Until that happened, there was a continued anxiety about what else could happen and what else would be said or done to prolong this agonizing experience.

The process of filing the paperwork and trying to get the divorce finalized was grueling. Throughout the process, it seemed impossible to get clear answers. I wanted to know what to expect, how long the process would take, and what the judge would do based on the circumstances. The lawyers I consulted with couldn't give me consistent answers, the court clerk didn't give me straight answers, and the internet was no help. I felt so alone, confused, and angry. The day I got the email with the final paperwork from the judge, I thought: *I can't believe it. It's over, I don't need to wait anymore.* Tears streamed down my face, angry I even had to endure the last year, that I wasn't able to grieve because of the tangible, concrete parts of the divorce process.

Any attempts to contact my ex to get access to the last of my valuable things were met with silence. Each attempt deepened the fear that I wasn't going to get those things back. The pit in my stomach grew as time went on. *Why can't we just give each other back the last things we have?*

The day I received the email confirming that my pictures, holiday ornaments, and other memories were gone, the grief became overwhelming. I was in disbelief. I stayed inside all weekend and couldn't imagine saying out loud to anyone what I just lost. I couldn't understand why he did it. I was left with my own decision of what to do with the last items I had of his. I struggled with whether to send them back or dispose of them as he did my things. I beat myself up about that decision for months, thinking I was a bad person if I threw them away. I wanted to be the bigger person. Eventually, I was able to move through the guilt and make a decision that liberated me by throwing those things away.

SAD AND LONELY

Some firsts after the relationship ended landed harder than others. The hardest were Thanksgiving and our anniversary.

The first Thanksgiving left me anticipating what I would feel. I was intentional about making room for any emotions that might surface. I told my family I wasn't sure if I would attend any family plans and that I wanted to allow myself space to cry and be alone. I came to appreciate hosting Thanksgiving for my ex and me, and now that was gone. The day came, and as I anticipated, I was sad. I allowed myself to cry and sit in my sadness but ultimately decided to see family, only to find it difficult to see all of the other couples in the room.

By the time our wedding anniversary came around, it had been a year since we separated. I was driving, barely aware of what day it was, heading towards my dad's house for plans we made. As soon as I got off the freeway,

I felt a wave of sadness, flooded by remembering the date. I had flashbacks of driving to my dad's to tell him the news, remembering it would have been six years of marriage. The lump in my throat was back. I started taking deep breaths as I knocked. My dad opened the door and hugged me hello, and I immediately started crying, telling him what I remembered.

"The greatest thing in the world
is to know how to belong to oneself."

~ Michel de Montaigne

Going through this process feels incomplete without acknowledging the act of forgiveness. It wasn't until writing this chapter that I was faced with the question, "What are you having a hard time letting go of?" during what was supposed to be a fun get-to-know-you card game. The first thing that came to mind was that I needed to let go of feeling guilty that I stayed in a marriage that wasn't working for longer than I felt I should've. Here is a letter I wrote to myself in response:

Dear Tiffany, it's okay. It turns out that you were only drawn to something familiar, although there was no way for you to know at the time. You found comfort in something you could rely on and trust in. It all made sense. You believed that someone else's "stuff" could stay separate, that it wasn't a reflection of you. But it all got so hard. You thought your loyalty was the most important thing, even if it meant blocking out your friends and family. You felt your body react to new information, which meant you could probably never feel safe again.

You were so scared, anxious, angry. You wanted so badly to be able to talk about what had happened. When you were met with silence, you tried harder. Nothing worked. You went inward as a way to protect your heart, your mind, and your soul. You were beaten down word by word, not deserving of any of it. You needed to pace yourself until the right time came. You chose you, even when you hadn't invited much support in. You faced your fear of what would happen next. You regained your life back, but more importantly, your Self. The pain and the loneliness you feel sometimes is okay. I hope that you seek out ways to feel held and comforted. You are safe. Be brave.

At the time of writing this chapter, it's been 21 months since I decided I could no longer stay married and eight months since the divorce was finalized. As more time passes, the painful reminders of the relationship become less frequent. Each holiday and anniversary get a little easier.

However, with time also comes new experiences of grief that can't show up until you face new chapters in your life, like feelings that arise when someone brings up your ex's name or when you consider dating again. I waited a year and a half before I was willing to put myself out there and was still hit with a tidal wave minutes before my first date: nausea, anxiety, panic, fear, sadness. *This is so weird,* I thought. *What am I doing? How do people even do this?*

Although getting divorced was the best thing I could've done for myself, there's still a tender part of me that continues to heal on its own timeline. The loss of my marriage didn't have to mean the loss of me.

THE TOOL

The following exercise will guide you through a process that has been incredibly helpful for me. This process uses self-awareness and intention.

When was the last time you went somewhere outside of your comfort zone? Or spend your day just being outside, by yourself, without your phone or music to distract you? Aside from talking about my feelings to family, friends, or my therapist, being outside has been the biggest teacher and healer as I navigate my divorce.

Why? It has forced me to slow down, get in touch with myself, and learn how I respond when I'm in unfamiliar territory. *When I see strangers, do I say hi? Do I avert eye contact? Do I become aware of my loneliness?* It brings me back to my existence and simplifies everything.

Take a moment and think about a place you have wanted to go but never made the time or even the environment that surrounds where you live. Find a place outside where you can spend some time: a beach, forest, mountain, trail, park, or lake.

Maybe you start by going for 30 minutes or throw yourself in and plan a hike in unfamiliar territory. No matter how you do it, as long as the intention is there, you can't go wrong. Challenge yourself to leave the headphones at home; no music, no podcasts, no audiobooks. Go alone; bring a journal if you want. Also, tell someone where you are going if you are going somewhere unfamiliar to you.

Before you go, ask yourself the following questions:

What are the strongest emotions for you at this time? This is not intended for you to dwell on the feelings but to recognize and accept where you are and know what you need to release to move forward.

What is my intention for today? This question forces you to pause and self-reflect. While you're outside, you can come back to this if you find your mind starts to wander or you feel anxious.

Where am I feeling lost? The answer to this is not as important as making room to be in the unknown. Allow space to not have all the answers in your life right now.

How do I feel anchored? This question should prompt you to connect with something that grounds you. It might be a memory, person, symbol, spiritual connection, or goal.

What do I wish were different right now? Maybe it's all the things you wish were different (e.g., how you're feeling, your work circumstances, your relationship status, other people's behavior), or maybe it's imagining all the possibilities and opportunities that are available to you now.

What am I open to receiving during this experience? Asking this question alone opens you up. You don't need a practical answer to this. Just ask and watch how your awareness expands.

Come back to this tool when you are feeling overwhelmed, detached, or sad. Let it guide you back to your truth.

Tiffany Thomas is a Licensed Marriage and Family Therapist and Certified Drug and Alcohol Counselor with over 12 years of experience. Tiffany's journey in the addiction field led her to delve deeper into understanding the root causes of human behavior.

With a Bachelor's Degree in Human Services and a Master's in Clinical Psychology earned in 2018, Tiffany's expertise spans various levels of care within the substance use field, including detox, residential, and sober living. She seized the opportunity to broaden her horizons by working with survivors of Domestic Violence and developing trauma-informed care programs.

Tiffany is not only a dedicated clinician but also a mentor, providing clinical supervision to pre-licensed clinicians and crafting training programs on diverse topics. Her passion lies in community outreach, where she educates others on supporting loved ones dealing with Domestic Violence/ Intimate Partner Violence and Substance Use.

In her private practice based in Los Angeles, Tiffany specializes in substance use, grief and loss, and interpersonal conflict. She envisions a world where people prioritize self-care and reconnect with their true purpose for a fulfilling and joyful life. Tiffany firmly believes that our relationships with ourselves and the world around us profoundly influence our sense of fulfillment.

Beyond her professional commitments, Tiffany enjoys a vibrant life, participating in soccer, exploring local and international destinations, hiking, and auditioning for exciting game show opportunities.

Connect with Tiffany:
www.tiffany-thomas.com

CHAPTER 15

CHASING YOUR RAINBOWS

STAYING CONNECTED WITH YOUR LOVED ONES

Kirby Kay L. Clark, MSED, Licensed Funeral Director

MY STORY

As humans in mourning, we often find comfort and encouragement in symbolism. Small, everyday things or occurrences we encounter may remind us of all the good times and experiences we've had with deceased loved ones. For me, that proved true on my wedding day. I had recently experienced the death of both of my grandparents shortly before my wedding. Knowing they would not be there at my wedding was very difficult. But that day, I experienced something remarkable that brought me much peace and comfort.

You may have heard the old wives' tale, "It's good luck if it rains on your wedding day!" Well, on this hot July day in 2016, there wasn't a cloud in sight! There was certainly no rain in the forecast. Although a little hot, it was a perfect, beautiful day atop the highest point in Albany County, overlooking the Hudson Valley below. After reciting our vows and saying our "I do's," everyone retreated to the air-conditioned reception hall for all the traditional wedding celebration festivities.

Twenty minutes after the reception began, a torrential downpour of rain came out of nowhere. As the rain poured down, everyone enjoyed the festivities and merrily discussed our new marital good luck found in the rainstorm. Then, all of a sudden, as fast as the rain began, it stopped! My maid of honor found my new husband and me and said, "Quick! Go look outside!" My husband grabbed my hand, and we rushed outside to see what all the excitement was about. We could not believe our eyes. There was an incredibly bright, beautiful double rainbow arching from one side of the sky to another. My husband turned to me with a big smile on his face and said, "That is your grandparents celebrating with us." *He's right! They are!* While I was obviously excited to be married, part of me dreaded the day because I knew two of the most important people in my life wouldn't be there. At that very moment, with my husband by my side, I felt a sense of peace and calmness I hadn't ever felt before.

Since my wedding day, inevitably, I have experienced some dark days and times in my life. When I see the brightness in the colors of a rainbow, though, it brings me an immediate sense of peace, comfort, and calm. It reminds me of the good times and all my grandparents did for me throughout my life.

Losing a grandparent may not seem like a significant loss. I was raised by my grandparents, who were essentially my parents. They both passed away within seven months of each other. Experiencing the death of a loved one is never easy. For me, losing both of them was an overwhelming loss. I had physical pain in my chest I thought would never subside. I couldn't imagine my life without them. I never thought they'd miss so many significant events in my life: my wedding, earning my master's degree, the birth of my children, and much more. All this left a hole in my heart that couldn't be filled. Learning to live with and process so much grief proves to be difficult. One method that significantly helped in my grief journey was journaling.

I was born in Sweetwater, Tennessee, in 1985. My parents were very young. My mother was only 15 years old, and my father was 18 years old when I was born. They were ill-equipped to be parents at such a young age. The commitment of raising a child while still children themselves proved too much for them. They quickly split up, leaving me with my mother's parents. When I was only 18 months old, my grandmother became ill and could no longer care for me. She called my dad's father, Eddie Konkel, and asked if he and his wife, Opal, could help. My Grandpa, Eddie, immediately jumped in the car and drove to Tennessee. Eddie and Opal picked me up and moved me back to Pratt, Kansas, to live on their small farm, which would become my home for the next 18 years.

Eddie and Opal Konkel were born to large families on farms outside Pratt, Kansas. After they married in 1956, they decided to stay close to their families and began a small farm in Pratt. They were married for 60 years and had four children. Unfortunately, one child died at a year old due to a heart defect. I became their fifth child. Grandpa Eddie was in the Army Reserves for 40 years and worked as a window and door installer for a glass company for 45 years. Grandma Opal, known as Granny O, was a manager of a local department store for 40 years.

Eddie and Opal were an average, hard-working, middle-class, down-to-earth couple raising a family in America's heartland. They were naturally hospitable, which made it easy for them to take me in when the need arose. They provided me with unconditional love and instilled morals and values I would never have received from my birth parents. They demonstrated what it meant to have a good work ethic and to be selfless. They were the glue that held our family together and were my compass for 30 years.

As it eventually does to all of us, age caught up to my grandpa. He was diagnosed with dementia and Alzheimer's disease. I watched him decline slowly over a decade as he tried so hard to fight against this terrible disease. Like many Alzheimer's patients, our family eventually had to make the tough decision to move my grandfather into a nursing home where he'd receive the care he needed. During the nursing home tour, Grandpa Ed looked at my aunts, my grandma, and I shook his head and said, "One condition. I don't want to be left here alone." That statement sealed the deal. Granny O knew she couldn't leave my grandpa's side. Even though she was perfectly healthy and capable of caring for herself, she made an incredibly selfless sacrifice and decided to move into the nursing home with him.

Eddie and Opal lived in the nursing home for two years until Eddie took a turn for the worse. I had just moved to New York, where my soon to be husband and I were settling into our new careers. One day, Granny O called very upset. Crying, she explained, "Your grandpa is not doing too well. I wish you were closer. Do you think you can come home soon?" I started crying as she was sharing more details about what had happened that morning. *I should have never left him.* "Grandma, I am on my way. Tell him to hold on until I get there." I booked the next flight out and left for Pratt, Kansas that afternoon.

When I arrived in Pratt, the nursing home had sent my grandpa to the hospital. As I arrived at Pratt Medical Center, I met the rest of my family at my grandpa's bedside. Shortly after I arrived, the doctor came in and explained, "Your Grandpa has suffered a massive stroke. He is completely paralyzed on his left side. Given his age of 85 and current condition, there is nothing left we can do for him here. The best option would be to return to the nursing home and be placed in hospice care."

My whole family was heartbroken. I was trying to hold my composure, but as soon as I looked at my grandma, we both broke down crying. We were devastated by the news. Even though he lived a wonderful, fulfilling life, it was clear to me that letting him go would be the hardest thing my grandma and my family would have to do.

I had the privilege of having my last coherent conversation with my grandpa two weeks before I moved to New York. He shared some stories from his time in the Army, memories from his life, and provided advice for my future. "Make sure to pack up your suitcase at least once a year and go see the world. There is a big world out there, sweetie. Don't be like me and work so much you never get to see much of it."

The strong man who hardly ever showed any emotion became overcome with sadness and concern. Tears filled his eyes when he asked me if he and my grandma did a good job raising me. I tearfully replied, "You did a wonderful job raising me, and I have never questioned your love for me." As we ended the conversation, he asked me to pray for the Lord to take him first. He did not think he could live without his Opal.

The Lord answered those prayers early on the morning of June 10, 2015, three days after suffering the stroke. I held his hand as I watched his love of 60 years, my grandma, Opal, say her final goodbye. Witnessing this was among the most challenging yet beautiful things I've ever seen. You could feel the calmness, love, and peace throughout the room as he took his final breath. In the end, it was just the three of us together.

As a funeral director and grief counselor, I understand the privilege of being at the bedside of someone who has lived a full and good life as they transition from this life to the next. Even though I understood this in my mind, and my grandpa's passing was relatively calm and peaceful, I was still utterly numb at that moment. The pain and details of that scene are cemented in my brain. I remember sitting on the floor weeping. I can still smell the lemony scent of the freshly mopped, cold tile floor. Even though I had dealt with loss before, my grandpa's death affected me differently.

Before we knew it, the new year was upon us. Even though my grandma, family, and I were still grieving the loss of my grandfather, we tried to look at 2016 positively and optimistically. I had so much to look forward to that coming year. The biggest and most anticipated event of my life would happen in July. I was getting married! I had always imagined my grandpa giving me away at my wedding. *I can't believe he's not going to be here to give me away.* My grandma was honored to stand in his place and was giddy with excitement about traveling to the "big city" for the festivities. Unfortunately, her body had different plans.

"Granny O" was diagnosed with thyroid cancer on September 7, 2015. She had a procedure to remove the tumor in early December 2015. From the beginning of the diagnosis, the doctors were very hopeful and optimistic about her recovery. Nobody expected all the complications she soon experienced.

Early on the morning of January 2, I got a call from my Aunt Brenda. She said, "Kirby, I think you need to come home now. Granny O was rushed to the hospital overnight. She lost consciousness and is unresponsive." They were still running many different tests to find a diagnosis. Hearing this news was shocking. I knew I needed to get on the next flight back to Kansas. I told my Aunt Brenda, "Tell Granny O to hold on until I get there." These are the same words I told my grandma to tell my grandpa seven months prior.

After Granny O was admitted to the hospital, the doctors conducted several scans and tests. They determined she had a blood infection, was bleeding internally, and found several more tumors throughout her body that didn't appear in her earlier scans. The doctors were concerned that additional surgeries to remove the tumors would be too dangerous and almost certainly be fatal.

When I arrived at her hospital room, she opened her eyes, gave me a big smile, and said, "Hi, number one kid." *She looks so scared, weak, and lifeless.*

That is what she always called me. "Number one kid" was always written inside every card she ever gave me. My family said she had been restless since arriving in the hospital. They believed she waited for me to get there.

I will never fully be able to describe the relationship she and I had. I believe God puts people in our lives at the right time for a reason. She was the person I shared everything with, without fear of judgment or retribution, even though sometimes there maybe should've been. As I sat by her side, holding her delicate hand, watching her try to beat the cancer, I started writing in a journal. I picked one up in the airport gift shop on my way to Kansas. Something told me I might need it.

I'm not entirely sure why I decided to start a journal. Maybe I felt that my grandparents deserved to be remembered in detail by someone. Maybe I thought I would be writing down memories of them that I didn't want to forget. Initially, that was true.

Journal entry from January 5, 2016, says, "Right now I feel like my mind is blank. Like this is a dream, and someday I will wake up, and she will be better." In a desperate attempt to remember as much about her as possible, I added a few of her catchphrases in that same entry: "Don't be a Freddy Free Loader," "What's the Gossip," and "That is so Awesome!"

After a couple of days of writing in my journal, I realized it was quite therapeutic. It became a way to process and organize the millions of thoughts running through my head. It provided a kind of order in all the chaos surrounding the passing of my grandparents.

On January 4, 2016, my journal entry read, "Today, the doctor came in and talked with my grandma and the rest of the family about how her condition continued to decline. He said there was no treatment and no hope that she would recover from all the tumors throughout her body and the blood infection. The best option was for her to be placed on hospice.

After hearing the news, she looked at the doctor and me and said, 'I have a few requests. I want all the ice cream I can handle while I'm still here. And I don't want those funny lines on my face at my funeral, so no oxygen masks! And lastly, I don't want to be left alone. I want to go peacefully, and I want to be loved until the very end.'

I assured her I'd make sure all her wishes were granted. She told the nurse, "She is my little buddy. I know she will make sure I'm taken care of.'"

Over the next several days, I sat by her side, writing in my journal, which brought me peace and comfort. I watched her day by day as she slowly declined and slept more and more.

January 11, 2016, entry says, "At 1:00 a.m., I was still awake watching Grandma try to hold on. The rattling noise of her struggling to breathe was hard to take. I just watched her, feeling horrible that she had to fight so hard all night. Around 2:15 a.m., I decided to lay my head down to try to sleep. I dozed off, still holding her hand. A little after 3:00 a.m., when the nurse came in, I woke up just as Grandma took her last breath. I could not believe she was gone."

I was so overwhelmed with grief I could barely function. *I don't know how I'm ever going to get over this.* Planning and attending my grandmother's funeral seemed an impossible task. However, I continued to write in my journal. I made it a point to write something every day. Eventually, the entries took the form of a letter to my grandparents. I wrote to them, keeping them updated on what was happening in my life. Sometimes, I would write about an experience I had that reminded me of a memory with them. After a year of faithful and deliberate journaling, the pain has eased, and each day has gotten a little brighter. Now, instead of dwelling in the painful rainstorm, I find joy in the memories I see through the rainbows.

THE TOOL

When my grandparents died, I kept a journal for a year. I wrote to them daily about what was happening in my life, whether it was good or bad. I felt that was my continuing bond with them. Somehow, I felt closer to them with each word I wrote down. This technique brought me a sense of peace during an extremely tumultuous period.

Journaling serves as an organizing force when everything else feels out of order and overwhelming. Through this medium, you can articulate your fears, express thankfulness, and explore your evolving identity or sense of purpose following the death of a loved one. If you're wondering how to begin or what to include, here are some straightforward prompts to kickstart your journaling journey:

- List three aspects of life you are thankful for.
- Summarize your loved one's life story in just six words.
- Describe a specific memory you cherish of your loved one. Focus on details like sounds, scents, and sensations.
- Document what you miss and treasure about the person who has died.
- Create a letter to your future self, explaining how you feel now and what you hope will change or stay the same.
- List any regrets or unresolved issues you may feel and explore how you might come to terms with them.
- Note any changes in your daily routines.
- Explore what resilience means to you and how you have noticed it showing up in your life recently.

Embracing the power of journaling can provide you with a unique and healing tool to navigate your own grief experience, helping you find comfort and strength in your cherished memories.

From a young age, **Kirby Kay Clark** was intimately acquainted with the reality of death. The significance of honoring those who have died was a lesson she learned early on. At just eleven, she faced the deaths of her great-grandmother and grandfather within a week of each other. It was the funeral director's genuine care for her grieving grandmother that inspired Kirby Kay to pursue a similar path.

In 2010, Kirby Kay completed her studies in Mortuary Sciences at Kansas City Kansas Community College. With over a decade of experience as a funeral director, she has been a cornerstone in her community for providing compassionate services. She furthered her education at Friends University in Wichita, KS, earning a Bachelor of Business Administration in 2013.

After relocating to Albany, New York, in 2015, Kirby Kay achieved her Master of Science in Clinical Counseling from the College of St. Rose in 2019. During her studies, she interned at the American Cancer Society's Hope Club, where she founded and led a grief and loss support group that has become one of the most impactful in Upstate New York. She also served as a bereavement coordinator for a hospice agency, orchestrating support for families dealing with the death of a loved one. Beyond her professional roles, Kirby Kay has volunteered her expertise at various grief-related camps and events.

Currently, Kirby Kay resides in Upstate New York and relishes her role as a stay-at-home mom to her two-year-old twins. She and her husband are avid outdoor enthusiasts, frequently exploring local hiking trails. In her spare time, she enjoys baking and decorating for the holidays.

To connect with Kirby Kay, visit The Grief Empowerment Group on Facebook:
https://www.facebook.com/groups/griefempowermentgroup/

CHAPTER 16

THE HEALING POWER OF ART

LEARNING HOW TO TRANSFORM THE PAIN OF GRIEF

April Hannah LMHC, MS.Ed.

MY STORY

I've been a mental health professional for over 20 years, a filmmaker and podcaster investigating life after death for more than a decade, and have had a lifetime of psychic experiences. None of this prepared me for the moment on October 19, 2019, when a State Trooper showed up on my doorstep, letting me know my mother was killed in a car accident.

I was fast asleep in my cozy LuLaRu blue peacock leggings and a navy blue tanktop when my doorbell rang and the sound filled my one-bedroom apartment. I jumped out of bed knowing it was still early in the morning by the lack of sunlight coming through my windows. I tiptoed slowly out of my bedroom, through my kitchen, to the front door to peek outside. I quietly stuck my fingers between the white mini-blinds and gently opened them to see who was standing outside my door, hoping to not be noticed in case I'd have to call the police. Once my eyes focused through the small slit of my mini-blinds, I realized I didn't need to call the police because one was standing on the other side of my door. A tall, caucasian New York State Trooper in a grey and purple uniform was there, holding a white piece of paper.

Okay, it's 5 a.m., and a state trooper is at my door. I dreamt of this a few months ago. My mother is dead.

The pit of my stomach was heavy. I knew why he was here. I'd been waiting for this moment for many years, knowing it was only a matter of time before my mother would die tragically and a police officer would be the one to notify me. But no matter how many times the scenario played out in my mind, I still wasn't ready for the wave of shock that hit me.

I knew I couldn't sneak back into bed and act like I hadn't heard the doorbell, so I opened the door.

"Are you April Hannah?" he asked in a caring voice.

"Yes. Is this about my mother?" I responded immediately.

The trooper looked surprised by my question.

"Yes. She's been in an accident," he answered.

"Is she dead? She's dead, isn't she?"

Bewildered by my comment, the officer stood there with a shocked look on his face, his eyes widened, and he tilted his head to the side like a dog would when it heard a funny sound. My question rattled him, and he was at a loss for words.

He began shaking his head in disbelief. Gasped in a large amount of air and asked in a shocked whisper, "How did you know that?"

Oh, if you only knew, sir, that I have been psychic my whole life and have had a gut feeling she was going to die soon. I also dreamt about a police officer coming to my door last month, and here you are!

I could tell by the perplexed look on his face that he knew there was no way anyone else had notified me of what had happened and wondered why this would be my first line of questioning when he never said she was dead; he just referred to her as being in an accident.

"I just had a gut feeling that's what you were going to tell me. Come on in. I'll be right back, I just need to grab a sweatshirt."

I turned around and left the front door open for the Trooper to enter my apartment. I quickly headed back to my bedroom. I ran over to my closet with shaky hands, opened the white sliding door, and grabbed my oversized, black Imagine Dragons concert hoodie. This hoodie was my rainy-day-lay-on-the-couch-and-put-on-a-Netflix-movie kind of sweatshirt. It immediately provided a soft touch to the hairs standing up all over my body. Once I was covered up, I walked back into the kitchen and sat down with the trooper at my two-person kitchen table. I realized I didn't remember the officer's name, so I inconspicuously glanced down to the left side of his chest and read, Stanley. Trooper Stanley is a name I'll never forget.

"What kind of accident was she in?" I asked.

"She was in a car accident, and unfortunately, she was dead at the scene."

I worked a few years on a military base as a Psychological Health Director, providing mental health counseling to active duty military. I knew their language was straight and to the point. Not much fluff, just the facts, so I didn't take Trooper Stanley's presentation of words personally. I spoke back to him just as direct and asked, "Was she driving? Did she kill anyone?"

"No, she didn't kill anyone; she was the only one who died in the accident."

I let out a loud sigh of relief. I was afraid her alcoholism and drug addiction would take the life of an innocent human being.

At this point, it still wasn't clear what happened, and the trooper stopped my questioning and began to give me orders on what to do next. I concentrated hard on the sound of the trooper's voice and the directions he gave me as he handed me the white piece of paper he was holding. Every word coming out of his mouth sounded like it was suspended in air and being spoken slowly.

"Here is the county coroner's phone number. I need you to call him right now. I will stay here with you while you make this phone call and will stay here until someone from your family can come and stay with you. Is there anyone you can call to come over and be with you right now?"

It's 5 a.m. I can't call anyone now and wake them up with this news.

"Everyone I know is sleeping, and everyone I know lives an hour or more away. Let me call the coroner first."

I picked up my iPhone; my hands were starting to shake even harder as I started pressing the numbers in slow motion to dial.

I can't believe this is it. I thought I was prepared. I'm not prepared. Am I dreaming?

Thankfully, the coroner picked up after one ring. I didn't wait for him to say hello. I blurted out quickly, "Hi, this is April Hannah. I am here with Trooper Stanley. I'm calling about my mother, Marian Hannah, who was killed in a car accident this morning."

He responded, "Hi, April; I am the coroner who was on the scene of your mother's accident. She was crossing the road of US 9 Highway in Castleton, New York, across the street from the SkyView motel near the Loves truck station. Around 1 a.m., a truck stuck and killed her."

Wait, what?! She was hit by a car? A truck! She wasn't driving? She was walking across the street? Why was she walking across the street so late? I thought she was driving a car and was in a car accident. Why didn't Trooper Stanley tell me she was hit?

My panic set in, and my voice began to tremble; tears started to well up in my eyes as I started asking more questions about what happened. The way she died was worse than what I imagined her fate would be. I was convinced she'd most likely die of an overdose of heroin or by drinking herself to death, not by walking across the street after midnight and getting hit by what I later learned from the police report was an SUV, not a truck. The questions I asked the coroner are still a faint memory, but I remember writing down short sentences the coroner was saying. The one I underlined was, "You don't want to see this."

The coroner reassured me my mother was properly identified by people living at the motel where she was staying, and she had her driver's license in the purse she was carrying. He said I wouldn't need to come to the morgue to identify her body and strongly recommended I not do so due to the trauma she experienced from the vehicle hitting her at a fast speed.

I remember his exact words being: "She will not be recognizable to you. All of the bones in her body are broken, and there is no bone structure holding up her face. It's hard to describe, but her face is flat. We do this for a living and see dead bodies all the time, and this one was hard for us to see."

The experience that morning was sowing the seeds of my grief, with this moment being the largest seed of grief that burrowed deep inside my body. The thought and emotions of not being able to see my mother one last time was a seed I wanted to bury and never find. I buried it well and chose to forget all about it.

My mother's accident investigation did not wrap up until the end of February 2020. A few weeks later, the world was thrown into the coronavirus pandemic. From March 2020 to January 15, 2021, I put my grief on hold and used my mental health private practice clients as a distraction. I went into caretaker mode with my clients and made *them* my priority, not my grief. I was happy to be working from home because I knew, on some level, I was grieving. I loved that I could work in my pajamas and sit on my brown couch, talk on the phone, and not be seen. The clients I talked to were now becoming my company on the tough days of solitude brought on by the pandemic. Everyone in my life was now individually grieving and in panic over the pandemic, and my grief process, the death of my mother, and what I was going through felt like a lost memory. My grief was no longer at the forefront of my mind—or anyone else's, for that matter.

As the months went by, I thought I was doing a wonderful job dealing with my grief. I wasn't crying, I didn't feel depressed, I was living life as much as I could with pandemic restrictions. I fell in love and met my husband-to-be in May 2020. I felt I had come to a great understanding that although my mother's death was tragic and traumatic, it was anticipated. For many years, my mother struggled with her addictions to alcohol, abusive men, and drugs. Little did I know, the grief that I wasn't acknowledging had an energy of its own and was finding nice cozy places to hide in my physical body.

Fifteen months after my mother's death, that seed I buried deep in my body was germinating and ready to grow. I woke up in the middle of the night with sharp pains in my left breast, and I found it hard to breathe and felt the strangest, knife-wrenching pain in my stomach. These symptoms went on for almost a year and brought me to the emergency room on three separate occasions. I went from having a primary care physician whom I saw once a year to a large medical team of doctors to find out what was "wrong with me." My medical team consisted of two integrative medicine doctors, a massage therapist, an acupuncturist, a pulmonologist, a cardiologist, and an otolaryngologist. I had a picture taken of every bodily organ. I also donated many vials of blood only to be told I had a slipped rib, and my blood showed high levels of inflammation. No provider asked me if I was grieving or having a hard time dealing with life because once I told them what I did for a living, it was assumed I was in good mental health. I'd be the one to mention, "My mom died pretty tragically a few months ago. Do you think the grief has anything to do with my symptoms?"

After the first few medical tests came back normal and I was cleared of breast cancer, a heart attack, and lung disease, I had more peace of mind. I came out of my fear state and turned to what I really believed to be true: we are not our physical bodies; we are energy, and energy follows thought. Therefore, thought can directly affect how our body feels. I knew deep down I wasn't processing the emotions of my mother's death, and my physical body was storing a large amount of grief energy. Energy doesn't die; it just transforms, and my grief was transforming into pain—a kind I had never felt before.

Since 2008, I have been investigating life after death, making documentaries, and interviewing over 400 of the top consciousness researchers and healers. I decided to reach out to one podcast guest who introduced me to the work of David Hawkins, a world-renowned author, psychiatrist, and researcher of consciousness, with his most famous work being *The Map of Consciousness Explained.* Hawkins teaches about the spectrum of human emotions and the energetic frequency each emotion holds. The lower frequency levels of emotions on the map include shame, guilt, and grief, and the higher frequency emotions move up the map, where you'll find courage, acceptance, and joy. I learned that love and joy had a higher frequency than grief, and I could choose to shift my state of mind and feelings to a higher frequency just by the thought I was thinking. Lower-frequency emotions make our body weak, and higher-frequency emotions make our body strong, according to Hawkins. The podcast guest who taught me about the Map of Consciousness asked me a question that changed my grief journey: "Do you want to stay in your grief, or do you want to choose joy? It's your choice."

I responded curtly, "Of course, I want to choose joy, but I'm in pain and really sad about the way my mom died."

He said, "Put your grief into a painting. Go into a meditation, give your grief a color, and paint what you see and feel. It will raise your frequency and heal your grief."

I did as he instructed, but I wasn't convinced it would make my physical symptoms go away. However, I was willing to stay open-minded and try.

I took a drive to my favorite lake and sat outside to meditate on my grief. It was a brisk, chilly spring day, and I wore my Imagine Dragons hoodie to set the mood. I meditated on my lungs and saw them crying. They were pink, healthy lungs, with blue tears dripping off them. I also saw a white light representing my mother's soul lifting up from the road and out of her body and into the universe. I then saw a pool of red, representing the accident. This vivid image stayed with me as I drove home, and when I arrived, I went to my basement and started to paint. The painting didn't come out at all as I saw it, but it was a strong representation of how my lungs felt. It captured the scene of the accident and the hope that my mother's soul was somehow saved by the quick transition into spirit. Twenty-four hours later, I was able to take deep breaths again, and the pain in my stomach and breast went away. The next day, I called and canceled my remaining medical appointments. I shifted the grief frequency in my body to acceptance of my mother's death, the love I have for her, and the joy I can still feel without her being here on Earth.

THE TOOL

The following tool is the process I used to move the physical pain of grief out of my body. It's a simple, abstract art technique anyone can do; no artistic ability is required. I gave my technique the name High-Frequency Healing Art. You can follow along and watch my process and listen to my guided meditation to help you connect with the grief in your body at www.HannahsHealing.com/HighFrequencyHealingArt.

Before you begin, you will need to buy a few art supplies: an 8x8 canvas, a package of acrylic paints, a paintbrush, a glass of water, and paper towels.

- Step one: Set up your space with the intention of healing. Bring a candle, a picture of your deceased loved one, a crystal, sage, or anything that brings you comfort.
- Step two: Begin to play the guided meditation on my website, as it will help you get into a meditative state. This meditation will connect you with your grief, help you face it, communicate with it, and give you a vision of how to represent it on your canvas in three separate layers. If you're unable to listen to the meditation, here are the series of questions to ask yourself before you begin your painting.
    - Layer 1: Where is your grief located in your body? What color is it? What shape has it taken? What is the size of your grief? Is there anything else your grief wants to show you? Open your eyes and write down the information that came to you on your canvas. You will use these words and color(s) as the first layer of your painting.
    - Layer 2: Ask your grief what colors it needs to begin to heal. Trust the colors that come to mind, even if they are colors you wouldn't typically select. Write these colors down as they will be painted over layer one.
    - Layer 3: What colors and shapes represent the feeling of love and joy? Write these colors down, as they will be the last layer of your painting.
- Step three: Apply your paint to the canvas in this order, and you will begin to create your own piece of High-Frequency Healing Art.

Use your painting as a reminder of what the higher frequency of grief feels and looks like every time you look at your painting. Allow your painting to be a reminder to choose joy over your grief.

To learn more about High-Frequency Healing Art, to see my grief paintings, and to listen to the guided meditation, visit my website:

https://www.HannahsHealing.com/HighFrequencyHealingArt

April Hannah, the founder and visionary behind Hannah's Healing Wellness Studio, is a multifaceted individual with a rich tapestry of accomplishments. Not only is she the co-founder of Path 11 Productions, a renowned media production company, but she has also embarked on her latest venture, expanding her wellness studio into a tranquil haven for sound healing nestled in the serene landscapes of upstate New York.

With a distinguished background as a licensed mental health therapist spanning an impressive two decades, April's journey is one of dedicated service to others. Drawing from her extensive clinical mental health counseling experience of over 20 years, April Hannah extends her wisdom and guidance globally. She offers a unique blend of spiritual coaching, holistic healing methods, and profound exploration of consciousness. As a seasoned Reiki Master Teacher, she has expertly mentored and enlightened more than 200 students while facilitating an astounding 12,000 Reiki sessions since 2005.

Situated in Malta, New York, her wellness studio is a hub of activity, hosting an impressive array of 95-100 wellness classes annually. These classes encompass a diverse range of offerings, including transformative Usui Reiki training, immersive sound baths, intuitive art sessions, serene meditation practices, soul-soothing grief and loss retreats, and engaging spiritual book clubs.

April is equally adept in the realm of podcasts, where she shines as a captivating host on the Path 11 Podcast. Her creative genius is most evident in the three thought-provoking documentaries she has masterfully produced, each delving into the profound themes of consciousness and the enigma of life after death. These projects bear witness to her unwavering passion for unraveling the intricacies of human existence and the ceaseless quest to unearth answers about the mysteries that await us beyond this life.

Connect with April here.
Wellness Studio: https://www.hannahshealing.com/
High-Frequency Healing Art: https://AprilAnneHannahArt.com
Documentaries: https://path11productions.com/vod
Podcast: https://path11productions.com/podcast/
Instagram: https://www.instagram.com/HHwellnessstudio/
Art Instagram: https://www.instagram.com/aprilannehannahart\
Facebook: https://www.facebook.com/hannahshealingwellnessstudio
YouTube: https://www.youtube.com/@hannahshealing

CHAPTER 17

THE ALCHEMY OF GRIEF

DISCOVERING THE SILVER LININGS IN A LOVED ONE'S DEATH

Amy Lindner-Lesser, MSW, Certified Life Transitions Coach

MY STORY

"Every experience, no matter how bad it seems,
holds within it a blessing of some kind.
The goal is to find it."

~ Buddha

We met on the first day of graduate school. I was starting at the School of Social Work and Social Policy at the University of Pennsylvania. I was minding my own business as I walked on the sidewalk in front of the school building. That's when I saw her, sprawled out on the ground. I ran over and immediately bent down, offered her a hand, and helped her up.

That was the beginning of a friendship that lasted 44 years! And, although she was ill and disabled for quite a few years, I never thought I'd get that call.

Liz, as I soon learned was her name, tripped on a patch of uneven sidewalk. I "rescued" her, and for the next 44 years, we were best friends. There was scarcely an evening that went by that we didn't share our feelings, thoughts, laughter, and tears. We shared stories of our work. I tutored her in statistics to ensure she'd pass and graduate. We shared heartaches, family stories, and relationship breakups. We drove from Philadelphia to Ohio together for another friend's wedding.

Liz was one of a small handful of guests who attended my wedding. We shopped together for my dress. When my late husband, Steve, and I decided to adopt our daughters, Liz not only was one of our character references, but she also became godmother to our two children. She was their Aunt Liz and took them on roller coasters when I refused.

Even when my family and I moved from Pennsylvania to Massachusetts, our friendship survived. We visited each other for concerts, birthdays, and holidays. Her parents were some of the first guests at my inn and came for Thanksgiving the year after my husband died when my mother was in Florida. We were as close as sisters.

Liz accompanied me to visit my daughters at sleepaway camp the weekend before Steve died and every year after. We always stopped at her old camp on the way home. She even helped me redo flowers for my older daughter's wedding that the florist messed up.

I remember speaking with her one morning as she drove to work. I was on my way to a massage. We were chatting when, suddenly, the call dropped. In and of itself, that wasn't unusual. Cell reception in the Berkshires wasn't great; I waited to call her back until after my massage. No answer.

I'm not worried since this isn't unusual. Our calls drop all the time.

I called her at work, an adult day treatment program where she was the director. Her assistant answered and told me, "Someone crossed the median and hit her head-on. She was pulled out of her car with the Jaws of Life and is in the trauma center in South Jersey."

After months of treatment, hospitals, and rehab centers, Liz was discharged. She couldn't walk and wouldn't be able to remain in her home or ever go back to work or drive. One of her brothers bought a house near him in Maryland and renovated it so she could live on one floor using her wheelchair. Down to Maryland, she moved.

A few years later, Liz fell in her bathroom and fractured her femur. It was hours before anyone realized and got help to her. She spent months in rehab, and then Covid-19 hit. Alone, with no visitors allowed, and with the new complication of needing dialysis, Liz decided to return home with 24-hour help.

Over the next year or so, Liz volunteered with a local hospice and a homeless shelter. She had home dialysis and made a life, although much smaller than before. She began asking me to take some of her things when I visited. I knew she was preparing for her inevitable death. I couldn't bear the thought that she wouldn't be around forever and kept putting it off.

She turned 70 in April of 2022. I asked her sister-in-law to pull together a dinner party to celebrate this milestone. Liz didn't want a party. She didn't want to celebrate. I remember saying, "Liz, you only turn 70 once. This is a reason to celebrate." And I thought: *This may be your last birthday. I want you to know how much you are loved by so many people. I want you to see it too!*

My last visit with her was at the end of July 2022. I was on my way to Virginia to help my daughter, who was about to give birth to her second child. I spent about four days with Liz in the hospital in a dull room with poor lighting and a view of a tar-covered gravel roof with a smokestack in the middle. She looked at me and, in her Liz way, said, "Go on Amazon and order some kind of decoration to make that view better." I wish I had taken her request seriously. She might have enjoyed looking out at the roof more. She was lucid most of the time but in lots of pain and not eating or drinking. We reminisced, and I told her how much she meant to my children and me. I said, "You are an amazing human being, best friend. I love you, and I'm so grateful you're in my life."

I stopped back to the hospital to see her a week later and spent two days with her. Things were looking worse; she was mostly incoherent when I left. A little less than two weeks later, just five days after my birthday, my phone rang. It was her sister, "Liz passed this morning. She died on her own terms." I was numb. I wanted to cry, but I couldn't. "The ambulance was on its way to bring her home, but she didn't make it. She said her goodbyes to the family"—her two brothers, sister, nieces, and nephew the night before and made her exit quietly from this world.

I stood at her graveside at the cemetery in New Jersey on a hot Friday in August, listening to her niece give a eulogy. She said, "Liz never met a stranger. She was a friend to everyone from the homeless person on the corner to the best-dressed person at the country club." A few weeks later, at her memorial service in Maryland, I made a promise to myself and to her that I'd figure out a way to honor her. Standing there at her brother's home on the water, I decided to pull all of my experiences (personal and professional) and sew them together into a legacy.

Recently, one of my friends called me the Queen of Silver Linings. I needed to think about that label for a few minutes, unsure if it was a moniker I wanted to own. With all the lifequakes (life transitions on steroids) I've experienced in my life, I decided it was a huge compliment, and I liked the title.

As I have long known, grief doesn't only happen after the death of a family member or spouse. We can grieve over the loss of an identity, loss of health or mobility, loss of a close friendship, and, unfortunately, so much more.

My life has been filled with so much joy and love; with that naturally comes sadness. It's all part of the journey.

Over the last 60 years, I've lost 14 of my closest family members to death, including my husband, father, mother, all my grandparents, my stepfather, and another 18 deaths of people who weren't as close. The 30 plus include only the human deaths, not the pets and other lifequakes (moves, infertility, diabetes, job changes, etc.) I've navigated which also caused grief. Yet it was Liz's death that hit me the hardest.

I had a choice to either start to feel sorry for myself and be very miserable or look at it in a new way. Instead of seeing things as happening *to* me, I began to see how things were happening *for* me. It's a mindset shift that's not always the easiest to do, but it's more positive and productive. So, I started to think about what I was supposed to learn from each of those lifequakes. What were my lessons and my takeaways from them? I started to see life in a different way. I began to feel grateful not for the entire experience but for parts of each, the parts that made me grow and become a better person.

I realized that each lifequake comes with a lesson or silver lining if we allow ourselves the time, space, and permission to keep examining it. I understand it isn't easy to think about silver linings when you're in the early stages of grief. Heck, we don't always even realize or identify the emotion we're feeling is grief.

What I do know is that as we're navigating through our grief, there's often a point when we're ready to acknowledge it and see there is life after grief. We realize that while our life will never be the same as it was pre-quake, we will go on and possibly even find a more enriching life. We become ready to find the silver lining, gift, or lesson we can embrace to help us understand and give meaning to the lifequake and help us move through and forward.

Here are some of the other lifequakes I experienced and what I can now identify as silver linings. I hope they will help you to begin to recognize them in your life.

With each death, I learned that nothing and no one was permanent and without knowing, began to live my life in the moment. When President John F. Kennedy was assassinated, his daughter, Caroline, and I were about the same age. I watched how she and John Jr. behaved. I remember feeling compassion. This experience normalized death for me, seeing I was not alone.

When my great-grandmother died, I learned the importance of family, play, laughter, and storytelling.

Ten months after my wedding, my father died. He was my biggest cheerleader, my source of strength, and believed I could do anything I set my mind to, which gave me the conviction that I could. Forty-two years later, I'm still working on being my own cheerleader, something I don't know if I would've done if he were still alive.

After a year of fertility treatments and lots of soul-searching, we became parents through international adoptions. Each of our daughters' adoptions, three and a half years apart, took five weeks of time away from our home, family, friends, and work. I wouldn't change our experiences for anything. We got to spend our daughters' first weeks of life in Mexico and experience the country as natives. We deepened our connection to the land of our children's heritage. My Spanish became almost fluent. We met and became close friends with a family there who became our extended family. And most importantly, we were able to add two bright, caring, funny, wonder-filled, and amazing daughters to our family.

When they were 11 and 8 years old, my husband and I decided to move and pursue new careers as innkeepers using money my husband inherited. We moved from Pennsylvania to Massachusetts and lost contact with many of our close friends and the community where we were very involved. I didn't realize at the time how difficult this would be or how much I'd grieve since I was excited by our new opportunity. The recent diagnoses of melanoma (skin cancer) for my husband and diabetes for me further complicated the move and my grief.

A mere two-and-a-half years later, I became a widow when Stephen's cancer returned and attacked his liver and brain. I was still trying to settle into a new community. Not only did I have to grieve the loss of my husband, but I was forced to assume new roles of single parent and solo entrepreneur, roles I never wanted.

I learned not to take anything for granted and not put off doing something until the time felt right. For the first time in my life, I became independent and learned to live alone (other than caring for my children, who were 11 and 14 at the time of Stephen's death and thought they were quite mature and independent). Even though I was an only child, I was always surrounded by friends. I began to enjoy my own company and the power of setting boundaries around my energy, desire to be alone, and ability to say no to doing things I didn't want to do. I wasn't there yet, but I was taking baby steps toward no longer being a people pleaser. I also found a spiritual home at that time.

In the following 15 years, I cared for the inn, my children, and then my aging mother and stepfather. When my mother and stepfather died less than three months apart, I felt lost without my role as a caregiver. Six months later, I became an empty nester when my younger daughter got married.

My next lifequake came during Covid. I was struggling to keep a business going while the world was mostly shut down to travel and tourism. I was committed to continuing the employment of my two very dedicated staff members. One day, right before Christmas in 2020, my doorbell rang. On the porch stood a man I recognized as a local realtor who asked me if I was interested in selling the inn. My immediate response to him was, "No." And then a voice in the back of my mind said, Amy, don't be a fool. Every business is for sale if the price is right. So, I told him I wasn't looking to sell, but as I knew, every business could be for sale, and I would be happy to meet his buyers. They came after Christmas, and by March 30, the inn had new owners, and I moved from the Berkshires to Saratoga County, New York.

The sale of the inn was neither inherently good nor bad. Every way you look at it, though, I was grieving its loss. I missed my assistant, the guests, the town that was my home for 25 years, the culture, and my friends. I missed the busyness of the inn, the people, and performing weddings. I loved my new home, and yet I was lost and lonely. I knew very few people (my daughter, son-in-law, and his parents). The world was still mostly shut down, so there weren't opportunities to meet people in person.

Then the proverbial shit hit the fan. My BFF died; it's the story at the beginning of this chapter. I felt completely alone—no parents, husband, or BFF. My daughters were busy with their own families and young children. The grief felt unbearable for a while. And then, I decided I wanted to be happy and focused on joy. I was no longer content with surviving; I wanted to thrive.

I learned to be resourceful and joined online groups, took professional development and self-improvement courses, attended Zoom calls, and attempted to start a coaching business for innkeepers. I kept busy, but I was lonely and still grieving my former life. I pushed myself out of my comfort zone and took on challenges, and I began to grow. I joined a few Meetup groups, made new friends, and decided to turn the lessons I learned from my grief into a living legacy to my friend Liz and my husband, Steve.

You, too, can find silver linings in your own lifequakes when you're ready.

"They always say time changes things,
but you actually have to change them yourself."

- Andy Warhol

THE TOOL

The first step is to allow yourself to feel all your feelings! Grief is normal, natural, and healthy. It's also painful and messy. Unfortunately, you have to go through it, or it will just rear up again, possibly stronger and in sneaky ways like anger and addiction. After you've taken the time to feel all the feelings, started on the work to settle any legal and financial matters (believe me, I know how tough this is), and are feeling like you're ready to move forward with your life, take some time to answer these prompts:

Describe the lifequake you're in the midst of or have experienced.

How would you describe yourself before the quake?

What dreams did you have for yourself when you were younger? Were they realized? What/who did you dream of becoming?

What activities did you love as a child? As a teen? Before your lifequake?

Why did you stop doing them?

What activities have you always wanted to do but never tried? What held you back?

What are your hobbies? Interests? What brings you joy? Are you including these in your daily life? If not, how can you integrate them?

Imagine yourself three years into the future; how would you like to see yourself (emotionally, spiritually, physically, job/career, friends/relationships)?

What is one thing you can do today/this week that will bring you joy?

What memories of life before the lifequake bring you happiness?

What are you able to do today that you couldn't do before the lifequake? What strength do you now have because of what you've been through?

Who is in your corner (family, friends, co-workers, clergy, therapist, coach)? Who bring you joy? Who makes you laugh?

____

____

____

____

____

One of the gifts I have found in navigating grief is that while life will never be the same as it was before your lifequake, in some ways, it's also freeing. This may be the perfect time to redefine yourself and decide who and what you want to be. You don't have to meet anyone else's ideas or expectations. Have fun. See what resonates.

Amy Lindner-Lesser, MSW, Advanced Grief Recovery Method™ Specialist and certified life transitions coach, is an expert in navigating through grief and loss.

She's taken her life and career experiences and combined them, forming INNtrospection to compassionately support individuals through the emotions and feelings of loss and grief that arise with major life transitions (lifequakes).

The name of her business reflects the love she has for innkeeping as well as the word, which means to look inward, introspection.

Whether it's the heart-breaking grief that arises from the death of a loved one or the disorientation felt when life suddenly shifts due to the loss of a job, relationship, identity, or a health challenge, Amy's passionate about guiding clients to understand and navigate the transition with self-compassion.

Her own journey of navigating 30 lifequakes in 60 years, including the losses of her husband and BFF, led her to the work she's passionate about today. Find her free guide, The 7 Phases to Navigating Life's Transitions, on her website at www.INNtrospection.com where you can also schedule a get-acquainted call.

Amy has a master's in social work with a concentration in families. She compassionately served clients in a variety of situations, including home health care, hospice, and women's health.

Her podcast INNtrospection: Grief to Growth may be found on all platforms and on YouTube.com/@inntrospectiongrieftogrowth. In it, she interviews guests on topics related to death, dying, living, self-discovery, mourning and grief as well as shares the thoughts that pop into her head while always striving to normalize death and grief.

When not working Amy can be found reading, enjoying flea markets, antiques auctions, concerts, sitting on her porch enjoying nature, or playing with her grandchildren.

Connect with Amy using the link below.
https://linktr.ee/INNtrospection

CHAPTER 18

A NEW BEGINNING

RECLAIMING LIFE BEYOND INFERTILITY

Alaina Bullock, LMHC

MY STORY

In our pursuit of love and family, destiny had other plans. "Unexplained infertility" confounded us, leaving our confidence shaken. *How could we solve a problem they couldn't even identify?* Our dreams of a simple journey to parenthood shattered and were replaced by a daunting reality. We envisioned a life together, filled with love and laughter, and two or three kids completing our family. Armed with assurance from annual checkups, we set out with optimism to conceive. However, nature's course proved unpredictable. Our efforts turned into a delicate balance of hope and uncertainty. Despite challenges, we clung to love, persistence, and the wonders of medical science.

When we started dating, we talked about our dreams for our future. Our dream looked like many couples'—we'd move in together, get engaged, get married, and have multiple children. Easy, right? In our 30s, we decided to try to conceive immediately. At my annual visit, I was told everything looked great, *"All of your testing looked perfect."* My doctors assured me I should have no problem conceiving naturally. We were both optimistic about getting pregnant quickly after my doctor's visit.

We tried conceiving on our own for 16 months. During the first six months, we were okay with not getting pregnant as we were both aware that not everyone conceives quickly. Ten months later, frustration set in after each cycle. After our wedding, I returned to my doctor, worried something was wrong. Again, I was told,

"You are healthy."
"Start using ovulation testing strips."
"Chart the best time to have intercourse."
"Use pregnancy tests monthly to help ease the anticipatory worry."

Still, with following all recommendations, I was not getting pregnant. I became obsessed with tracking my cycle by using the ovulation strips, taking my basal temperature every morning, planning when we should have intercourse, and writing it on our calendar. I researched everything I could about how to conceive a child naturally.

After more than two years of trying, my doctor prescribed me medication for the subsequent several cycles. The medication had multiple adverse side effects, which I was willing to risk to finally become pregnant. Unfortunately, I experienced many of these side effects, both physical and emotional. I became obsessed with taking pregnancy tests throughout my cycle to the point where I began to have a trauma response just looking at the unopened test. My relationship with my husband started to suffer because I could only think or talk about becoming pregnant. Sex was becoming an obligation, and we both felt awful.

Unfortunately, I didn't conceive while taking the oral medication and was referred to a fertility specialist. We had our first appointment in January 2015, almost three years after we started trying. I underwent a battery of lab tests, ultrasounds, and medical procedures in the hospital. We scheduled a consultation with the fertility specialist and anticipated finally getting a diagnosis so we could fix the "problem!"

They couldn't find a medical cause for why I wasn't getting pregnant. It was another blow to our confidence. If they couldn't find the problem, how would they fix it? I immediately felt anxious and panicked again.

What did this mean?
How would I become pregnant?
Would I ever become pregnant?
Why is this happening to us?

I felt like a failure. I was fearful my husband would leave if I couldn't give him children. I was fearful our parents would be disappointed if I couldn't give them grandchildren. I had ruminating and intrusive thoughts about getting pregnant.

After our consultation, we were given a few treatment options. We went home to think about what the best decision would be. Fertility treatments take a toll physically, mentally, emotionally, and financially for not just the person getting pregnant but also for the partner. We determined our treatment plan and how much we were willing to go through to have a child.

We decided to start fertility treatments for my next cycle. I thought I was prepared for what this meant, but I wasn't. I got bloodwork and ultrasounds every other day until I triggered (or forced) ovulation. Then I went to the specialist during the dreaded "two week wait" for more testing to ensure everything was going as planned. I took multiple days off from work for appointments. My social life became non-existent. When I felt okay seeing friends and family, I had to remember to pack all of the medications with me to take them on time.

Ultimately, we decided to do three treatment cycles because of the enormous toll. I had many side effects from the medications; we drained our savings and suffered individually. As a couple, we didn't tell many people what we were going through, so trying to "act normal" became harder. I was exhausted by the entire process, and our three-month plan didn't go as expected—something I was unprepared for. Every other month, my cycle was canceled by the fertility specialist because my body wasn't reacting to the medication as they hoped. Each time they canceled a cycle, I wanted to scream.

Again!
I don't know if I can keep doing this!
How much more do we have to go through?

It was another blow to our confidence. I felt like my body was failing me, and I was failing others. I was crying all the time.

After our third, complete treatment cycle, or seven months total of canceled and uncancelled cycles, I was convinced I would get the same call from my nurse saying, "Alaina, I'm so sorry. Your blood test is negative again. We will try again during the next cycle." Instead, my nurse excitedly called and stated, "Alaina, you have a positive blood test!" My first response was to ask if she had the correct number. Then I broke down in tears. After all this time, I had my positive (blood) test. She encouraged me to take a pregnancy test at home because I'd finally see the two lines I always dreamed of seeing. I couldn't bring myself to do it. I never took that pregnancy test.

It was one of the best days of my life, telling my husband I was pregnant. He was equally surprised and delighted. We were cautious during the beginning of the pregnancy and waited well into my second trimester to announce the news. I was wrought with fear and worry during the entire pregnancy. Finally, in 2016, we welcomed a healthy baby boy into the world, almost five years after we started trying to conceive him.

Since then, we've talked about expanding our family, and decided not to return to the fertility specialist because of the toll it took. I don't think I could ever go back to that office without having a negative reaction. Since we were "healthy," we'd try on our own. It has been over seven years, and I've been unable to get pregnant since. There were times when I thought I was, but I couldn't bring myself to take a pregnancy test. Eventually, my cycle came each month. We came to accept that we will only have our son, and our dream of having two to three children is something we have had to grieve over time. I still grieve this dream today, especially when my son asks if he can have a brother or sister.

THE TOOL

THINGS TO CONSIDER WHILE UNDERGOING FERTILITY TREATMENTS

Going through fertility treatments is an ongoing cycle in which we grieve the loss of our dream of becoming parents every month. At the beginning of the cycle, there is hope; during the two-week wait, there is anticipation, fear, worry, and panic, and when you get the blood test results, there is immense sadness, grief, and hopelessness. A week later, the cycle starts all over again. During this time, it's essential to acknowledge, talk about, and hold space for all these feelings.

BE AWARE OF YOUR BOUNDARIES

You will be in contact with individuals who have difficulty accepting your boundaries when it comes to your fertility. They won't think about how asking personal questions about when you will have a baby may negatively impact you. Personally, I had a lot of worry and fear around getting together with family and friends, especially those I hadn't seen in a while. I wanted to avoid these questions. I didn't need to be reminded I wasn't pregnant. I was already worrying daily about this and fearful it would never happen to us.

When we were in the middle of fertility treatments, it seemed everyone was announcing their pregnancies and births. Give yourself permission to decline baby showers and gender reveals if you find it too difficult to go. It may be too difficult to celebrate others' pregnancies when we're in a constant cycle of grief. You don't have to explain to anyone your decision not to attend.

INTIMACY

Your sex life changes with your partner during fertility treatments. For us, sex became a series of ever-changing dates on our calendars. Sex felt like an obligation that was no longer fun or spontaneous. My husband and I considered this a loss of the intimacy we once shared, and we had to process our grief around this, individually and as a couple. It's important to remember that you can have a healthy and enjoyable sex life again.

TAKE A BREAK

There is more to life than just your fertility. During fertility treatments, I became obsessed with researching and talking to providers about anything related to getting pregnant. I was unaware that I sacrificed the rest of myself while undergoing treatments. I wasn't socializing with my friends or engaging in the hobbies I once loved. I know it's hard to close the internet searches and put your phone down, but taking a break and focusing on something you truly enjoy will help you stay more present.

LISTEN TO YOUR BODY

My friends and family tried to be as supportive as possible, but it wasn't easy to accept their support because I didn't know what I needed. I also didn't know anyone else experiencing difficulty getting pregnant. It was lonely and isolating for me and my husband. It also became less of me expressing how I was feeling and more of me giving them medical information they couldn't understand. It's important to identify what you need and express these needs to feel supported.

Take care of and listen to your body. When I was doing fertility treatments, I experienced many different physical symptoms, such as pain, soreness, weight gain, bruising, night sweats, and bloating. I also experienced emotional symptoms, including tearfulness, sadness, panic, worry, fear, and hopelessness. Take a quiet moment and listen to what your body is telling you it needs, and nurture that part of your body.

What am I feeling today?
How is my mood?

You know your body the best, and you are the best one to advocate for yourself. Speak up to your medical providers if something isn't feeling right to you physically, emotionally, or mentally. It's important that they know you and not just what is written in your medical chart.

UTILIZE YOUR SUPPORT SYSTEM

Reach out to trusted positive supports. Talk to them about how you're feeling and what you need from them to feel supported. They want to be there for you but may need guidance on how best to help. You may want to keep this circle small to avoid having to talk about it all the time. Share with them that you want to be the one who brings it up when you feel comfortable. Postpartum Support International is an informative website where you can find many resources from individual therapists, how to join specific support groups, and find informational articles.

ACTION STEPS

FIND A THERAPIST WHO SPECIALIZES IN MATERNAL MENTAL HEALTH

There are wonderful individual, couples, and group therapists that can help you during this time. Maternal mental health therapists can help you process your feelings and learn coping skills to improve your overall well-being through this difficult process. Many maternal mental health therapists have experienced their own struggles with fertility, and they may relate to what you're experiencing.

MEDICATION OPTIONS

Consider talking to your medical provider about safe medication options while trying to conceive and during pregnancy. This may help decrease unpleasant symptoms. Going through fertility treatments can feel unbearable, and medication options may help to improve your overall daily functioning.

PRACTICING MINDFULNESS

Practice self-compassion, gratitude, and grace with yourself and your partner. Making statements such as," This is hard" or "I'm scared" can be helpful for both you and your partner to feel less alone. Identifying, validating, and talking about your feelings can help you feel more connected to each other and can create a new form of intimacy within the relationship. Starting a daily gratitude journal of things you normally take for granted may help you think about something other than your fertility and help with staying in the present moment.

LEANING INTO GRIEF

There is an immense amount of grief with infertility. For the loss of the dream you pictured for your family, the loss of a pregnancy or pregnancies, the loss of the relationship you had with your partner, the loss of friends/ family who may not have been supportive toward you during this time and all of those failed cycles and negative pregnancy tests. Try to be aware of how you are feeling. Allow yourself to grieve these losses. If you're comfortable doing so, talk about how you're feeling with one of your trusted supporters or therapist.

SOCIAL MEDIA

Limit your social media activity. If you're comfortable doing so, delete social media during this time. It's hard to see people on your feeds announcing they're pregnant or had a baby. This may lead to increased intrusive and ruminating thoughts due to comparing ourselves to others on social media. Instead of scrolling through social media, try engaging in one of your hobbies, call a family member or friend, or take a walk. If you're having a hard time walking away from or limiting social media, when you're thinking about scrolling your feeds, identify how you feel after scrolling social media versus engaging in a hobby that brings you joy. If you know you will feel negatively after scrolling, do something you know will make you feel good.

Avoid or limit your internet searches. If you have a question about your lab results, ultrasounds, or even a comment you overheard someone else say, email your provider or call them. I also started carrying a notebook to appointments, where I wrote out my questions and left space for their answers. This helped me challenge intrusive and ruminating thoughts after the appointments because I could read back what providers said to me.

MANAGING EXPECTATIONS

Try to manage your expectations during this time and make a treatment plan with your partner. The treatment plan can include:

- What you're willing to do regarding the fertility treatments, and for how long. Think about how this will impact you physically, mentally, emotionally, and financially for you and your relationship.
- Identify who specifically in your support system will know that you're trying to become pregnant and try to keep this group small.
- Make a list of boundaries to protect yourself and your relationship while going through this process.

As I reflect on the rollercoaster that was our quest for parenthood, I find solace in the fact that life often takes unexpected turns, and sometimes, those twists lead us to the most beautiful destinations. Our journey, fraught with uncertainties and heartaches, eventually rewarded us with a precious gift: our son.

Becoming parents brought overwhelming joy and fulfillment. We held onto hope, navigated the treacherous waters of fertility treatments, and, against all odds, celebrated the miracle of life. The tears shed during the trials were washed away by the flood of happiness that our little one brought into our arms.

Though our dreams of having two or three children won't happen, we've come to a place of acceptance and peace. Our family may be smaller than we envisioned, but it's overflowing with love and cherished moments. We've learned that sometimes, life has its own plans, and in the end, what truly matters is the love we share.

Our journey taught us valuable lessons: to listen to our bodies, to set boundaries, and to prioritize self-care. We discovered the significance of finding supportive allies in friends, family, and, most importantly, in each other. We learned that grief and loss are an integral part of the journey, and it's okay to embrace those feelings with compassion and grace. As we embrace the road ahead, we do so with the knowledge that life's most beautiful surprises often come when we least expect them. Our family may be small, but it is a family built on love, resilience, and the belief that miracles are possible, even in the face of "Unexplained infertility." And so, our chapter continues with open hearts and a spirit of gratitude for the blessings we have and the ones yet to come.

For those facing similar struggles, I offer the wisdom gained from our experience: seek support from maternal mental health therapists, manage expectations with your partner, and remember to care for yourself amidst the emotional whirlwind. And though it may be challenging, try to find moments of mindfulness, joy, and gratitude to carry you through the darkest times.

Alaina Bullock is a licensed mental health therapist and owner of Bullock Mental Health Counseling. Alaina graduated from Sage Graduate School with her master's degree in Community Psychology and Counseling. Alaina has worked in a substance abuse program, a community mental health program, and a group private practice. After experiencing her own fertility struggles, she made the decision to help other women and couples navigate their own fertility struggles and made maternal mental health the focus of her career. In 2021, Alaina opened Bullock Mental Health Counseling, and she offers both in-person and virtual appointments. Though she specializes in maternal mental health, Alaina also helps individuals who are experiencing depression, anxiety, life transitions, and relationship difficulties.

Alaina lives in upstate New York with her husband, son, and their two dogs, Lola and Pepper. Alaina spends her free time reading books, spending time with family and friends, and taking trips to the beach.

Connect with Alaina:
alaina@bullockmentalhealth.com

CHAPTER 19

THE LAST RESPONDER

CONTINUING FOR THE DEAD

Brittany DeMarco-Furman, Licensed Funeral Director

MY STORY

I was Googling "adorable, baby Halloween costumes" when the funeral home's phone rang.

"Brittany, it's Mrs. Jones", followed by a long *familiar* pause. She didn't need to say anything more, I felt her pit in my own stomach.

There has been a death, and my services are required. My colleague and I prepared our funeral vehicle to transport the loved one into our care.

Stretcher, check! Headrest, check! Gloves and safety gear, check! Transport stretcher, check! White rose, check! Deep Breaths, *easier said than done.*

We never truly know what to expect when we drive to a private residence on a death call. Even when deaths are expected, no one is truly prepared for someone's passing. As much as I wish we could all pass away like "Titanic'" Rose Dawson — long-lived and cozy in our own bed, surrounded by loved ones and photos of our life adventures — that's not the typical case.

As my colleague and I approach the deceased's colonial house, Christmas lights, and candy canes lining the driveway strike notes of cheer. Driving closer to the home, we see reindeer and snowman fixtures in the windows, and Santa Claus is on the roof. I look around in disbelief; I pre-ordered my daughter's Halloween costume only minutes ago.

My knock on the door is followed by the sound of shuffling inside, and a muffled voice: "The funeral home is here." It feels like an eternity before the door opens. I get it: no one wants to face reality—the last responder.

To my surprise, it was Mrs. Jones opening the door. Along with her bravery, I was overcome by the smell of pine and Christmas. An hour ago, Mrs. Jones was married. Now, she's widowed. To me, however, she will forever be the brave wife who watched her husband plan his own funeral as he clung to life in a wheelchair.

The two of us hug, I feel her heart thumping in anxiety. My head is organizing what I must say next to help her in this difficult moment, but before I can utter comforting words, she nervously shouts, "He is in the bedroom!" Removing a loved one from their home, especially when it is their cherished forever home, is one of the most challenging responsibilities honored by my profession. It is a funeral ceremony all on its own. My heart, too, skips a beat, acknowledging how unforgettable this moment will be for the family.

Entering the bedroom, I see him. He has withered away from pancreatic cancer. He was in front of me only a month earlier, asking me, "Would you like a ride on my wheelchair?"

His charm still shined through his sickness.

Typical end-of-life pre-planning is full of tears, and the family is doing the arrangements, without the person nearing death. The meeting for Mr. Jones was different; there were no tears or regrets.

Our meeting started with him exclaiming, "Fuck this Cancer!", followed by a chuckle that made me chuckle.

"I have a feeling you are a lot of fun."

At that moment, I knew Mr. Jones wasn't going to hold back, *he knew he was going to die.*

He continues, "So, how much is it going to cost me to die?!"

I am watching his face turn up into a smirk. As a funeral director, I am approached with this direct question multiple times a week, and every time I have to read the room to figure out if I should laugh with them or go directly to the itemization sheet. Nobody wants to meet with a funeral director, but my job is to make it comfortable. I laughed back.

"So, I see I have my work cut out for me today," I told Mr. Jones. "Where did you get your big personality?"

This simple response led to hours of conversation. I was captivated by his history. When we arrived at his recent timeline, I nearly forgot he was terminally ill, and we were here today pre-planning his funeral. *I think he did too, and that made me happy.*

Mr. Jones left my funeral home *stronger*, with that unforgettable smirk of his; he had remembered who he truly was. As he faced his own mortality, he gave me the story of a lifetime, *his story.* Someone I would never have met if it wasn't for my profession, but for God's sake, I wish it wasn't why we met.

I learned about his ancestral history in Italy and how his father influenced his integrity and strong will. He talked about his beautiful mother, and even though our conversation wasn't led by faith (to be honest, he was more of an atheist), I grasped that he knew he was going to see her again, giving him peace. I learned about his struggles, his triumphs, his wishes for his children, the interior stitching inside his favorite Cadillac Coupe DeVille, Christmas being his favorite time of year, and how he won the heart of his bride.

My manila folder was buried with words, his words. He shared a quote with me that reminds us humans of the beauty of being mortals, "Memories are treasured when you get closer to the horizon."

The Jones family name popped up on the funeral home caller ID several times before Mr. Jones died. I was always relieved to hear his voice. "Brittany, I have another story for you," he invariably launched the conversation.

I admired his capability for storytelling. My favorite story was about his college days.

"Holy Shit! I thought I was crazy in college, you must…"

Mr. Jones cut me off and snipped back, "Your generation has no idea what fun is! There is more to life than video games and Kardashians."

The last time he called, he asked me to officiate his funeral, "I don't want my family to have to tell a stranger things about me and have him/her stand up there on my behalf." I paused.

I've written and officiated services countless times in the past where I am the stranger he is talking about. He trusts me with his life story.

"Mr. Jones, it would be my honor."

"Thank you, Brittany. Oh, and make sure you tell Mrs. Jones how much I love her."

"Mr. Jones, give your bride a kiss, and tell her yourself," I catch my breath, "I'll take good care of her."

We said goodbye, for the last time.

I'm shot back to reality. He is dead. This brilliant, spirited man is gone from this life. Those who were a part of his life would call me a stranger. But, I feel like I knew him.

Hold it together, Brittany, don't get too emotional. You are here for his family. You have to be strong.

Being a funeral director is weird. It is a business, but you wish the phones didn't have to ring.

I'm not ready to take him out of the house yet. I need to make this experience positive for the family.

"He looks peaceful," I quietly say as I grab Mrs. Jones' hand.

Looking up from Mr. Jones' motionless body, my eyes find the fireplace mantle, it is filled with stories. These are the memories and people he wanted to see before he died. I grabbed a familiar story by its frame, "Is this your home on Long Island?"

She replies, "Yes, that is where we raised the kids."

"I also believe you mentioned it was the 'party house'."

"Brittany, you wouldn't believe how many people we fit into that tiny house."

"It is beautiful, just as this home. Full of love."

I put the frame down and saw Mr. Jones' handsome obituary photo from his son's wedding. When Mr. Jones gave me a copy of the photo, he told me how he wished to attend one more soiree in a tuxedo. As if on cue, Mrs. Jones withdraws a garment bag from the closet.

"He decided he wants to go out in style," she says as she unzips the bag revealing a tuxedo.

Even as a *stranger,* I knew these were *his words* that he asked her to say to me.

Mrs. Jones and I walk out of the bedroom to introduce me to their children. Feeling Mr. Jones' presence throughout the house, I follow her down the hallway and notice all of his art. He was a collector.

I remember his raspy voice, "Kids these days don't have good taste."

I responded matter of fact with a side of sass, "I'm 29, and I collect art". His shocked expression was delightful, but his cackle laugh that came next was my favorite.

I continued, "Yeah, but my kind of collecting occurs on cruise ships after day drinking. My husband and I were confused as to why a giant Park West shipping container showed up at our front door one day."

He was beside himself with laughter, "Oh, I've been there. Free champagne is dangerous!"

We pass One-Two-Three Christmas Trees, and the sound of Christmas music is getting louder and louder. I approach the children, who are a decade older than me. I see the music coming from a turntable, I point to the antique, "Well, you don't see these too often."

The oldest son responds, "It was my great-grandfather's."

"What a beautiful piece of history to have in the family."

With a renewed sense of what I must do next, I find the strength to ask an important question. I grab Mrs. Jones' hand, "Are you ready for me to take Mr. Jones into my care?" Her eyes swell up as she looks around to her family.

I look up from the ground trying to hold my composure. The twinkle of the Christmas lights reflects off my watery eyes. It is the first week in October, and I'm standing in a snow globe. My brain travels back to the conversation with Mr. Jones on the topic of Christmas. *Oh, I remember now.* He proposed to his wife on Christmas, and their home on Long Island was the designated Christmas house. It was the only calendar day he would allow fish in the house. True Italian.

Find the words, Brittany. Find the words!

"It feels like Christmas morning in your home. You made his final day, his favorite day."

She embraces me and gives me a nod to take him into my care.

After securing him onto the stretcher, I look back towards the empty bed. Typically, I'd leave a single white rose, but Mr. Jones wasn't a flower kind of guy. Instead, I find a photo of his family from Christmas on the mantle and place it on his sunken pillow.

As I walk Mr. Jones towards the front door, I stop in front of his family to give them the opportunity to say goodbye before I graciously cover him with a blanket and exit his home for the last time. They each kiss him goodbye.

I am now outside in the removal van. Mr. Jones is in my care. I scroll to my Spotify playlist. I put the car in drive.

As I head out of the holiday-infused driveway, "Have Yourself a Merry Christmas" by Frank Sinatra begins to play. This is dedicated to you, Mr. Jones, my vibrant, Christmas-obsessed, unexpected friend.

THE TOOL

BUCKET LIST

Meeting Mr. Jones was one of my most memorable human experiences, not only because it was the first funeral pre-arrangement I made for someone who was terminally ill but for his lasting imprint on my heart. He opened my eyes to what it means to leave your mark on the world, as a funeral director and a person living for today. In this business, you see death all the time— I know we aren't promised tomorrow. Mr. Jones, however, helped me understand that the beauty and story of all my yesterdays can inspire someone else's tomorrow.

I am grateful but saddened that Mr. Jones is not the only grief I've experienced as a funeral director; each loss has given me unique heartbreak and influence as my community's last responder.

After losing a loved one, you are in uncharted waters in the deepest depths of grief, and no life vest can immediately bring you back to the surface. No matter how many deaths you've experienced, you never get used to what comes next. Whether that loss is a best friend, parent, spouse, pet, or your second cousin once removed, you must face the reality that your life is moving forward without them physically here.

As I face death on a daily basis, I prepare myself for the front lines of grief. In the first 48 hours, a grieving family will answer over 150 questions to create a beautiful goodbye and celebrate an entire life.

You can have multiple weddings, but only one funeral.

After the funeral, the next month is filled with another 100 questions to move forward financially and legally, "Do we sell the house?", "Where is the life insurance policy?", "Did he/she have a safety deposit box?", "Who is the beneficiary?" All things you wish you didn't have to take care of while you try to hold yourself together emotionally, mentally, and physically.

One month officially passed. There are no more sympathy flower deliveries, your mail is thin, no new voicemails, and your family and friends are back into their normal routines. Your life exploded, and it was overwhelming with "I'm sorry for your loss", to becoming disturbingly quiet and lonely.

Some may say this is when the grieving begins, but if that is so, then the funeral service didn't serve its purpose as the beginning of your grief journey.

As a funeral director, my purpose is to create peace and, most importantly, to guide the family through the early stages of grief when their bodies are functioning only to survive. And when the time is right, I can help them put the word "loss" aside, and focus on appreciation for the life that was here. An affirmation that helps me personally is as follows, "I am grateful for his/her life. And I am grateful for my life. He/she will continue within me."

A bucket list isn't something new, most people just call them goals. Bucket lists are created somewhere in the middle of ordinary life, typically without deep thought, just desire. However, when faced with your own mortality clock, let's call a spade a spade since we all kick the bucket one day.

The kind of bucket list I want you to implement is one with love and purpose behind it. Let these goals steer you towards happiness and fulfillment, and test the strength of the new version of you.

Many people in my personal life and those whom I have honored have inspired me in different ways; my love for writing, desire to travel, obsession with oysters, and appreciation for sailing, fishing, and listening to Fleetwood Mac, all originated within the funeral home.

The dying and the dead have a lot to teach us. Luckily, I have a front-row seat to all the master classes — and the forum to share all I've learned.

You may be reading this and not know where to begin. Start by examining yours and your loved ones yesterday, and plan you're tomorrow. Here are some prompts:

What in my past did I love to do, and why am I not doing it anymore?

What did he/she do that I never have tried before?

What did he/she do with me that I can continue tomorrow with?

What did he/she want to do that he/she never got the chance to do?

What is something he/she taught me?

What is something he/she wished they could do one more time?

The fact is that love never dies. Heartbreak will come and go for the rest of your life. And then, one day, our life is over. And someone else will have to endure the heartbreak as we have. And when we no longer write our own story, it becomes the responsibility of our legacy and people you wouldn't ever expect to celebrate your memory—the last responders. As you continue your grief journey, please honor your loved one daily by living for today, hoping for tomorrow, and appreciating the past.

"There are no goodbyes for us.
Wherever you are, you will always be in my heart."

~ Gandhi

Brittany DeMarco-Furman is a fourth-generation funeral director at her family-owned and operated firm, Glenville Funeral Home in Upstate New York. She is proud to be the first female licensed funeral director in her family's 100-plus-year history, even though she always said, "I am not getting into this business." Brittany didn't know enough about life to know about death to enter the funeral profession. After graduating from the University at Albany with a Bachelors in Business and Communications, traveling throughout Europe, soul-searching, working in marketing, and experiencing a few broken hearts, Brittany found herself back home, where a grieving family altered her life plan. She returned to college to earn her Mortuary Science Degree, completed her national boards and residency, and became licensed in 2019.

Today, she navigates between familiar traditions and new-age healing practices to serve all faiths and beliefs in our evolving world. When people think of a mortician, they think of a morbid and unfamiliar individual in society—she is the complete opposite. Brittany faces death as a beacon of light, promising to be there for you during your darkest days. As a certified celebrant, Brittany cultivates unique funeral services through storytelling, engaging with survivors, and fostering inspiration; she will remind you that every life has a story to tell.

Brittany lives in Saratoga, New York, with her husband and daughter. Her zest for life is evident in all she does, from being the first, and sometimes only, person on the dance floor to creating magical fundraiser events for her community. Brittany strives to leave her mark on the world—with glitter!

Connect with Brittany:

LinkedIn: www.linkedin.com/in/brittany-demarco-a86a1158

Instagram: https://www.instagram.com/buriedinconversation

Instagram: https://www.instagram.com/glenvillefuneralhome

Website: https://www.glenvillefuneralhome.com/

CHAPTER 20

LETTERS FROM THE HEART

TRANSCEND STUCKNESS WITH SOULFUL WORDS

George Garcia, PhD, LMFT

MY STORY

"You're going to be a great father one day."

Maybe not; you don't know the whole story.

"You're going to be a great dad someday."

Not likely. It doesn't look good right now.

This is the tension I was forced to live with as I fought to make my dream a reality, regardless of what the future held for fatherhood.

I was told over and over again how good I was with kids. How children just seemed to gravitate towards me. How I had a special ability to connect with children and make them feel seen. How all this would come together to make me a great dad someday.

If only it were that easy.

It was a well-intended sentiment I heard a thousand times over—comments that, at one point, made me smile and excited for what the future had in store.

Little did everyone know, myself included, that these kinds of sentiments were not likely to come true and that there was a direct threat to my own dreams of fatherhood. It was a foe not easily recognized by the human eye, a rival that was invisible yet capable of infiltrating the most private parts of my life.

The foe was named infertility.

The same thing that most often gets associated with women is also applicable to men.

Even the healthiest of men. Even the most successful of men. Even the most resilient of men. Even to me.

Infertility was now part of my story. This diagnosis hit me like a freight train and thrust me into a battle that changed my life completely.

Ill-prepared, I quickly found myself on the ropes, struggling to stay afloat, challenging everything I once believed to be true about myself. This nemesis brought with it a continuous struggle, ambiguous losses, and a time of isolation and confusion.

THE INTRODUCTION

I remember that day like it was yesterday.

A routine check-up. That's all it was supposed to be.

I drove in a sea of red lights, trying to keep the sweat from flooding my face as I navigated the infamous rush hour traffic that L.A. was known for.

I hate being late.

The music in the background was barely audible over the sound of my pounding heartbeat. The anxiety that sat with me was mainly focused on getting to the appointment on time, thinking traffic would be the worst part of the whole ordeal.

After all, I was young, in good health, and, at the very least, resilient enough to find my way through the toughest of challenges.

Finally, I arrived. *This will be quick. I take pretty good care of myself and have never had any major health issues come up before.*

This was why I was so neurotic with exercise. With eating well. With taking a few supplements.

My daily routine basically keeps me well, I boastfully thought to myself.

Annoyed at the nearly two-hour drive, I checked in at the desk. 55 minutes later, I was called into an old dingy office. There I waited again, more annoyed at having to wait so long for what would likely be a typical appointment. Finally, a small, scruffy man walks in.

With a mere introduction of his name, he buries himself into my chart and says, "Something's not right."

"Oh," I respond shakily.

"We're going to need to run more tests."

"Okay."

I sat there, taking in what the doctor said.

"Well, this is annoying," I said as I thought about the hassle of scheduling additional appointments, still believing there could be nothing wrong with me.

The weeks come and go, the tests are completed, and I find myself back with the scruffy old man. I sat there confused as he uttered a word I'm sure Google never heard of.

"What does that even mean?"

That was the moment I first heard of the word infertility. The air seemed to grow heavy as the words echoed in my mind. "I'm sorry, but the test results confirm that you have what's called male infertility." The doctor continued on in his never-ending monologue about infertility, though at this point, I struggled to take in his words. My eyes welled up with tears as the doctor explained further what that diagnosis meant and what treatment would entail. I was still unaware of it all, but something didn't feel right.

Even if I did everything right, it was still a mere roll of the dice. At least, that's how I understood it.

Male infertility?

The words hung in the air like a dark cloud, casting a shadow over my hopes and dreams. Images of fatherhood, once so vivid and radiant, now seemed distant and unattainable.

As I stepped out of the office and made my way through the empty parking lot toward my car, the weight of the diagnosis began pressing me down. The world seemed to move in fast-forward while I remained stuck in slow motion. Every passing driver seemed blissfully unaware of the storm raging within me.

All hope seemed lost.

But I had to try, right? If I work hard enough, I can right this ship. I've always done that. That's who I am.

From that day forward, I obsessed with every possible advantage I could give myself.

My eyes, weary from the hours of research, tried to maintain a picture of hope for the future. My Amazon cart was full of recommended vitamins and supplements I found online. I was intentional about managing stress. And I was neurotic with the regimented poking and prodding of injections ordered by the doctor.

One by one, I'd count them out, pretending to believe that the thousand vitamins actually made a difference. Bracing myself each time, I loaded the syringe with the prescribed medication, hoping it would do whatever it was meant to do behind the scenes.

And yet, none of it seemed to matter. Nothing seemed to change. No improvement. No way to see even the smallest steps of progress. Still, I tried to stay the course.

Days turned into weeks, and the grief continued to settle deep within my soul. I found myself retreating more and more into the solitude of my own thoughts, constantly wrestling with a torrent of emotions. I endlessly mourned the loss of a future I always envisioned, one where I'd proudly watch as my child took their first steps. Dreams of going to dance class and soccer practice. Sharing in the joys and challenges of parenthood. I carried the guilt of the burden that was now placed on my wife and the shame of robbing her of a dream she had always longed for.

Everywhere I turned, I saw reminders of what I believed I could never have. Friends and families announcing pregnancies and parents doting on their children. Even the smallest of interactions became painful reminders of my own self-perceived inadequacy and relational failure.

Grief became a constant companion, a haunting presence that consumed my every waking moment.

As I tried to navigate the depths of my grief and the demands of the treatment regimens, the heaviness continued to weigh me down. Communication with others, even my wife, was strained as I feared burdening others with my own insecurities and fears. I feared acknowledging my fears would only bring them to fruition.

Unable to articulate the storm brewing within, I threw myself into my work with relentless determination. I worked long hours at the office as a means to escape and numb the pain. The pursuit of excellence in my work became an obsession, a shield to hide behind as I yearned to prove my worth in a world where my infertility struggles had no power.

Driven by a desperate need to compensate for my perceived inadequacy, I chased every validation in every success I achieved. Promotions, accolades, good grades, and recognition all served as temporary measures to sooth the storm.

High-level work success, excelling in my doctoral studies, hitting athletic milestones—all a means to show that I brought some value to the table and prove I was healthy.

Yet, the emptiness persisted, unquenchable no matter how many external achievements I garnered.

I questioned my own masculinity, my very essence as a man. I struggled to reconcile the image of myself that society had ingrained within me with the reality of my own infertility.

Men are supposed to be strong. Yet I feel so weak.

Men are supposed to be resilient, yet I feel so broken.

I was supposed to be an overcomer, yet there was nothing I could do to change my situation.

To make matters worse, every month continued to be a reminder of my failure. There was an open-endedness to my situation—circumstances with no clear ending or resolution. I was left to hold onto an ambiguous hope that something would change.

If I believe hard enough...long enough...something will change. It has to.

But I apparently never reached a belief that was sufficient enough. Week after week I was left with disappointment, as signs of improvement were scarce.

As the walls constructed around me, fortified as they may have been, began to crumble, I found myself at a crossroads. The realization that burying my pain beneath layers of work and isolation would only lead to further disconnection and happiness set in.

It was time to make a change. That was the moment I turned my behemoth of a writing project, my dissertation, into an opportunity to participate in the internal dialogue.

After all, I was already writing about male infertility, spending hours at a time researching all there was to know about the topic. I wrote from an academic perspective about the topic of infertility. I journaled about my own thoughts, beliefs, and even past behaviors related to infertility. It was all laid out on the table so I could limit my research bias and write a better dissertation, but it also helped me become more aware of the internal dialogue raging on the inside.

The awareness was pivotal. The journaling helped me shift my thinking and gave me an idea for the grief dialogue going on in my head.

For so long, I was afraid and even unable to articulate my grief. But I knew it was time to start breaking through the taboo. And that is where it started.

I grabbed a piece of paper and a pen and wrote down the word infertility. That was the beginning of the process for me—the name of the thing that was raging war within me. Naming it helped me distance myself a bit more from it, separating my identity from this diagnosis. This was lesson number one: *I am not infertility. Infertility is something I experience.*

I took the writing a step further and listed the limiting beliefs that ravaged my mind. Sometimes, they came out as just a word or two at a time.

Inadequate.

Broken.

Less than.

A failure.

Undesirable.

These were just a few of a lengthy list. If I'm honest, I was shocked at some of the beliefs I wrote down. My heart ached for the torment that some of those sentiments caused. It was revealing to reflect on how influential those beliefs were.

As I sat there in my chair, reading over what I wrote, I had a revelation. I began to think about how loud these beliefs were over several months and subsequently, how silent I had been. It dawned on me that it was a one-sided conversation all along. It was at that moment that I decided to enter into the conversation and speak back.

I began to write down what I would've said, what I wanted to say, and what I wished I had said back to infertility from the start. I spoke my truth to those ill-fated beliefs. I took that opportunity to correct some of those negative, unhelpful, and even false beliefs. I even offered my own grief what I needed all along—love.

This whole experience sucks. I wouldn't wish it upon my worst enemy. Being a father is one of the biggest dreams I have. And you are threatening to take that away. What would be worse is giving up. Letting you win without a fight. And that is not who I am. I am a fighter. I am resilient. I don't need awards to prove that. I just need to be.

This is an example of what was in my letter. I spoke from the heart and to the heart.

There are real strategies for overcoming grief, even the ambiguous and invisible kind, to grieve resiliently and induce growth amidst adversity. It begins with awareness and understanding. It involves the sharing of our stories. It entails a readiness to move towards growth and develop a new life stance in the face of adversity.

THE TOOL

STEP 1

The first part of this strategy is all about awareness. If we can't see it, we can't heal it. Grab a pen and some paper, and find a place that you can focus on.

We all have an internal dialogue going on, that inner voice that speaks loudly to us. It's a voice that often gets it wrong and gives unhelpful commentary on life. Taking the internal dialogue and bringing it outside in front of us often gives a different vantage point to consider.

Start with naming that adversary that stands before you. As I mentioned in my story, infertility was my foe—the challenger who pushed me to my limits and changed my life as I knew it. That opponent who forced me outside my comfort zone and forced me to reconcile the life scripts I previously clung to so tightly. Naming my challenger brought this battle outside of my head and helped separate it from my own personhood. It helped me manage the distance so I could better manage the damage and assess what was happening.

STEP 2

Just like I did above, take a few moments to write down any past limiting thoughts or beliefs that have stuck with you. This helps with better understanding these beliefs through awareness and seeing the choices in front of us. At the very least, it can help guide us to where and what we need to speak to.

Write it all out. Don't hold back. The conversation and the statements are already happening whether we acknowledge it or not. They don't always have words, but the conversations are going on even in the inaudible. This step is just about putting words to the conversation. So, put it all on the table.

> **Example 1:** One limiting belief I held onto was that I was inadequate—that I was a failure because I wasn't able to overcome this adversity. Because having biological children was not likely.

Example 2: A second belief I held was that the estranged relationship with my own father was essentially for nothing. That the experience I was viewed as a means to equip me to be a better father was, in fact, a mere pain point in my life, holding no redemptive value, reinforcing the belief that was just a mere failure.

STEP 3

Time to write the letter. I want you to literally treat this as a letter you'd write to a friend and put in the mailbox. Write to that foe you identified in step one. Tell them what you would say if they were literally sitting across from you.

Speak from the heart. Say the things they and you need to hear.

STEP 4

I want you to switch roles now. I want you to write a letter to an earlier version of yourself. For me, this would've been the version of me that sat in that doctor's office and first heard the words male infertility.

I would tell him that he's going to be okay. That he doesn't need anything more than his presence in the world. That he himself is enough-despite the infertility.

This is where we can give ourselves what we needed all along—assurance, love, support, and truth.

STEP 5

This is the last step. I want you to read the letters out loud. This will access a different part of our brain and allow us to experience the words in a different way.

You deserve a part in the conversation. You deserve a seat at the table.

Dr. George Garcia, LMFT, Ph.D., is a licensed Marriage and Family Therapist in the States of California and Ohio. He completed his bachelor's degree in Print Journalism from Biola University and his master's and doctorate degree in marriage and family therapy from Hope International University and Northcentral University, respectively. He has worked in community outreach programs, private practice, and has taught at the master's and doctoral levels.

His relentless passion for guiding others into greater healing and health is evident in the endeavors he's engaged in. Whether he is teaching graduate and doctoral students, training other therapists, or caring for his clients, George brings strong support and genuine commitment to helping others discover healing, health, and the best version of themselves.

His passion for seeing the world change, and his belief that the change needed requires each person's unique personhood, drive him to pursue excellence in his craft and self-discovery. He shares his journey, wisdom, and passion with bold transparency and tactful delivery.

When not in the office or classroom, you can find him being active in some capacity. Whether it be rolling on the mats in a Jiu-Jitsu academy, attempting to hit a decent drive on the golf course, or chasing his young daughter and son around, he keeps active to stay healthy physically and mentally. He pursues learning through reading and maintains a close circle of friends.

Connect with George:
Email: drglmft@gmail.com
LinkedIn: www.linkedin.com/in/george-garcia-621b2632
Instagram: https://www.instagram.com/drg_mft/

CHAPTER 21

TRAUMATIC GRIEF: YOU ARE NOT ALONE

A JOURNEY OF HEALING THROUGH FEELING

Rebecca Johnson, LPC

MY STORY

"Hey, Becca, you are going to drive me home, right?" Tuck said.

"Yep," I said. "I will take you home after this."

"Promise you will get me home?"

"No problem, Tuck. I promise."

"Okay, I just have to go to the restroom. I will be right back."

Those were the last words I spoke with my friend. Tragically, he never made it back to my car that night. I didn't get him home.

Growing up, I don't remember experiencing many losses. I was fortunate for that! I don't remember learning much about death and grief, let alone trauma and grief.

The year 2002-2003 was a year I endured more losses than I remember experiencing in my entire life before age 22. This chapter intends to provide hope, knowledge, and connection in a time that feels incredibly isolating, numb, and disconnected.

It was a fairly warm night in March 2002. I was the designated driver and took several friends to hit up a favorite bar downtown. It was a night of fun and laughter. I drove to my friend's home. At the first stop, everyone got out except Tuck. I was taking him home last. After everyone got out, Tuck made me promise to get him home.

Tuck said he needed to use the restroom. Tuck smiled and bounced out of the car. He went across the parking lot, and I remember a pep in his step. My other friend was in the parking lot as well.

"Tuck, go into the apartment," we both said. But boys will be boys, and he decided differently.

I was sitting in my car, watching as Tuck started walking back. That's when I saw the other car's lights in my rearview mirror. It happened so quickly. The car was racing up the parking lot. I could see Tuck was still in the parking lot. *They are going fast,* I thought. I quickly started yelling at Tuck inside my car, doing anything to alert him.

"Watch out Tuck, watch out. There's a car!" My friend was outside yelling at him as well.

As Tuck walked across the parking lot he finally turned and saw the car, but it was too late. There was a second of silence. Of shock and disbelief. Then, chaos and deep despair.

The chaos: *What do I do?* A friend in the apartment called 911. I crawled under the car, reaching for Tuck. *Is he breathing?* I placed my hand on his body. Nothing. His body was lying lifeless.

So many thoughts were running through my head. I wanted to help but didn't know how. I grabbed the phone from my friend. I explained to the 911 operator what happened.

"What do I do next? How can I help? We need to help our friend right now!"

The woman said "You just need to wait. Responders are on their way. Don't move anything. Don't touch him."

That was the hardest thing to do, not to do anything. At the same time, your friend is buried under a car. But then, reflecting, I knew he was already gone.

The early morning was filled with police, medics, and a group of friends in shock. Tuck's roommate and friends also came to the scene to try and conceptualize what happened. There was screaming, yelling, and crying.

For me, I remember walking around in a daze. I was cocky and refused help or support that night. I kept saying to myself: *I have a degree in psychology; I should know how to deal with this!* The victim's advocate asked me if I wanted to talk. I refused, saying to myself again: *I got this! I know how to deal with this because I have a degree.*

Although I spent the following day and week describing the details of what happened to Tuck's family, I found myself shutting down and not talking to anyone about my feelings. My close friends tried to help. Even hugging me, I refused. I was afraid I would fall apart. Inside, I hid a multitude of feelings.

Anger: I was angry at one of the firemen—his lack of empathy in telling us. "Tuck is dead." No, "I'm sorry," no compassion. As a therapist, I know first responders do things to protect themselves, but that response, the image of the fireman, his wide dark eyes while flatly telling me, "He's dead," has burned in my mind for years. I was so angry at him for his lack of empathy. He was the first person to confirm what my mind was telling me. Tuck was gone.

Blame: It's normal to ask who is to blame. I wanted to blame the one that hit him. He was driving too fast; was he drinking? But no. He was driving too fast but completely sober. That's when I turned the blame inward.

Why did I park the car there? Why didn't I take the time to find a spot? I created a blind spot for the driver. He didn't see Tuck because of my car. I was the reason Tuck didn't get home that night. I am responsible.

The day after, I replayed the moments of the night to Tuck's father. I stood in the parking lot, reliving each moment. I was only partially present. I answered questions, but my body was spinning around slowly as I was on an isolated merry-go-round while everyone was watching me. Everyone questioned what happened. I tried to answer as best as I could. *Did I say the right thing? Was that correct?* I felt like I was alone on an island with nothing to hold onto. And then my inner critic entered. *I should've done this differently. I shouldn't have allowed this to happen.*

Literally, the same feelings and judgments washed over me at Tuck's funeral. Tuck's mother walked me into a room and we sat on a piano bench together. She too wanted to hear what happened. I held back feelings because Tuck's mother didn't need to console me. But who was I to decide what she needed at that moment?

My guilt and judgment were in the way. I was stuck in a mindset of not upsetting anyone further. A mindset-based assumption that I hurt other people by sharing my difficult feelings. Today I understand people need feelings brought up to be connected. While I was desperately trying to protect her, I now realize I missed out on an opportunity to share my feelings, to connect while offering support and comfort.

Blame is a normal response to trauma and grief. Although we know it's "normal," it certainly doesn't feel good, no matter how much those who love you tell you over and over that it wasn't your fault. We feel it, especially if we have some preconditioned beliefs about ourselves that we're responsible for things or carry deep feelings of self-blame. The feelings are there, and we need to give ourselves grace while we allow ourselves to heal.

Sadness: I was so incredibly sad. A friend was killed. Watching others in their grief was devastating. Our group of friends shared such a special friendship with Tuck. My focus went outward. *How can I help them? What can I do to make things a little better?*

Shock: In the following weeks, I went through the motions. I was in shock. Saying to myself: *I need to get back to a normal routine.* Although I tried, I remember functioning in a cloudy haze, numb and detached. I went to play volleyball one night, which I did every week. I love volleyball! But that night, I felt such a disconnect. I was playing but not fully aware of what I was doing. My teammates asked me if I was okay and noticed a difference in me.

I want to say that after the funeral passed and life resumed, I started taking care of myself. But I didn't. The year of 2002, I experienced one death after another. Another friend, multiple family members, and family of close friends. I just went through each death as I did with Tuck: Be there for family and friends, but continue to push away thoughts and feelings. And partying—what a good way to not feel, right?

I carried on through the years, grief compounding in the background. I enjoyed time with friends and learned much at a job I deeply cared about. However, deep inside, remained this numbness, despair, and intense amount of grief, guilt, and shame. I remember saying to myself: *This is how things will be. This is my punishment.* I didn't seek any help or treatment until I moved away to graduate school.

I was sitting in my practicum supervision class, presenting a school case, providing therapy for a young girl who had experienced a traumatic event in a car. My supervisor caught on to my hesitation with the client.

"Becca, why are you being so cautious?"

"What are you protecting?"

"What is keeping you from helping your client to heal?"

Out of nowhere, I started sobbing. An image of Tuck came into my head, and I was transported back to the night of the accident. I reluctantly shared that I witnessed my friend getting killed in a car accident.

I was so mad! *How could I break down like this in class?* I was mad at my professor. *Why did she push me like this?* But it needed to happen. That realization that the trauma I experienced was still very well present and impacting my work and well-being.

So finally, after three years, I sought out treatment from a kind and supportive therapist. It was a beginning and helped me verbally process the accident and childhood experiences. It felt good and as I permitted myself to heal, I experienced some breakthroughs with my client.

I successfully graduated and began a career working in child welfare. I started as an intake worker, obtained my license, and then worked as a therapist. However, I struggled anytime I experienced a case with a car related to it or a client with feelings of responsibility. Any time there was an intense trigger or flashback, it felt like I was punched back to that moment in a deep hole. It would take me days/weeks to recover. I relived the moment of the accident and the events of that week. I stopped talking to others and withdrew.

I started telling myself: *I am tired of this.* I felt trapped and hopeless. I didn't know how to alleviate the distress from the memories. I was lost in how to treat myself. *How do I keep myself from going back to that hole every time I experience a trigger?*

I opened up and talked with other therapists on my team. I shared my difficulties, frustrations, and inability to move forward. I remember one saying:

"Have you ever tried EMDR?"

"No. What is EMDR?" I said.

"You should try it; EMDR will help."

Finally, there is hope! I may find some relief!

So, I went to therapy again around 2009, about seven years after the accident. Eye Movement Desensitization and Reprocessing (EMDR) is an evidence-based trauma treatment. With the use of bilateral stimulation, the therapy helps your brain reprocess a traumatic memory and move from negative thoughts (I am unsafe, I am responsible) to adaptive thoughts (I am safe, that was in the past; I did the best I could).

In preparing for EMDR, a therapist utilizes different resources or coping skills to prepare for reprocessing. Creating a safe place was a significant resource for me. In that process, I found that my boyfriend was my safe place, and now he is my husband. I found a connection with him that was safe and reliable.

I'm not sure if I can truly describe how much relief I experienced with EMDR. I gained a sense of reconnection with myself and others.

As I move through life, I still reflect on that night. I grieve the life Tuck would have had. The first couple of years, we had different gatherings to honor and remember him. Now I see friends continue to grieve when they don't have him to stand up at their wedding or see the life that Tuck would've created for himself. The trauma is still there. The memories go dormant at times. The distress and the dysregulation are manageable.

EMDR was an effective treatment for me and because of the changes I experienced, I was moved to get trained so I can provide this therapy to my clients. Through the years, I experienced many more deaths. Some were expected, others were unexpected and traumatic. I learned how to cope with these deaths in a healthier manner. I gained tools to use whenever those grief bursts or triggers show up in my life unexpectedly. One tool I remain connected with is the butterfly hug. Although EMDR treatment allowed me to regain connection again, this treatment takes time. The EMDR Butterfly Hug method for self-administer bilateral stimulation is a resource I learned in EMDR treatment. I've found relief whenever I use it. It can be used in treatment sessions or in moments when you are experiencing overwhelming feelings of sadness, anger, and/or despair. It's a tool of comfort, care, and relief. It's a way to connect with yourself.

THE TOOL

The Butterfly Hug (BH) is a beautiful therapeutic exercise created to help lower the intensity of high distress when experiencing a trigger, memory, or overwhelming emotion; when self-soothing techniques are ineffective.

Lucina (Lucy) Artigas originated the BH during her work with the survivors of Hurricane Pauline in Acapulco, Mexico. If you'd like to read the full updated article on the BH, understand the multiple uses, and appreciate the science behind the method, please go to Jarero, I., & Artigas, L. (October 10, 2023). The EMDR Therapy ButterflyHug Method for Self-Administered Bilateral Stimulation. Technical Report. Research Gate. https://tinyurl.com/2dv4yakr.

The following is a brief description of the BH method that can be used outside of therapy. Follow this link for a video: https://youtu.be/27tD6Iuv7YU

STEP 1

If possible, find a quiet space to administer the BH to yourself. It could be somewhere in your home, a private place outside, or your workspace. You can be creative in finding this space. You can lie down, sit in a chair, or even walk around. Find what is comfortable for you and works for the current situation.

STEP 2

Notice and observe your body. What images, thoughts, sounds, smells, feelings, and sensations are coming up? Notice all of these without judging or changing them.

STEP 3

Cross your arms over your chest. Place your hands so that your fingers are underneath your collarbone. Fan out your fingers and interlock your thumbs to form the shape of a butterfly.

STEP 4

Pick what feels comfortable to you: Close your eyes completely, keep them partially closed, or look toward your nose. Whatever feels safe and comfortable.

STEP 5

Begin tapping your hands. Alternating each hand. Like a butterfly. Notice your thoughts, feelings, images, sounds, smells, or body sensations. Pay attention to your breathing and use slow deep breaths from your belly. Just observe whatever comes up without judging, changing, or pushing away.

STEP 6

Observe whatever is coming up, as if you're watching a train pass by, watching a movie, or a storm moving through and passing. Use whatever tapping speed is comfortable for you and stop when you feel it has been enough in your body.

Repeat these steps as many times as you need.

If you would like another method besides interlocking hands, here are alternative options:

- ➢ Cross your arms and alternately tap each side of the arm.
- ➢ Fold your arms and alternately tap each side of your arm around your elbow.
- ➢ Place your arms on your legs and alternately tap each side of your leg.
- ➢ Place your feet on the floor and alternately tap them.

It should be noted that research has only been done on the BH method, not the modifications. However, for those times when you cannot utilize the BH, modifications can still provide a form of relief.

Navigating my experience of traumatic grief and all its components has been a long journey. There are moments when it can take your breath away! Although the message in our society is improving, there continues to be a message that grief and trauma are something to "get over" or "overcome." However, grief and trauma can be never-ending. It can show up at different times in your life, no matter how much you thought you processed and healed. You can learn to ride the waves as they come and go without feeling suffocated or secluding yourself to that island again.

My biggest lesson has been how to heal and move forward while experiencing grief or memories of the trauma. For me, the memories are still very present even though Tuck's accident happened over 20 years ago. The images and flashbacks are frequent, especially as I write this chapter. But the distress is not immobilizing. I remember the hole I was in, but I remain present to the moment. Being around kids certainly exacerbated my fear of seeing someone else get hit by a car. I never thought dropping my kids at school could be so triggering! But if you've ever experienced the hug-and-go lane at a child's school, you might have an idea of what I'm talking about!

Finding a treatment that incorporated all components of a memory; images, thoughts, feelings, and body sensations worked. It helped me find relief and hope for an enjoyable life. Currently, many therapies include body-focused treatment. Utilize this book for ideas and ask questions. I hope this encourages you to talk with others, find connections within yourself and support system/community. May this inspire relief and increase your sense of support during whatever journey you are facing.

Remember you are not alone!

Rebecca Johnson is a Licensed Professional Counselor with a heart for serving children and families. Since her teenage years, Rebecca has been committed to making a difference in the lives of those who need it most. Her passion for helping others led her to earn a master's degree in professional counseling from the prestigious Chicago School of Professional Psychology.

For over 14 years, Rebecca worked in child welfare, dedicating her time and expertise to supporting children and families in need. As an intake worker and later a therapist, she provided assessments, professional collaboration, parenting education, trauma processing, and healing to families working toward permanency. Throughout her career, Rebecca worked with families facing a wide range of issues, many of which involved trauma, grief, attachment, guilt, and accountability.

Rebecca's dedication to supporting families through difficult times has led her to open a practice in Broomfield, Colorado. While her primary focus is being present with her own family, she remains committed to her passion for providing therapeutic support to individuals who have experienced grief, trauma and life transitions. Rebecca also continues her passion to serve individuals involved in child welfare by contracting with a child welfare agency. She is trained in Eye Movement Desensitization and Reprocessing (EMDR), which she utilizes to assist in the treatment and healing of her clients.

Rebecca's personal experiences with grief and loss inform and guide her work with clients. Her empathy and understanding create a safe space for individuals and families to heal and grow. Whether you're facing a difficult life transition or struggling with the aftermath of trauma, Rebecca is here to guide you on how to enjoy the present moment when experiencing an array of overwhelming feelings.

Rebecca enjoys time with family, new experiences, connecting with the community, and challenging herself, family, and friends to do different things like running races and, most recently, triathlons.

Contact Rebecca here: Email rljohnsonlpc@gmail.com

CHAPTER 22

THE POWER TO GO ON

FINDING CONNECTION, MEANING, AND GROWTH IN LOSS

Susan Settler, LCSW

MY STORY

It was my junior year in high school. My guidance counselor, Mr. Mednick, came into our classroom to share information about college applications. After concluding his presentation, Mr. Mednick approached me with somber admiration, "All things considered, you're doing a great job, kid."

He was right; I was doing a great job. I was a straight-A student, had many friends, and actively participated in several after-school clubs. All these successes followed the death of my mother, who passed from pancreatic cancer only three months prior. His comment took me aback because, at that point, I felt fine. Unfortunately, my guidance counselor's appreciation for my success would soon turn to concern. By that summer, my grief set in; I could no longer avoid the pain, and I completely fell apart.

Then came my senior year, the worst year of my life. My mother, the foundation of my world, was gone, and I was no longer safe. Struggling to get out of bed in the morning, I rarely attended school, and my grades plummeted. My friends were planning their futures, attending prom, and experiencing the joys of senior year as I sat back and watched, sinking further into hopelessness and despair. Any attempt at teenage normalcy felt fraudulent and shallow. I felt like I had aged a thousand years in merely a few months.

During this time, my siblings and I became deeply intertwined, becoming exactly what the other needed—sometimes a sibling and sometimes a parent. It was this incredible bond, along with my faith in God, that granted me the courage to crawl out of the hole I was descending into. I finished high school, attended college, and slowly made my way back to myself.

Years later, I'm sitting in a bar with friends when this handsome guy wearing a black leather motorcycle cycle jacket and ripped jeans catches my eye. I can't recall what we discussed, but I remember smiling to myself later that night, thinking, *this guy is going to be in my life for a really long time.*

I was right. He was confident, considerate, and incredibly charismatic. Eventually, he became my husband. Rob made me feel safe and loved like no one else had. He believed in me and saw me for everything that I was. With his support, I achieved a master's in social work while raising two young daughters. We raised them in a beautiful home filled with love and laughter. He was my best friend.

My life as I knew it changed on Superbowl Sunday, 2017. Rob and I began our day on our favorite walking trail. Breathing in the crisp February air, we dreamed about our future and reminisced about our past. Although we loved being parents, we enthusiastically embraced the next phase of life. Walking hand in hand, Rob turned to me and said, "Sweet Thing, you and I are going away, just the two of us." I smiled back at him and replied, "Somewhere tropical, we could use some sunshine." We discussed our plans to retire in Florida and travel throughout Europe. I felt grateful to be planning a life with someone I loved deeply and who was eager to grow old with me.

Later that day, Rob approached me with a look of panic, "I need you to drive me to the emergency room right away." His breathing became so labored he could barely walk up the stairs. The urgency in his voice was incredibly concerning. We rushed to the hospital, and several hours later, the doctor informed us they had found fluid in Rob's lungs. We hoped it was as simple as pneumonia but later discovered the fluid contained cancer cells.

Two weeks later, Rob had exploratory surgery to confirm his diagnosis and determine the extent of his cancer. I sat in the waiting area with Rob's brother, Michael, and my nephew, Ryan, as we waited for news. The surgeon approached us with a solemn expression, leading us to a private room. This couldn't be good news. Michael grabbed my hand as the surgeon shared the results. "I'm sorry to tell you this: your husband has stage four lung cancer. His lungs are covered in tumors. Unfortunately, his options are limited." I sat in shock, staring at the surgeon's compassionate eyes as he shared the bleak prognosis. I made futile attempts to ask useful questions, but I couldn't avoid the reality of this life we built together falling apart.

Later that evening, I sat in my car at the hospital and cried explosively. *How can this be happening? Wasn't losing my mother at a young age enough? Why do my girls have to go through what I went through? How can I shield them from this? How will I tell them? How am I going to live without my best friend and partner in life? Why is God doing this to me again?*

Following the exploratory surgery, Rob was put on a ventilator in the ICU. Unable to speak, he motioned for a pen. The first thing he wrote was, "Where am I?" I knew I had to be strong. I told him the procedure went well and that he was in recovery. He then wrote the words "Sing *Landslide* to me." I'm a singer, and my husband always loved my voice, so I stood in the intensive care unit as the nurses watched me sing *Landslide* to my husband.

After receiving the conclusive results from the surgery, we knew it was necessary to share the news of Rob's cancer with our daughters. We called our youngest daughter into the family room and phoned our oldest, who was at college. I sat on the couch as my youngest daughter clung to me with tears rolling down her face. The very next day, our oldest daughter surprised us by driving five hours to be with her father. Rob was moved to tears as he saw her walk through the door. The four of us were now able to process the news together.

Two weeks after learning of my husband's diagnosis, I received more devastating news. After successfully battling depression and addiction for years, my youngest brother, Brian, had attempted suicide by overdosing on his prescribed medication. Soon after, he regretted his decision and asked to be taken to the hospital. Unfortunately, it was too late. Although Brian could walk into the hospital, he soon became immobilized and ventilator-dependent, losing his ability to move anything other than his thumb.

On the car ride to visit Brian in the hospital, my sister warned me, saying, "Be prepared; this is hard to see." I held her hand and cried. Nothing could've prepared me for what had become of my brother. He was hooked up to machines and had tubes everywhere. My family gathered around Brian, expressing their love for him as he lay helpless in his bed on life support. I cannot say with certainty what my brother was feeling, but in his big blue eyes, I saw what I believed to be fear and regret. It was heartbreaking.

I traveled to visit my brother often while continuing to support Rob with his doctor's appointments and chemotherapy sessions. For three months, I watched as my brother slowly deteriorated and eventually died at the age of 43. My husband was at my side, comforting me during my brother's funeral. I mourned the loss of my brother while anticipating the loss of my husband. It was all too much.

Even with cancer, Rob made the best of every moment he had left. Fortunately, he tolerated the chemotherapy well and remained capable of doing many things he enjoyed. Three months before his passing, we planned a huge birthday celebration for him. Rob was beyond excited, but I was dreading it. I just lost my brother and was mentally preparing to lose my husband. I simply wanted to get through each day. Despite my hesitation, the party was a huge success and a beautiful memory, both for Rob and everyone who loved him. People from every chapter of his life showed up for him and our family. Rob started the day with a golf outing and a pool party with great food, music, and games. We sang "Happy Birthday," and Rob gave a speech I will cherish forever. He stood there, looking at our home filled with so many people who loved and supported him. Then he flashed his radiant smile and said, "How lucky am I?"

Soon after his birthday party, Rob's condition escalated rapidly, and he was back in the hospital. The cancer had now spread past his lungs and into his bones. I had never seen anyone in so much pain. The doctors let me know there was nothing more that could be done, and when we left the hospital this time, we'd be taking him home to die. Knowing this, I wanted to cherish every moment Rob and I had together, even if we were stuck in a sterile hospital room. I shut off the lights, placed fake candles on the windowsill, played his favorite music, and together, we dreamed about a future I knew would never come.

Three weeks later and just seven months after his initial diagnosis, Rob died. It was excruciating to see his once strong, athletic body deteriorate and his outgoing and lighthearted personality become voiceless and distant. I witnessed my teenage daughters suffer as they watched their father slowly disappear like I had with my mother at their age. There were no exchanges of life-altering words of wisdom, just pain and sadness. My husband was slowly detaching from this world, and there was nothing I could do but watch him leave us behind. I held his hand as he took his last breath. And just like that, Rob was gone.

A few days after my husband's funeral, I sat on my couch, struggling with the idea of not being able to communicate with him. I missed him so desperately already. In a moment of intense loneliness, I used a technique I suggested for many of my clients struggling with grief. I wrote a letter to Rob. Almost every line expressed the same sentiment, "I just need to know you are okay." I felt a great sense of relief after getting my feelings down on paper. This was the first of many letters I have written to Rob since his death, and I expect to write many more in the future.

After writing the letter, I found Rob's watch on the kitchen counter and went to put it back in his office. On the floor of his office was a fluorescent blue business card with big white letters. I thought to myself, "Maybe this is a sign?" I picked up the card and read the words, "It's fun here." This gave me tremendous peace. It was a sign that wherever my husband was, he was okay, still being Rob and still having fun.

This is one of many signs my husband sent me in the weeks and years that followed. The most powerful sign I often get from my husband is the song I sang to him during that first hospital stay, "Landslide." The song seems to come on the radio during moments when I need him most. It has evolved into a "hello" from the other side. My husband was a brilliant communicator in life, and I believe he finds ways to break through whatever is between us.

Everyone I've loved and lost has left an imprint on my soul. I've learned from their lives, and the pain of losing them has inspired tremendous growth in me. When confronted with death, I learn to value life and experience a deeper, more meaningful spiritual connection. I view life as a training ground for the soul and the experience of death as part of the lesson plan. Finding meaning in the loss can help with the healing process.

So, how do we make sense of multiple losses that seem incredibly unfair and untimely? How does it influence our life? I believe the connection we have with our loved ones is never lost. I'll always have an attachment to my husband. I equate it to holding a rope with him on the other end. As time passes, I can loosen my grasp, but I will never let go. His love of life and decision to live every moment for what it's worth will always inspire me. My experiences with grief led me to a deeper spiritual faith and an exceptionally close bond with my siblings and ultimately inspired me to pursue a career in helping others. I knew from my experience that my daughters would survive the loss of their father just as I survived the loss of my mother. I couldn't shield them from this pain or any tragedy they might encounter in the future. It's part of their physical and spiritual journey, just as it was mine.

When I began this project, I didn't intend to share details of my brother's death. My family is private, and I planned to honor their wishes. I later realized that hiding the story of Brian's death was not honoring his life. My brother was kind and unselfish and remained sober for many years. He often shared his journey towards sobriety in hopes of inspiring and motivating others. If he thought the story of his death by suicide would help one person, he would want it shared. He is not defined by his death but rather by the impact he had on the people he loved. I'm so lucky to have been in that category.

Acknowledging the lessons of loss doesn't diminish the pain which accompanies grief. It has been several years, and I still have moments where I struggle with the reality of what I have lost. The road to healing is long and challenging. Over time, it has become less overwhelming. Throughout this process, I've allowed myself to embody my emotions and express my pain. At first, the pain was debilitating. In time, the severity has lessened. I'll never stop missing those I have lost, but I chose to honor their lives by living mine.

There is no shortcut through the grieving process. We walk through the pain to get to the other side. Ultimately, healing and growth can come from allowing the loss to inspire and transform us. In this way, we maintain the connection with our loved ones. We give meaning to their journey on this Earth, and on some level, they live on through us.

THE TOOL

One of the most painful aspects of losing someone is the loneliness you feel at the thought of being unable to connect with them again. Writing to Rob gives me peace because it allows me to release my feelings and express thoughts to him that I desperately need to share. I encourage you to write to your loved ones as often as you like and whenever you need to connect. It can be a tool to encourage closure for more complicated relationships or an opportunity to feel more connected, depending on your relationship with your loved one.

STEP 1

Choose a medium such as a notebook, journal, stationary, or laptop.

STEP 2

Find a comfortable place to write, such as a quiet room at home, a place that is special to you and your loved one, or somewhere in nature.

STEP 3

Write the letter. Allow your thoughts to flow freely, and do not filter them. Write everything you wish to express to that person, all the things you've been holding on to. Keep writing till you've gotten everything off your mind. Don't hold anything back, even if it's something negative.

If you struggle with where to begin, here are a few sentence prompts:

- "I want you to know..."
- "I need to know..."
- "What I miss most is..."
- "I have been feeling..."
- "I am angry that..."
- "I regret that..."
- "What I have learned from losing you is..."

What you can do with the letter:

- Read it out loud. This might be done at home, or you might want to visit your loved one's gravesite or another significant place where you feel especially close to them.
- Save it on your electronic device to add to it whenever you are inspired.
- Keep your letters in a journal.
- Destroy or delete the letter once your feelings are released.

Susan Settler, L.C.S.W, is a psychotherapist who owns and operates a private practice, Restorative Springs Counseling Center, LLC. She is licensed to practice in New York and New Jersey. Susan graduated with a bachelor's degree in psychology from the State University of New York at Purchase and a master's degree in social work from the State University of New York at Albany. Susan provides psychotherapy for individuals struggling with anxiety, depression, grief, and trauma and couples experiencing relational problems. Susan has a particular passion for helping clients navigate through the grieving process. She uses her own experience with overcoming the challenges of grief to inform her practice and provide clients with tools to manage the pain of their loss. She utilizes a psychodynamic, strength-based, collaborative, and empathic approach to her work, including curiosity, warmth, and humor. She is originally from Brooklyn, New York. She and her late husband, Robert, raised their family in Ballston Lake, New York. She now resides in Highlands, New Jersey. When Susan is not practicing psychotherapy, she enjoys participating in community theater, singing, and spending time with her two daughters.

Connect with Susan:
https://linktr.ee/ssettler

CHAPTER 23

THE SOUND OF HEALING

USING MUSIC TO PROCESS AND TRANSFORM DELAYED GRIEF

Cheryl Nix, LCSW

MY STORY

You are flat on the hospital bed.

Why isn't the head of the bed raised?

Your skin color is white and grayish.

Where's your pink, healthy, glowing face?

Your eyes are closed.

Come on, open those twinkling, laughing eyes!

There are no tubes in your body anymore.

This is way too quiet; let's get some movement going.

The room smells of antiseptic and is cold enough that I sense a shiver coming on.

Let's turn the thermostat up and hear some of your fun stories.

Everything around me is blurry, a dense fog.

That must be my mother and sister to the right and left of me.

My body feels frozen and rigid, my feet glued to the linoleum floor.

This cannot be real, and I must be dreaming; I'm really not here.

The doctors had called us and said you died.

I just want to scream noooooooooooooo!

At the age of 19, I experienced the sudden and unexpected death of my father, who was only 59 years old. He left behind a wife of 30 years, a son aged 21, myself, and a 17-year-old daughter. The tragic sequence of events began with my father undergoing a planned major surgery. Although the surgery initially seemed successful, he went into cardiac arrest 24 hours later. Despite being revived, he was transferred to intensive care after throwing a massive clot that resulted in a severe stroke, leaving him profoundly paralyzed on his left side.

Over two agonizing weeks, my father's condition deteriorated, and he ultimately passed away. His final days were spent on a ventilator, rendering him unable to verbally communicate. The haunting sounds of cardiac and medical monitors persist in my memory, a constant, alarming backdrop to the ordeal. The entire experience was nothing short of horrific.

I have always thought it was ironic—my father, a man who survived the perils of being shot down over Germany during World War II, ultimately succumbed to complications following a major surgery in America. He parachuted down after his B-17 was shot, breaking five ribs in the process. Upon regaining consciousness, he found himself facing a young boy with a bayonet, marking the beginning of days of interrogation. Subsequently, he endured 21 months in two German prison camps and participated in the infamous winter march from Stalag Luft III to Moosburg, Germany, aptly named the "Long March" or "Death March."

There were many chances for death to come previously in his life. Why now? A successful businessman, married for 30 years with three children, my father was on the brink of semi-retirement, with dreams of pursuing his hobby interest in gold mining.

To better understand my story about my father's death and the ensuing grief, it's essential to look into the background of his life. He was born as the eldest son in a family of six children in The Dalles, Oregon. His father, an immigrant from Denmark, sought to forge a new life in America, with my father's mother later undertaking the challenging journey across the Atlantic.

Growing up in Oregon allowed my father to engage in various outdoor activities, including watching the local Native Americans fish at Celilo Falls. He often took on jobs on local farms, such as picking cherries and baling hay. But an enduring family interest was music, and my father, with his beautiful baritone voice, later made our car rides memorable with family singing during road trip vacations. His passion for music persisted even in challenging circumstances; he sang in the Catholic choir, performing in Handel's Messiah while held in prison camp in Germany during World War II. Music seemed to sustain him.

As a prominent businessman in our small Oregon town, my father played a vital role in local fundraisers. His vocal talent became a centerpiece of these events, contributing to the success of various programs. The echoes of his baritone voice not only filled our family car but also resonated through the community, illustrating how deeply intertwined music and his life were.

The days following my father's death formed a disorienting blur, marked by a tumultuous time of emotions and physical sensations. Stomach upset became an unwelcome companion, while a profound sense of loss, helplessness, shock, numbness, and disbelief enveloped me. Energy deserted me, leaving me unable to concentrate and prompting withdrawal from some social interactions. I moved through many days like a robot, consumed by confusion.

Sleep became an elusive refuge, as nightmares haunted me with the vivid image of my father's wide eyes, filled with fear in his hospital room amid the relentless clamor of alarming monitors. My bed sheets bore witness to my tormented nights—twisted and damp with sweat. Hours passed before my heart slowed and allowed me to return to a semblance of sleep, though it was far from restful. This pattern persisted over months, etching the image of my father's fearful eyes into my consciousness.

In the 1970s, discussions about emotions were not commonplace, and I lacked the clarity to comprehend the range of emotions that gripped me. The magnitude of the loss was overwhelming, and the prospect of delving into my feelings seemed like an insurmountable task. Additionally, family social support was scarce, as my mother sought solace in alcohol to cope with her grief. My siblings had their grief to face.

Amidst this turmoil, I resumed my summer job at a nearby state park, overlooking one of my favorite beaches. Managing the main registration for the evening shift provided a welcome distraction, but without my father's insightful discussions about life, I grappled with a pervasive sense of aimlessness. Throughout the summer, physical manifestations of my grief persisted—stomach discomfort and headaches.

Grief support was minimal, and the prevailing attitude urged me to "move on and get over it." Struggling with emotional pain, I called in sick to work, only to be met with a supervisor's directive to "move on in life after death." Taking this advice to heart, I suppressed my feelings, weathering the storm in silence.

Returning to college in the fall after my father's death, several months passed, and the expectation seemed to be that I should leave that chapter to the past and refrain from discussing it further. As life progressed into adulthood—marriage, completion of nursing school, the joy of having a son, and employment at a local hospital—a facade of normalcy prevailed. However, beneath the surface, the real struggles with my grief were about to unfold.

My initial nursing position on a surgical floor, working the swing shift, introduced me to a group of wonderful women with whom I felt a profound connection. We shared adventures, hiking the local trails leading to high lakes, engaging in regular craft gatherings, and enjoying potluck dinners together. The camaraderie and activities painted a picture of what seemed like a perfect life. Yet, as the exterior of normalcy persisted, the unresolved grief from my father's death was ever-present under the surface.

I have a distinct memory of a particular day on the surgical floor when an elderly woman returned from surgery. Complications arose post-surgery, leading to cognitive changes, and she was not the same as before the procedure. The details are somewhat hazy, but I recall witnessing the woman's gradual decline, culminating in her death. Many family members visited her room to bid their farewells before she died. At that moment, my mind involuntarily flashed back to the familiar scenes during my father's last days, and the impact on me was profound. My heart rate increased, and my stomach became upset. I felt disconnected from myself and everything around me. I felt numb.

Upon returning home that day, I found myself overwhelmed with emotions—intense tears, and a deep sense of sorrow. It struck me as excessive for the situation at hand. *This is confusing, I don't understand, why is this so strong.* I realized that this experience had triggered a wellspring of unresolved grief related to my father's death. The parallel between the two scenarios became clear. Suddenly my body became tight, full of tension, and I trembled slightly. *Here is that fear and anxiety from my past.* This marked the beginning of a hint of understanding of the enduring impact of loss on my emotional well-being.

The echoes of my father's last days became even more intense during my time on the surgical floor when a telemetry unit was introduced. These units involved continuous cardiac monitoring, where electronic signals transmitted from electrodes on a patient were centralized and observed. Throughout my father's entire post-operative hospitalization, similar monitoring was in place, and the presence of these units triggered vivid flashbacks to those agonizing final days of his life.

The relentless beeping and electronic hum became an unintentional soundtrack, resonating with the haunting memories of my father connected to similar monitors. At times, I felt startled by the sounds. Each beep, each electronic pulse, seemed to transport me back to the hospital room where my father lay, hooked to the machinery that measured his deteriorating health. The emotional weight of these flashbacks added an extra layer of complexity to my work on the surgical floor, underscoring the enduring impact of the traumatic experiences surrounding my father's death.

Recognizing the need for emotional support, I reached out to a compassionate social worker who specialized in grief and loss counseling. This professional had extensive experience in the field, and over time, a foundation of trust was established that allowed me to open up about my feelings. What set this therapeutic relationship apart was the deep respect for my personal loss, creating a safe space where I felt heard and understood. Many years had passed since my father's death, yet I had never truly discussed my emotions or the entire experience surrounding his death.

Through our sessions, the social worker helped me understand that I was contending with unresolved or delayed grief, coupled with symptoms of post-traumatic stress disorder (PTSD). The therapeutic journey, though challenging at times, became the starting point for a healthier adaptation, allowing me to integrate the profound loss of my father into my life. Additionally, the use of Eye Movement Desensitization and Reprocessing (EMDR) played a pivotal role in my healing process. EMDR is designed to process upsetting memories, thoughts, and feelings related to trauma, providing relief from PTSD symptoms by facilitating the integration of these experiences. This comprehensive approach marked a significant turning point in my lifelong grief journey.

In parallel to my father's reliance on music for solace, I, too, discovered the therapeutic power of music in my life. I turned on the radio or played a CD, using the melodies and lyrics as a means of emotional expression and healing. Sometimes, as a way to honor my father, I deliberately chose songs he loved or had sung during his lifetime. In those musical notes, I found a source of comfort, a connection to the past, and a pathway to navigate the complex landscape of grief and remembrance.

Personally, I discovered the profound impact of music as a tool for navigating through my grief. It served as a poignant connection to my late father, as certain songs had the power to transport me to specific times and places in my life. These musical triggers stirred deep emotions, often bringing tears. While not everyone expresses grief through tears, for me, the act of shedding tears became a cathartic release.

In the initial stages of confronting my loss, there was a fear that allowing myself to cry would be endless, and I could never stop. To manage this, I adopted the strategy of choosing a song and allowing myself to cry only within the song's duration. This method became a practical tool to temporarily halt the tears, providing a necessary pause in the grieving process. Tears, in this context, became both a response to the moving nature of music and a means of balancing my overwhelming emotions.

Music has an incredible ability to pierce through numbness and connect with our emotions, offering solace and healing. The shift in the tone of my life, from the haunting beeping of the cardiac monitor to the melodies and human connection that music brings, underscores the profound impact that intentional engagement with music can have on one's emotional well-being.

The therapeutic nature of music allows it to become a powerful ally in navigating grief, bringing about a change. So may the melodies and human connections continue to be sources of comfort and growth as you navigate the complexities of loss and healing.

In the words of Hans Christian Andersen, "Where words fail, music speaks." This sentiment captures the profound ability of music to articulate and express emotions when language falls short.

THE TOOL

Using music as a means of processing and transforming grief can be a powerful and therapeutic approach. Grieving is a unique and personal journey, and finding effective tools to navigate this process is crucial. Music, with its ability to evoke emotions and memories, can be a powerful aid.

1. List three songs that provide connection or memories of your loved one.

   ____

   ____

   ____

   ____

   ____

2. Create a personalized playlist. A list can have specific themes, such as songs that remind you of your loved one, songs that bring comfort, or those that uplift your spirits. Or you can compile a memorial playlist of songs that hold special meaning or were favorites of the person you are grieving.

3. Choose a song that holds significance for you about your grief. Select a way to play the song you have chosen: CD player, vinyl record, computer, Pandora, Spotify, or any other platform of your choice. Find a quiet and comfortable place where you won't be disturbed. Close your eyes if you feel comfortable doing so. Take a deep breath and exhale slowly, letting go of tension. Listen without judgment.

Pay attention to any feelings, memories, or thoughts that arise. Stop the music at any time if needed. After the song concludes, take a few moments to reflect on the experience. Journal any emotions, memories, or insights that surfaced during the listening session.

4. Use music for reflection and mindfulness. Mindfulness is a mental state achieved by focusing one's awareness on the present moment while calmly acknowledging and accepting one's feelings, thoughts, and bodily sensations. Set aside dedicated time to listen to music mindfully. Pay attention to the lyrics, melodies, and emotions evoked.

5. Express yourself through music. Write or compose a song expressing your emotions. This can serve as a therapeutic outlet for your grief. Sing along, as this can be a cathartic experience. Joining in with songs that hold emotional weight for you can provide a sense of release.

6. Use music as a companion. Let music be a constant companion in your daily activities. Having it play in the background can provide comfort and solace. Explore the calming effect of instrumental music. It can serve as a soothing backdrop for moments of reflection.

7. Attend concerts or musical events. The communal experience of music can create a sense of connection and shared emotion. Joining a choir or participating in singalongs can be a way to engage with others through music.

Conclusion: Remember, there is no right or wrong way to use music for grief. Find what resonates with you and allow the sound of healing to guide you through the transformative process.

Cheryl Nix, BS ed, ADN, LCSW, is presently a licensed clinical social worker operating a private practice in Oregon. Her academic journey began with a focus on education, but then she pursued an associate degree in nursing. After over 30 years in the nursing field, Cheryl decided to shift her focus to trauma therapy. In her mid-50s, she returned to college and earned a master's degree in social work from Portland State University. Following her degree completion, she dedicated a decade to working at two hospices, specializing in case management, as well as providing bereavement and grief counseling for individuals and groups.

Cheryl's current focus is on individual therapy, with a particular emphasis on Eye Movement Desensitization Reprocessing (EMDR). Despite conventional retirement norms, Cheryl is driven by a strong desire and passion for her work, anticipating to continue beyond the typical retirement age of 65. She attests that her profession not only keeps her feeling younger but also energized.

Residing in rural Oregon with her husband and their active yellow lab, Lily, Cheryl cherishes her connection with the beach and ocean, rooted in her upbringing. However, her many years in central Oregon have instilled in her a profound love for the mountains and breathtaking sunsets. Beyond her professional commitments, Cheryl enjoys spending time with her husband, her adult children, and numerous friends, taking walks in diverse outdoor settings, exploring art, reading, watching "Wheel of Fortune," and immersing herself in the world of music.

Connect with Cheryl
Email: cherylnlcsw@gmail.com
Facebook: https://www.facebook.com/cheryl.nix.716/

CHAPTER 24

DEATH OUT OF ORDER

RECOGNIZING AND EMBRACING THE BOTH/AND

Misti Klarenbeek-McKenna, LCSW, LMFT

MY STORY

I spend my workdays helping couples work to, as many of them describe, "find us again." I love this work. It often includes hearing stories of trauma, loss, and pain, but one of my favorite parts of the work is hearing how people met and fell in love. For most, this is a story of fun and flirtation that grows over time into something deep and beautiful. These stories present a contrast to my own love story, in which the fun and flirtation were cut short by trauma, loss, and pain after the Oklahoma City bombing, which is why I enjoy that part so much.

Friday, April 7, 1995, was a beautiful spring day in Albuquerque. The sky was blue, everything was in bloom, and everyone wanted to be outside. I was a sophomore at the University of New Mexico, enjoying my best semester so far. Classes ended early that day, and I did not have to go to work until later that evening, so I laid out on the field outside my on-campus apartment to study, where vigorous volleyball games were happening nearby.

In the evenings, I worked at a steakhouse, and Friday nights were my night to close, which meant I collected the servers' money and reconciled the books in a small office in the back we called "the cage." I shared that space on Fridays with the cute bartender, Ken, who got to leave early. On that Friday, though, he waited around for me to finish work, and we had our first date later that night.

The next day, I got a phone call from my best friend, Cartney. It was a rushed call because one of us was running out somewhere, but she called to let me know that she was home from Haiti, where she had been deployed with the Air Force for several months for Operation Uphold Democracy. I was thrilled she was home and safe. She was engaged to a fellow Airman, Shane, and was planning a wedding back home later in the year.

Cartney and Shane decided to get legally married on April 15 in order to get paperwork submitted to the Air Force in hopes they would not be deployed separately again.

Wednesday, April 19, 1995, was one of those days I appreciated living in New Mexico, where the spring comes earlier than my hometown in the Black Hills of South Dakota. I got home from my last class in time for the soap opera I watched and turned on the TV. A special report had broken into regular broadcasting. I went to the kitchen to make myself a sandwich, figuring that the show would be back on by the time I returned. It was not. I realized the images of the bombed building they were showing were in Oklahoma City. I immediately thought of Cartney; she was stationed at Tinker Air Base nearby. I listened long enough to hear that the building was in downtown Oklahoma City and that the bombing had occurred at 9:00 a.m., so I turned the TV off.

She's fine; she works at nine a.m., and she works on base. I'll call her tomorrow to see what's going on there, I thought, since I had to work that night. Besides, we had just talked the night before. These were the days I had to be aware of what time I made long-distance calls to avoid expensive rates.

The next day, I was fresh out of the shower after my ballet class around 3:30 pm, and I was in my room with my hair wrapped in a towel when the phone rang: it was my mom. It was very unusual to get a long-distance call from her so early, so I immediately tensed, fearing something was wrong. She engaged me in some small talk, so I relaxed. *She must just miss me.*

"I have to tell you something, okay?" She asked if I had seen the news about the bombing. My heart sank. My mom was a teacher at the local high school. She informed me that Cartney's mom had taken her younger brother out of school, and they were headed to Oklahoma City. Cartney was unaccounted for, and she was believed to be in the building. *Why would she be downtown at nine a.m.?*

I kept trying to call her number, not caring about long-distance rates, but each time, I got a recording that all circuits were busy. Finally, Shane called later that night. He explained that the Murrah building was indeed her destination that morning; she had gone to the Social Security office to have her name changed.

I am not sure how anyone can process that kind of news, but at twenty years old, I was not prepared. Ken was working that night but came over late when he got off work and brought me chocolate; I knew Cartney would have approved. Days stretched out as I awaited news. *Surely, I'll hear something today,* I thought day after day. I was a thousand miles from home or anyone who knew Cartney. The phone in my room was like Grand Central Station, with people calling to see if I had news or to offer support. I kept going to work and school. Ken and I spent time together, and I was not sure what I would have done without him. I wished I could tell Cartney about him and everything else I was feeling. I prayed and believed there would be a miracle.

If I just have enough faith, she'll be okay.

I sat by the phone, awaiting a call I half eagerly anticipated, and half dreaded. It got to the point where I braced myself every time the phone rang, preparing to hear Shane's voice.

I did not get the news that her body had been found until May 1. I answered the phone to hear a friend's voice. I was expecting her call, but she was crying, so I knew immediately. It had been twelve days, and despite having a moment of not wishing anyone to be buried alive in the rubble, I could not allow myself to entertain the thought that she would die. I was not prepared for this kind of out-of-order loss. And then there was the way she died. I had never heard of domestic terrorism and never imagined someone would hate their own government enough to kill fellow Americans. When I thought of terrorists, I thought of hijacked airplanes and embassies across the world being bombed. It turned my view of the world upside down and robbed me of my innocent belief that the world was a good place and people were good. Despite trying to prepare myself for any scenario, when that phone call came, I came apart at the seams.

I heard from others and told myself all the usual platitudes at her funeral and after, with a twist for this situation: *She helped the kids from the daycare in the building find their way to heaven; God needed another angel in heaven; she's in a better place.*

Her funeral was on Monday during the week of finals. I missed my first final and had to create a test based on the material. Tuesday, I flew back and tried to take finals like everyone else. Like nothing happened. Until Friday, when I slept through my last final, fortunately I was able to drop that grade and maintain an A in the class. Sleeping through school became a pattern. I was so tired, and before I knew it, I slept all the time. I found myself falling apart with Ken, and although he handled it well, how many new relationships must carry that kind of emotional weight? I felt needy, and I was taking so much more from him than I had to give. *Am I just overemotional or blowing this whole thing out of proportion? I am such a wreck right now. I am constantly on the verge of tears. Mood swings from hell. I'm not myself.*

It is astounding now to think that no one pulled me aside to check on me. I was majoring in sociology and minoring in psychology, and none of my professors told me this was a huge trauma or encouraged me to seek support. I just thought I was supposed to go back to my regular life, which is what I did. A year and a half later, when I finally sought counseling, I felt like a mess. I was sleeping all the time, I barely weighed a hundred pounds, and my relationship with Ken was more than tumultuous. I was not the same person I was before. I was no longer fun or carefree. I felt like I was 50 rather than 20 years old. I no longer fit in or felt like I could relate to my peers.

My paternal grandfather died a few months after the bombing, and I remember my dad telling me he could finally relate to my experience around Cartney's death. I was astonished to realize that at twenty years old, I had an experience he had not yet had in life. Despite the psychology courses I took, I had no ability to see what was happening to me or understand how grief impacted me. Cartney's mom calls us pioneers because back then, people did not talk about grief or trauma like we do now. We were on our own. Grief is lonely because no one has the exact same relationship, even when they have a person in common who was lost. I was a thousand miles from anyone who knew her and from the community in Oklahoma that experienced this together. I had family and friends who tried to support me, but how could they know how?

In a real testament to the love we have for one another, Ken and I were married in 2000. We missed the fun, light, flirtatious time in our relationship. The bombing happened a week and a half after we started dating, and he quickly became my biggest support. We fell in love quickly because of the intensity of that time, but there was also a heaviness to it all and he was with me every step. It was hard for him to understand what was going on with me (I sure didn't!) and painful for him to see me struggle. I'm forever grateful for the way he was able to be there for me, and I also lament the loss of how I would have liked the beginning to be for us.

Experiencing traumatic out-of-order death so young has defined me in so many ways. Grief is a part of my life, and it's hard to remember my life before that was true.

Every year, April is a month I can feel approaching. The anniversary of the bombing is always a heavy day. I've come to see grief as a both/and experience. April reflects this: It's both a beautiful time as spring emerges, and it has a weight to it from the reminder that another year has passed without my closest friend.

The anniversary in 2019 offered a lightness I didn't usually experience on that day, thanks to a process group with some fellow therapists. They gave me the gift of hearing my story and feeling seen, recognizing that Cartney and I had a deep connection, that of soul mates.

Several days later, Ken called during a fundraising dinner I was attending. *This is strange,* I thought. His words to me, "Louis died today." Louis was our oldest nephew, seventeen years old with good grades, who played football and loved to ski. He was so responsible and funny in a quiet way.

My experience with grief has led me to try to reach out and be with people I know who have experienced a death. I often felt so harmed by the well-meaning things people said and believed, so I am aware and intentional about just trying to be with people and offer space for them to feel whatever is coming in that moment. There was a kind of muscle memory Ken and I had that allowed us to galvanize to support his sister, the rest of the family, and each other. Despite my own grief experience and my career as a therapist, I often felt like I had nothing to offer or to say, and I wished I could offer more.

Ken and I were a rock-solid team during that time. We had been through all the darkness and heaviness together in a very imperfect way at the start of our relationship, but we were much better prepared this time around. It made the weight easier to carry, being in it together. This time, it was more than just the two of us experiencing this grief, and the impact on the whole family was a seismic shift.

On Ken's birthday in September 2020, we got the awful news that my sister's youngest son, five-year-old Brendan, died. "Brendan fell in the water, and we can't find him," she sobbed on the phone. Brendan was very precocious and smart. He could crack anyone up, often with something very grown-up he would say. There were parallels with the bombing; Brendan's body was not found for three days, and the tragedy caught the attention of the media.

Once again, I was surrounded by my broken-hearted family, on the other side this time. Ken and I were now grieving two children in our family, seeing grief through the eyes of those we love and continuing to support each other and those we love.

After these two losses so close together, yet so long after the bombing, I found myself in tears frequently and unable to stop. Tears would be triggered by something that reminded me of Brendan, Louis, or Cartney, and suddenly I was crying about all three of them at once. Sometimes, I couldn't distinguish what brought the tears on, and I was surprised how intensely I felt the grief for Cartney because I felt like I had already grieved and integrated that experience. I became familiar with the term "cumulative grief" through Dr. Joanne Cacciatore. It gave me comfort knowing there was an explanation for the experience and that it could be true that I integrated that long-ago loss *and* was feeling a brand-new intensity after these two other traumatic grief experiences.

In my grieving process after Cartney's death, I had to learn to hold both/and. I tried to think positively and find comfort in believing she was in heaven, and we would see each other again one day. But that was harmful, and I ended up suffering because I didn't honor my sorrow, anger, and guilt. I had to learn how to hold both and honor all the feelings that were there. I both lost my best friend and gained a new one in Ken. Ken and I struggled mightily at the beginning and built a solid foundation for an incredible relationship. April is both a beautiful month and one of incredible sorrow, now the anniversary of both Cartney and Louis's deaths. Ken's birthday is a day I celebrate that he was born and grieve that it's the day Brendan died.

I have always kept journals. I have pages upon pages from after Cartney's death. I journaled after both Louis and Brendan died. It's helped me name and express the emotions I didn't feel I could express elsewhere. I didn't know in the early days after Cartney's death how to process that trauma or how to get support. Those around me didn't know how to support me. I didn't know what I needed. No one around me knew then the things we now know about trauma and loss. Writing my narrative in a journal has helped immensely.

THE TOOL

Write a journal entry or narrative that captures your person in story. Write about what is special to you, what you most miss about them, and what you most appreciate about them. Some prompts for your writing include:

Tell me about a loss in your life (who died, but also secondary losses like loss of control, who you were before, dreams and hopes, future experiences with your person, etc).

How do you mourn for the life you and your loved one didn't get to live and hold joy for the life you shared?

What do you miss about the old you (before) and appreciate about the person you are now?

What do you miss about having your person here with you, and how do you maintain a connection to them and carry them forward?

When you read your narrative, what emotions come up? Notice what happens in your body. Where do you feel the sadness? Where do you feel guilt? Where do you feel shame?

Write down each emotion as it comes up and what it feels like in your body (pit in the stomach, heart hurting, tightness in the chest, etc.).

Give yourself permission for all the emotions that come up. Give voice to the parts that may be contradictory, like one part that feels guilty, while another part has compassion for yourself or one part that longs for things to be the way they were and another that feels selfish for feeling that, etc.

Write what you notice about yourself when you think about your person. Write about you without this person. Allow yourself to experience all the emotions that come up. This is a way to include both your memory and love for them and compassion for yourself.

Misti Klarenbeek-McKenna is a Licensed Clinical Social Worker and Licensed Marriage and Family Therapist. She is an ICEEFT Certified Emotionally Focused Therapist and Supervisor as well as an AAMFT Approved Supervisor. She has a private practice in Denver, Colorado, where she specializes in working with couples and EFT supervision. She is on the faculty at Denver Family Institute, where she loves having the opportunity to share her passion for EFT and relational work with eager students.

Misti has been living in Colorado for 26 years with her husband. They have two sons and a Black Lab mix who is obsessed with playing fetch. She attends multiple ballet classes every week to keep her balance and loves all Colorado has to offer.

Connect with Misti at www.thrivingconnectionsco.com

CHAPTER 25

Moving Through Grief

RECONNECTING TO SELF THROUGH CONSCIOUS MOVEMENT

Jean Trewhella

MY STORY

Kicking off my shoes and flopping onto the bottom bunk of the retreat center dorm room, I see the time on my phone: *6:45, less than an hour before the evening session starts. Should I close my eyes for a minute or change out of these sweaty clothes? What about a hot tub? Yeah, I want the full retreat experience.*

Just then, I feel the buzz and hear the old-fashioned telephone ringtone. I set it special two years ago when going through my divorce.

"Hello, Jean, are you sitting down?" Tim, my ex-husband's voice is quivering, "It's Tai, she, I mean, they really did it. Jean, I'm sorry," his pause transitions into sobs, "Tai's gone."

"No, no, no, no, no!" my screams resonate in the dorm room and out into the hall. The joyful chatter of my roommates getting ready for our next session goes quiet, still, dead.

What happened next is a blur.

Tai was our younger child, raised female until age 18 when they came out as non-binary. We still get the pronouns wrong sometimes.

This was Tai's fifth or sixth suicide attempt; we never knew which episodes the doctors were counting.

Tai was twelve years old the first time the emergency room doctor told me they couldn't come home; they needed help. Help we couldn't give them.

Now, nine years later, I sit knowing it's over. This nightmare of constant worry at what the next phone call will bring. Of trying to understand, trying to help. Searching for reasons. It's over. I'm numb. It isn't supposed to end this way.

My roommates squeeze into my bottom bunk, hugging me, holding me, and rocking me as the tears flow down my face.

It can't be. Maybe it's not. How do they know for sure that it's Tai?

Tim continues as if he can read my thoughts, "Terrance found them first thing this morning. He didn't have a way to reach us."

Tai hung themself from the railing of Terrance's fire escape in Brooklyn.

"I'm so sorry, Jean. We have to identify the body tomorrow. I'm driving up to Amherst now to give the news to Catherine in person."

This is real. I feel numb and cold. I tell him I'll meet him at our daughter's school. "See you at Amherst Coffee in a few hours; wait for me, let's tell her together."

I drop the phone and look up to see Mother Jan sitting right next to me. I can't believe it, an Episcopal priest, right here, right now. My church had always been fundamental in keeping me sane through Tai's struggles. Now this.

Looking into her eyes for answers. "Did I do something wrong? I couldn't keep them safe. I tried. I really tried."

She responds clearly, and calmly, "God doesn't blame you; it isn't your fault. God is here for you and for Tai." I feel my body go limp in her arms.

Joni, one of the JourneyDance™ trainers is on the other side of me, talking. I hear my wife Susan's voice on the phone. "I'm on my way. It'll take me an hour." Susan goes into protective mode. "Hold Jean tight. Put pressure on her body. It'll help her feel safe. Stay with her."

As they hold me, my mind scrolls back over the past 15 hours. That day started before sunrise, around 4:00 a.m. I woke up startled by a dream; my heart was racing. Little did I know then that this was probably the time of Tai's last breath.

I tiptoed out of the dorm room and found hot tea in the empty, cold cafeteria. I sat for a few hours drinking ginger lemon tea with honey, writing in my journal about my fears, my hopes, and my dreams. Trying to capture all the insights I had during the weeklong training.

I remember looking out the window and starting to see trees taking shape out of the darkness. I headed up to the Sunrise Room to soak in the experience. Another retreat guest was sitting cross-legged in quiet meditation, grounding the energy of the room.

Watching the sunrise, there was a thin silver line of clouds over Lake Mahkeenac. The serene beauty of nature's transition from cold darkness to warm, bright sky was amazing. I felt at peace as I rocked. I pulled out my phone and captured a few photos to remind me of this deep feeling of gratitude, awe, and love for Mother Nature.

After breakfast, I entered the daily personal practice session. Surveying the options—art, journaling, yoga, meditation—I opted for the divination station. Laying out a full reading of *Sacred Rebels Oracle Cards: Guidance for Living A Unique & Authentic Life,* by Alana Fairchild. I noticed one card in particular, my challenge card, "Release the Dark Wound: Let Love Live."

A card of change, encouraging me to let suffering end and allow the transformation of energy into love. It resonated with me and aligned with the direction of growth and healing I walked through during my training. In retrospect, the card was signaling the challenge I'd face, accepting that Tai's suffering had ended, and their energy was freed to pure loving spirit.

I signed up to lead embodiment in our first dance of the day. I put the microphone on as I queued the playlist with the song "Here In The Now" from *Talisman* by Murray Kyle.

Slowly, I began grounding the group with the beat of the drum and the chant:

"Here in the now I am hearing the now, as I listen, and I listen.

To the sound that grows on up from the ground, can you hear now in the here and now?

Can you hear that the song of the Earth, she be singing in a cycle, in a circle

In a circle round with a sound that carries the ancient memory, constantly, gracefully.

Calling us to heal now stewards are we, from the inner world to the world we see.

Raising up our voice for unity."

I invited the group to connect their feet to the ground to drop slowly down, sinking into the floor, stretching, and rolling. Feeling the connection of each part of the body to the floor. Feeling the weight and releasing, releasing into the Earth. Allowing Mother Earth to support us.

It was deep. I was in it fully, in my body, reconnecting to the energy of motherhood. The words I led the dance with seemed to come from spirit, from God, through me. I cried tears of release as I allowed my fears to melt into the floor.

I turned over the dance to the other facilitators in training to take us through immersion, funky connection, evocative emotion, celebration, and heart, closing the flow with prayer and rest.

I remember that day continued to be spirit-filled and in retrospect ominous. After lunch, I sat drinking coffee, telling the facilitators, Toni, Joni, and Joy about my child Tai—about my struggles as a mom to understand Tai's recent identification as non-binary, and Tai's request to be referred to with the pronouns *they/them.*

I taught them my trick of reminding myself that I don't know. When we don't know someone's gender, we naturally use the pronouns *they/them.*

For example:

Child: "Mom, can my friend come over after school?"

Mother: "Sure, what kind of snack would *they* like?"

So, when someone in front of me is presenting as male or female, I just remind myself, "I don't know," then it's easy to use.

I was surrounded by love. I had just spent the whole week with my tribe, sharing our vulnerability, and reclaiming our strength and our joy together.

We opened new pathways for healing and connected with each other. We did this without words, communicating through our shared movement, reconnecting to ourselves, and connecting to our inner spiritual guides.

I realize now that Tai had been with me all that day, I could feel them. I honestly think Tai chose that day subconsciously, knowing I was in the best place I could ever be to handle their bodily exit from the Earth.

After Tai's death, I took a three month leave of absence from work, and I danced regularly. I did a JourneyDance™ every Tuesday at noon and an Ecstatic Dance every Thursday night.

When I danced, I saw Tai, I felt Tai. I laid Tai in the ground, and I held Tai like a baby. I felt them with me, guiding me to process the grief and the pain.

This was so helpful for me that when I returned to work, my psychiatrist wrote me a prescription for Tuesday noon dance as my grief therapy. I took that script. I brought it to HR, and I got a medical accommodation to take every Tuesday at noon off to go and dance.

To tell you the truth, I didn't need the script. My boss would have given me the time. But I did it for me.

I needed to remember that this was real medicine for me—that this was something I needed to continue the work of grieving.

I knew myself; I'd get busy and not think I had time. And sure enough, I did. I did get busy; life started up again, and work priorities crept in. *It's just this one time; It's a really important meeting; So-and-so is only here for one day.* Or worse yet, *I don't feel like dancing today.*

You know how it is.

That's why the medical accommodation was helpful, to keep my priorities in check. To remind me that healing from grief is a process that continues over time.

That was six years ago. I still do JourneyDance™ almost every Tuesday at noon followed by Ecstatic Dance on Thursdays. But now I have my own space in Insights Studio that is a haven for healing and learning through movement, art, and music. I lead grief workshops, 12-step recovery dances and so much more. I even got the chance to bring a Movement Insights JourneyDance™ to the 2022 "AFSP Long-Term Suicide Loss Survivors Conference".

Helping others reconnect to their inner wisdom and gain insight through the transformative power of movement has become a purpose from my loss.

As human beings, we hold experiences in our bodies. We hold trauma, fear, hurt, and grief as well as joy, gratitude, pleasure, and safety. The issue is when these experiences get lodged and stuck in our bodies and minds. They can build up leaving us feeling out of natural balance.

We compensate for the imbalance, but this requires extra energy and we become tired, stressed, and overwhelmed.

The amazing thing is if we allow our bodies to lead, to respond to natural stimuli like music, and let our minds take a little rest from being in charge, we begin to unlock our stuck emotions, expressing them through movement. We create new pathways for healing and growth.

Our bodies are very wise, and they will show us how to release what needs to be released, how to make space for new experiences, and how to allow for a new mission and purpose to emerge.

I offer you the following tool as a step toward reconnecting to your embodied self.

THE TOOL

The tool that has helped me in my grief process and in many aspects of my personal growth is conscious dance. I prefer the term conscious movement avoiding the intimidation factor of the word "dance". All movement in essence is dance.

Fundamentally, conscious movement is the practice of exploring the connection between mind, body, and spirit through expressive movement. This exploration opens new pathways for energy to flow; allowing for profound insights that can propel personal development.

A heightened awareness of the body's sensations, reactions, and impulses, resulting in being more present in the moment, slowing down, and listening to the body's cues and reactions.

To get started just for a moment imagine yourself as a baby. Before you learned what dancing was. Your body just moved. Your legs kicked, your fingers and arms wiggled and reached. Your belly and bottom squiggled and rolled. Exploring the space around you. Feeling where your body begins and ends.

As a young child you may remember moving freely, swinging your arms, rolling around, skipping, jumping, twirling just for fun. This is intuitive movement, and it's a natural part of us all.

Even now you may experience an urge to tap your foot or bop your head when you hear a rhythm or beat. This connection to music can help draw your body out of stillness back into play.

Conscious movement invites you to tune into your innate urge to move and allow your dance to emerge without judgment. To play with each movement, each sound, and each breath.

Ready to give it a try?

For a free guided experience go to https://www.Movement-Insights.com or choose a five to ten-minute piece of music that resonates with what you are feeling. Something with a flowing melody, soft rhythm, and without distracting lyrics.

You can be seated, or you can be standing.

Close your eyes if you are comfortable with that.

Take a breath and feel your feet on the ground.
Imagine energy flowing through your feet deep into the ground.

With a few more breaths begin to allow movement.
Start with slow movements almost too small to be seen.

Notice any tightness or holding in your body.
Allow your breath to open these areas.
Imagine your breath flowing freely within you.

Allow a little sway to start to emerge.
Notice your body in space.

Put a hand on your heart and the other on your belly.
And breathe in and breathe out.
Just sway.

Let your head rock from side to side.
Release any tension or holding.

Feel your feet. Feel them grounded to the earth.
Breathe.

With each exhale feel your energy flowing down into the earth.
Allow any stress to ripple through your sway and melt down into the earth.

Maybe bend your knees if it feels right.
Breathe out as you bend down and breathe in as you rise.

Let the breath come up and roll into your shoulders.
Notice how the slow movements feel in your body.

Make a sign of openness. Reach one arm out and then the other.
Imagine you're opening a curtain in front of you.
Open, open, open.

There are no wrong movements.
Your movements are perfectly yours, perfect for this moment.

Open deeper into your body.
Feel your heart open.
Welcome breath and spirit to enter you.

Make a motion of calling in.
Calling in the energy of the universe.
Calling in from the heavens.

Calling in from the ground beneath your feet.
Calling in from of the souls who love you.

Calling in.

Calling in.

Calling in.

And hold that energy within you.

Let it swirl with your body with your hips, maybe a circle or a figure eight emerges. Allow movement to happen without judgment.

Play with starting your movement from different parts of your body.
Maybe your elbows, your shoulders, your chest, your back.
Let the movements grow bigger. Start traveling through the space.

Play.

Play.

Play.

Come back to your center.
Touch your hand to your heart, your other hand to your belly.
Connect to yourself.

Imagine letting go and allowing yourself to float in the air.
You're supported.
Moving through the air.
You're flying like a free bird. Effortlessly.

Is there something holding you back?
Somewhere in your body where you feel tight?

Move into that space.
Pushing back, pushing left, pushing right.
Pull yourself forward and give a wiggle into the tightness.
Let go of the holding.
Release the tension.

Return to center.
Connected. Once again. To you.

Feel the movement of your body.
Always feeling your breathing.
Notice your movement even in stillness.

Connecting. Internally. Externally.

Calling energy up from the earth, through your body, and up to the sky.

Feeling the connectedness through your feet to Mother Earth. Mother Earth who cares for you. Who supports you.

Trusting.

Connecting,

Knowing.

That you are whole.

You are loved.

You are love.

Namaste.

Jean Trewhella

My dance practice evolves from my own deeply personal experiences, diverse training, and various stylistic traditions. While studying Physics at Antioch College, I was introduced to dance and found that dancing each semester was a great way to balance my heavy coursework with creative, intuitive embodiment. I gained a foundation of body awareness through the practice of Alexander technique®, modern dance, and improvisational performance arts.

I am trained in leadership and diversity, including Stephen Covey's *The 7 Habits of Highly Effective People®*, Judith Humphrey's "Taking the Stage®", and Pat Heim's "Gender Awareness". I have practiced implementing these tools and driving change as leader of the IBM Research Diversity Council, President of the IEEE Electronic Packaging Society, and as a speaker on diversity and inclusion in engineering.

My personal growth has been shaped by the philosophical writings of Eckhart Tolle, *The Power of Now,* and Robert L. Leahy, *The Worry Cure,* through the dance practices of Mary Starks Whitehouse's Authentic Movement® and Gabrielle Roth's 5-Rythms®, through the spiritual teachings of the Episcopal Church, *The Rule of St. Benedict,* and through the empowerment experience of Mama Gena's School of Womanly Arts "Mastery Program".

After a lifetime of struggle with their mental health, my younger child died by suicide at the age of 21, which propelled my work in processing grief through dance. I became a certified JourneyDance™ Facilitator and founded Movement Insights, dedicated to using the power of movement to energize and inspire others. Today, I lead dances in person in Malta, New York, on Zoom, and at special events such as the American Foundation for Suicide Prevention's "Long Term Loss Survivors Conference", the Princeton Theological Societies "Women in Ministry Conference", and at Wellspring domestic violence support center.

Connect with Jean Trewhella:
Website: https://www.movement-insights.com/
Email: MovementInsights@gmail.com
Instagram: https://www.instagram.com/JeanTrewhella
Facebook: https://www.facebook.com/MovementInsights/

Closing Chapter

As we approach the final chapter of this collaborative book on grief and loss, I pause to reflect on the profound journey we have shared. Throughout this book, our diverse group of 25 authors has fearlessly opened up, sharing their grief experiences, vulnerabilities, and invaluable tools for acceptance, resilience, and connection amidst the complexities of grief.

A resounding theme that permeates these pages is the understanding that grief is an intensely personal experience, taking on various forms for each individual. By bearing our souls and recounting our personal narratives, my aim was to create a sanctuary where you, as a reader, could find solace, connection, understanding, and validation in your own unique experience with grief.

It's crucial to emphasize that grief defies a linear path and cannot be confined to a predetermined timeline for "moving on" from a loss. Instead, grief becomes a lifelong journey, transforming and evolving in diverse ways as you integrate it into your life and carry it with you through time. The intention behind sharing the tools and strategies in this book is to provide ongoing support as you navigate the ever-changing challenges of your grief experience.

I extend my deepest gratitude to you for joining me on this transformative expedition. I acknowledge that delving into the depths of grief through literature can be difficult and emotionally challenging.

You can always return to the stories and tools shared within these pages to foster a sense of continued support and empowerment. It provides you with an ever-present sense of connection and a nurturing community in the midst of your grief. While grief can feel isolating, it's essential to remember that others have traversed similar terrains and understand the intricate nuances of the grieving process.

In that vein, this book is unique in that every single one of these authors is available to connect with you on a 1:1 basis. I invite you to connect with those whose stories impacted you the most deeply, spoke to your heart the most profoundly, or felt like a mirror of yourself.

While grief can be arduous and painful, it also holds the potential for profound transformation and meaning. Within the realm of grief, we discover wisdom, savor life's precious moments, tap into our inner strength and resilience in the face of adversity. My aspiration in sharing our experiences is to ignite a spark within you, inspiring you to uncover your own purpose and meaning amidst grief while finding solace, hope, and healing along your path of loss.

May this book continue to be a wellspring of support and a tether to humanity as you navigate the intricate complexities of grief. Being safely anchored in this community allows more freedom and confidence to trust the natural flow of what life brings us, forge deeper connections with those who have died (and those who offer us solace), and come into deeper acceptance of ourselves.

As we near the end of this book, it is crucial to acknowledge that the journey of grief is perpetual and constantly evolving. While the tools and strategies shared within these pages are immensely valuable, it's important to recognize they do not provide a one-size-fits-all solution. I encourage you to explore and seek additional support and resources that resonate with your unique needs, guiding you on your personal grief expedition.

Finally, I express my heartfelt gratitude to each author who contributed their authentic stories and experiences to this book. I recognize the immense courage it takes to reveal one's vulnerabilities and struggles. I'm profoundly grateful for their willingness to do so. Through their collective contribution, we've created a resource that illuminates the path for others embarking on their grief journey.

FINAL TAKEAWAYS

- Grief is not an experience to "get over" but rather an integral part of our life story. As you progress through your personal grief journey, you can learn to integrate your losses in ways that feel authentic and meaningful to you, allowing your story to unfold with grace.

- The tools and strategies conveyed within this book have equipped you with the necessary guidance to navigate the challenges of grief in a healthy and constructive manner. Allow the ones that deeply resonate with your individual circumstances to empower you to forge ahead on your unique grief experience. Know that you can always come back to these pages to tweak your personalized road map as you evolve and grow.
- Remember that there is no singular "correct" way to grieve. Your voyage through grief is inherently distinct and profoundly personal. Allow this book to be an anchor of validation, support, and connection as you navigate the challenges of grief. May it remind you that you are not alone in your struggles and that there is always an opportunity for growth and resilience amidst grief and loss.

I'm deeply honored by your willingness to open your heart to explore the contents of these pages and embrace the insights they hold. I'm grateful and humbled to be your guide as you navigate this complex journey. I ask that you pause to acknowledge yourself for embarking on this journey, absorbing and embracing the emotions and ideas presented in this book, and carving out time for your own well-being. And don't forget…

"Just like the lotus, we too have the ability to rise from the mud, bloom out of the darkness, and radiate into the world."

~ Unknown

With Gratitude

With heartfelt gratitude, I extend my thanks to all the grieving individuals reading this book and placing their trust in the wisdom shared within these pages. Your willingness to embark on this journey is courageous, and I want you to know that you're not alone in your grief. May this book serve as a guiding light, offering insights, compassion, and hope for your future. Embrace the stories, absorb the wisdom, and know that even in the darkest moments, a collective of understanding hearts is standing beside you.

I extend my sincerest gratitude to each and every author of The Grief Experience for displaying immense bravery and courage by sharing your vulnerable stories with us. Your willingness to open up has touched my heart, and I'm profoundly grateful you trusted me to lead this project. The connections forged through this book are invaluable, and I'm forever thankful for the profound impact it has had on all of us.

To all the grieving individuals I've had the privilege of working with throughout my career, I want to express my heartfelt gratitude for the lessons you've taught me about grief and loss. It's been an honor to be part of your grief journey.

To my husband, Kevin, I am forever grateful for you. Your unwavering support, the thought-provoking questions we share during our morning coffee time, your meticulous attention to detail (Details Matter), and the inspiration you provide have played a pivotal role in my journey of writing this book. You are truly my rock. I've grown to embrace my own capabilities and face every challenge with newfound strength and determination because of your love, support, encouragement, and belief in me. I cherish every moment we spend together. All of me loves all of you.

To my dad, thank you for pushing me to join the teen grief support group at our local Hospice all those years ago. That decision was a turning point in my life, propelling me into a journey that has allowed me to assist countless grieving individuals. Your unwavering support has meant the world to me, and witnessing your personal growth and resilience since Mom's death fills me with immense pride. Our relationship today is a testament to the changes you have made. I love you.

My genuine thanks also go out to my sisters, Mary and Ann. The journey of grief we have undertaken over the past 29 years without Mom has been filled with both challenges and blessings. Your presence, love, and support have been a source of strength and comfort, and I am forever grateful to have you by my side.

I must acknowledge and appreciate the remarkable impact of Renee, the incredible hospice social worker who guided me as a grieving teenager. Your compassionate presence and the safe space you provided made a world of difference on my grief journey. Thanks for believing in me and for inviting me to help with the children's group, which propelled me to the beginning of my journey of helping other grieving individuals.

I'd like to convey my heartfelt gratitude to everyone who offered me support during my challenging teenage years of grief. Your kindness, generosity, and empathy will forever be etched in my memory. Special thanks to the Gilroy Family, Banicki Family, Powell Family, Ganzi Family, Schlicht Family, and all of my friends from Seaford, St. Williams, and SHA.

I'm grateful for my support network, including my friends, family, and colleagues who encourage me, listen to me vent, and, most importantly, share laughter with me. Big thanks to everyone at Malta Commons Suite 21. Your support, our lunches, and our chats really mean a lot.

Gratitude also goes to Laura Mazzotta, whose invitation to contribute to Holistic Mental Health was a pivotal moment in my life. Your support and encouragement fueled my ambition to become an author, and I am forever indebted to you for making this dream a reality.

Thank you to Laura Di Franco and Brave Healer Productions for giving me the opportunity to share this book with the world. Your guidance, support, and wisdom have been indispensable throughout this journey, and I am deeply appreciative of your instrumental role in bringing this project to fruition.

CENTER FOR INFORMED GRIEF

TOOLS & RESOURCES FOR GRIEVING INDIVIDUALS & THE PROFESSIONALS WHO SUPPORT THEM

WWW.CENTERFORINFORMEDGRIEF.COM

1 GRIEF JOURNALS

Discover a collection of heartfelt **journals** tailored to children and teens navigating the difficult journey of grief, including the death of a loved one and the challenges of divorce and beyond, providing them with a safe space to *express their emotions and find solace in their healing process.*

2 ONLINE COURSES

Explore the wide range of **online courses** tailored to *empower educators and therapists* in effectively assisting bereaved children, to deepen their understanding and skills.

For those personally navigating the complexities of grief, we also offer a free self-care course. Register today to take the first step toward empowered coping.

3 FACEBOOK GROUPS

Join the exclusive **Facebook communities.** *Supporting Grieving Students* is dedicated to school personnel and therapists providing resources and insights to enhance your work with grieving children.

The Grief Empowerment Group focuses on helping individuals on their personal grief journey, offering resources and support.

4 TRAINING & CONSULTING

Are you in need of **professional guidance** to foster a grief-informed environment in your school or agency? Are you considering offering staff development training on grief and loss? *Your search ends here!* Contact Kelly Daugherty at kelly@centerforinformedgrief.com to schedule your in-person or virtual training for your staff.

Printed in Great Britain
by Amazon

40844940R00155